WAR:
HOW CONFLICT
SHAPED US

WAR:
HOW
CONFLICT
SHAPED
US

MARGARET
MacMILLAN

RANDOM HOUSE
NEW YORK

Published in the United States by Random House,
an imprint and division of Penguin Random House LLC, New York.

RANDOM HOUSE and the HOUSE colophon are registered
trademarks of Penguin Random House LLC.

Originally published in the United Kingdom by Profile Books,
London. Published in Canada by Allen Lane, an imprint
of Penguin Random House Canada.

LIBRARY OF CONGRESS CATALOGING-IN-PUBLICATION DATA
Names: MacMillan, Margaret, author.
Title: War : how conflict shaped us / Margaret MacMillan.
Other titles: War, how conflict shaped us
Description: New York : Random House, [2020] | Includes bibliographical
references and index.
Identifiers: LCCN 2020014498 (print) | LCCN 2020014499 (ebook) |
ISBN 9781984856135 (hardcover) | ISBN 9781984856142 (ebook)
Subjects: LCSH: War—History. | War and society.
Classification: LCC D25.5 .M285 2020 (print) | LCC D25.5 (ebook) |
DDC 355.0209—dc23
LC record available at https://lccn.loc.gov/2020014498
LC ebook record available at https://lccn.loc.gov/2020014499

Printed in the United States of America on acid-free paper

randomhousebooks.com

246897531

First U.S. Edition

Book design by Barbara M. Bachman
Title-spread illustration: Albrecht Dürer, The Four Horsemen of the Apocalypse
(1498, woodcut), image © Bridgeman Images

For
Ann and Peter

CONTENTS

INTRODUCTION

===

"War remains, as it always has been,
one of the chief human mysteries."

—SVETLANA ALEXIEVICH,
The Unwomanly Face of War

W AR. THE WORD ALONE RAISES A RANGE OF EMOTIONS
from horror to admiration. Some of us choose to avert our eyes as
if the very act of remembering and thinking about war somehow
brings it closer. Others of us are fascinated by it and can find in
war excitement and glamour. As a historian I firmly believe that
we have to include war in our study of human history if we are to
make any sense of the past. War's effects have been so profound
that to leave it out is to ignore one of the great forces, along with
geography, resources, economics, ideas, and social and political
changes, which have shaped human development and changed
history. If the Persians had defeated the Greek city-states in the
fifth century B.C.; if the Incas had crushed Pizarro's expedition in
the sixteenth century; or if Hitler had won the Second World
War, would the world have been different? We know that it would
although we can only guess by how much.

And the what-ifs are only a part of the conundrums we face.
War raises fundamental questions about what it is to be human
and about the essence of human society. Does war bring out the
bestial side of human nature or the best? As with so much to do
with war, we cannot agree. Is it an indelible part of human society,

somehow woven in like an original sin from the time our ancestors first started organizing themselves into social groups? Our
mark of Cain, a curse put on us which condemns us to repeated
conflict? Or is such a view a dangerous self-fulfilling prophecy?
Do changes in society bring new types of war or does war drive
change in society? Or should we even try to say what comes first,
but rather see war and society as partners, locked into a dangerous
but also productive relationship? Can war—destructive, cruel and
wasteful—also bring benefits?

Important questions all, and I will try to answer them, and
others that will come up along the way, as I explore the subject. I
hope to persuade you of one thing, however. War is not an aber-
ration, best forgotten as quickly as possible. Nor is it simply an
absence of peace which is really the normal state of affairs. If we
fail to grasp how deeply intertwined war and human society
are—to the point where we cannot say that one predominates
over or causes the other—we are missing an important dimension
of the human story. We cannot ignore war and its impact on the
development of human society if we hope to understand our
world and how we reached this point in history.

Western societies have been fortunate in the last decades; since
the end of the Second World War they have not experienced war
firsthand. True, Western countries have sent military to fight
around the world, in Asia, in the Korean or Vietnam Wars or in
Afghanistan, in parts of the Middle East or in Africa, but only a
very small minority of people living in the West have been touched
directly by those conflicts. Millions in those regions of course
have had very different experiences and there has been no year
since 1945 when there has not been fighting in one part of the
world or another. For those of us who have enjoyed what is often
called the Long Peace it is all too easy to see war as something
that others do, perhaps because they are at a different stage of
development. We in the West, so we complacently assume, are
more peaceable. Writers such as the evolutionary psychologist

Steven Pinker have popularized the view that Western societies have become less violent over the past two centuries and that the world as a whole has seen a decline in deaths from war. So while we formally mourn the dead from our past wars once a year, we increasingly see war as something that happens when peace—the normal state of affairs—breaks down. At the same time we can indulge a fascination with great military heroes and their battles of the past; we admire stories of courage and daring exploits in war; the shelves of bookshops and libraries are packed with military histories; and movie and television producers know that war is always a popular subject. The public never seems to tire of Napoleon and his campaigns, Dunkirk, D-Day or the fantasies of *Star Wars* or *The Lord of the Rings*. We enjoy them in part because they are at a safe distance; we are confident that we ourselves will never have to take part in war.

The result is that we do not take war as seriously as it deserves. We may prefer to avert our eyes from what is so often a grim and depressing subject, but we should not. Wars have repeatedly changed the course of human history, opening up pathways into the future and closing down others. The words of the Prophet Muhammad were carried out of the deserts of the Arabian Peninsula into the rich settled lands of the Levant and North Africa in a series of wars, and this has had a lasting impact on that region. Imagine what Europe might be like today if Muslim leaders had managed to conquer the whole continent, as they came close to doing on a couple of occasions. Early in the eighth century Muslim invaders conquered Spain and moved north across the Pyrenees into what is today's France. They were defeated at the Battle of Tours in 732, marking the end of the surge northward. Had it continued, it is possible to imagine a Muslim and not a Catholic France shaping French society and European history over the next centuries. Some 800 years later the great Ottoman leader Suleiman the Magnificent swept through the Balkans and most of Hungary; in 1529 his troops were outside Vienna. If they had taken that great city the center of

Europe might have become part of his empire and its history would have been a different one. The spires of Vienna's many churches would have been joined by minarets and a young Mozart might have heard different forms of music played on different instruments. Closer to our own times, let us imagine what might have happened if the Germans had wiped out the British and the Allies at Dunkirk in May 1940 and then destroyed Britain's fighter command in the Battle of Britain that summer. The British Isles might have become another Nazi possession.

War in its essence is organized violence, but different societies fight different sorts of wars. Nomadic peoples fight wars of movement, attacking when they have an advantage and slipping away into vast open spaces when they do not. Settled agricultural societies need walls and fortifications. War forces change and adaptation, and conversely changes in society affect war. The ancient Greeks believed that citizens had an obligation to come to the defense of their cities. That participation in war in turn brought an extension of rights and democracy. By the nineteenth century the Industrial Revolution made it possible for governments to assemble and maintain huge armies, bigger than anything the world had seen before, but that also created an expectation among those millions of men who were conscripted that they would have a greater say in their own societies. Governments were obliged not only to listen but also to provide a range of services, from education to unemployment insurance. The strong nation-states of today with their centralized governments and organized bureaucracies are the products of centuries of war. Memories and commemorations of past victories and defeats become part of the national story and nations require stories if they are to be cohesive. Such centralized polities, whose people see themselves as part of a shared whole, can wage war on a greater scale and for longer because of their organization, their capacity to use the resources of their societies and their ability to draw on the support of their citizens. The capacity to make war and the evolution of human society are part of the same story.

Over the centuries war has become more deadly, with greater impact. There are more of us; we have more resources and more organized and complex societies; we can mobilize and engage millions in our struggles; and we have a much greater capacity to destroy. We had to come up with new terms to describe the two great wars of the twentieth century: world war and total war. While some threads run consistently through the history of war and human society—such as the impact of changes in society or technology, attempts to limit or control war, or the differences between warriors and civilians—I will be paying a lot of attention to the period since the end of the eighteenth century, because war has become not just quantitatively different but qualitatively. I will also draw many of my examples from the history of the West, because it has pioneered so much in the recent past in war, as well as, it must be said, attempts to keep it under control.

Yet in the majority of Western universities the study of war is largely ignored, perhaps because we fear that the mere act of researching and thinking about it means approval. International historians, diplomatic historians and military historians all complain about the lack of interest in their fields, and of jobs too. War or strategic studies are relegated, when they exist, to their own small enclosures where those called military historians can roam away, digging up their unsavory tidbits and constructing their unedifying stories, and not bother anyone else. I remember years ago, in my first history department, we had a visit from an educational consultant to help us make our courses more appealing to students. When I told him that I was drawing up plans for a course called "War and Society" he looked dismayed. It would be better, he urged, to use the title "A History of Peace."

It is a curious neglect, because we live in a world shaped by war, even if we do not always realize it. Peoples have moved or fled, sometimes disappeared literally and from history, because of war. So many borders have been set by war, and governments and states have risen and fallen through war. Shakespeare knew this well: in his plays war often provides the mechanism by which kings rise and fall while the ordinary citizens keep their heads down and pray that the storm will leave them unscathed. Some of our greatest art has been inspired by war or the hatred of war: the *Iliad,* Beethoven's "Eroica" Symphony, Benjamin Britten's *War Requiem,* Goya's *The Disasters of War,* Picasso's *Guernica* or Tolstoy's *War and Peace.*

War is in the games children play—capture the flag or the fort—and one of the most popular video games of 2018 in the United States was *Call of Duty,* based on the Second World War. The crowds who go to sporting events sometimes treat them as battles with the other team as the enemy. In Italy those who are known as Ultra fans arrive at soccer matches in highly organized groups with a firm hierarchy of command. They wear uniforms and give themselves names such as Commandos, Guerrillas and, much to the dismay of many of their fellow Italians, some borrowed from the partisan bands of the Second World War. They come to do battle with supporters of the rival team more than to watch the match. The modern Olympics were meant to build international fellowship but from almost their first moment they mirrored competition between the different nations. The games were not war but they took on many of its attributes, with the awarding of medals, the playing of national anthems and teams in uniforms marching in unison behind their national flags. Hitler and Goebbels famously envisaged the 1936 Berlin Olympics as key in their campaign to show the superiority of the German people and, during the Cold War, tallies of medals were read as showing the superiority of one side over the other.

Even our language and our expressions bear the imprint of war. After they defeated the Carthaginians in the Punic Wars the Romans continued to use the expression "Punic good faith" (*fides Punica*) sarcastically. In English we say dismissively that someone or something is a flash in the pan without realizing that the expression originated with early guns, when the gunpowder meant to ignite the charge flared to no effect. If the British want to be rude they will call something French or Dutch, because those nations were once enemies. Taking French leave means departing rudely and abruptly, while Dutch courage means drinking gin. (And the words "British" and "English" fill the same role for the French and the Dutch.) So many of our favorite metaphors come from the military, for the British especially from the navy. If we are three sheets to the wind, eating a square meal might help. If we run into a spot of trouble we can wait for it to blow over or give it lots of leeway. If you don't believe me you can always say, "Go tell it to the marines!" Our conversation and writing are sprinkled with military metaphors: wars on poverty, on cancer, drugs or obesity (I once saw a book entitled *My War on My Husband's Cholesterol*). Obituaries talk about the deceased as having "lost the battle" with their illness. We speak freely of campaigns, whether in advertising or to raise money for charity. Business leaders read a Chinese work on strategy written 2,000 years ago for tips on how to outsmart the opposition and carry their enterprises to victory. They boast of their strategic goals and their innovative tactics and are fond of comparing themselves to great military leaders such as Napoleon. When politicians go to ground to avoid questions or scandals—firestorms, they are often called—the media report that they are in their bunkers trying to rally their troops and planning an offensive. In December 2018 a *New York Times* headline read: "For Trump, a War Every Day, Waged Increasingly Alone."

War is there too in so much of our geography. In the names of places: Trafalgar Square in London after Nelson's triumph; the Gare d'Austerlitz in Paris after one of Napoleon's greatest victories; Waterloo Station in London after his final defeat. In Canada there is a town which was once called Berlin-Potsdam because it had been settled in the nineteenth century by German immigrants; when the First World War broke out, it suddenly became Kitchener-Waterloo. Our towns and cities almost always have their war memorials with the names of those who died or monuments to long-gone heroes. Nelson stands on his column in London; Grant's tomb is a popular meeting place in New York's Riverside Park. Increasingly in the past century, memorials have appeared to the rank and file, the often anonymous participants in war, such as nurses, pilots, infantry soldiers, marines, ordinary seamen and even, in the case of the United Kingdom, to the animals used in the two world wars. Reminders of past wars are so much part of the scenery we often do not see them. I have walked up and down Platform 1 at London's Paddington Station more times than I can remember, never noticing a large memorial to the 2,524 employees of the Great Western Railway company who died in the First World War. At Paddington too is a striking bronze statue of a soldier who stands there, dressed for war, reading a letter from home. Without the commemorations of the hundredth anniversary of the war I would not have stopped to see it, or taken the time at Victoria Station to search for the plaques to the vast numbers of soldiers who entrained there on their way to France, or the one to the body of the Unknown Soldier which arrived back in 1920.

If we pause to reflect on our own histories we can often find traces of war in our memories. I grew up in a peaceful Canada but many of the books and comics I read were about war, from the seemingly inexhaustible supply of G. A. Hentys, with stories of noble and heroic boys in most of the major conflicts before 1914, through the intrepid pilot Biggles and his crew in the Second World War to the Black Hawk comic books, which had started out in that war but moved seamlessly into the Korean one. At Brownies we sang songs—much cleaned up, I later realized—from the First World War and learned semaphore and how to make bandages. At school in the early 1950s we collected string and foil for the war effort in Korea. We also practiced sitting under our desks in case nuclear war broke out between the United States and the Soviet Union.

Many of us will have heard stories told by older generations who knew war firsthand. Both my grandfathers were in the First World War as doctors, the Welsh one with the Indian Army at Gallipoli and in Mesopotamia, and the Canadian one on the Western Front. My father and all four of my uncles were in the Second World War. They told us some but not all of what they had experienced. My father, who was on a Canadian ship escorting convoys across the Atlantic and into the Mediterranean, mostly had funny stories, but once and only once he told us how close they had come to being sunk. His voice shook and he could not go on. His own father never told him much about the trenches, but as often happens he talked to a grandchild, my sister, who was too young to understand much of it. Our grandfather also brought back a hand grenade as a souvenir which sat in my grandmother's curio cabinet along with such treasures as a miniature Swiss cottage and a tiny wooden Scotty dog. We played with the grenade as children, rolling it around on the floor, until someone noticed that it still had its pin. Many families must have such stories and mementoes, the packages of letters from war zones, artifacts picked up on battlefields, the old binoculars and helmets, or the umbrella stands made out of shell casings.

And the souvenirs keep coming as the battlefields around the world give up their debris. Eurostar has had to put up signs to remind passengers who have been to the battlefields of the First World War not to bring on board shells or weapons they have collected as souvenirs. Every spring Belgian and French farmers along what was once the Western Front pile up what they call the Iron Harvest. The winter frosts have heaved the land, bringing to the surface old barbed wire, bullets, helmets and unexploded shells, some of them containing poison gas. Units of the French and Belgian armies collect the munitions for safe disposal, but the war still claims its victims, among farmers and the bomb disposal experts, workers who dig in the wrong place or the woodcutters who build a fire for warmth on top of a live shell. Construction in London and Germany still turns up, from time to time, unexploded bombs from the Second World War. And relics surface from much older wars. A ship dredging Haifa harbor in Israel found a magnificent Greek helmet from the sixth or fifth century B.C. A retired schoolteacher out for a walk with his metal detector found a Roman helmet buried in a hill in Leicestershire. Scuba divers on a routine training exercise on the Shannon River in Ireland found a Viking sword from the tenth century.

Many societies have war museums and days of national commemoration when they remember their dead. And the dead themselves make unexpected appearances to remind us of the costs of war. On the quiet Swedish island of Gotland archeologists unearthed the body of a local soldier in his chain mail. He had been killed along with many of his fellows fighting Danish invaders in 1361. Bodies can be preserved for centuries if they are buried in mud or mummified in hot countries. In the summer of 2018 archeologists surveying land near Ypres for a housing development found the remains of 125 soldiers, German mainly, but also Allied, who had lain there since they fell in the First World War. In 2002 thousands of corpses, still dressed in their blue uniforms with buttons bearing the numbers of their regiments, were discovered in a mass grave outside Vilnius. They had died during Napoleon's retreat from Moscow in 1812.

When we pause to remember war we think of its costs—the waste of human beings and resources—its violence, its unpredictability and the chaos it can leave in its wake. We less often recognize just how organized war is. In 1940 Germany tried to force Britain into surrender and for nearly two months London was bombed day and night. Many nonessential civilians were evacuated to the countryside. Those who remained slept in makeshift shelters or the Underground. The British Broadcasting Corporation—the BBC—which was based in the center of London, sent several departments away. Music went to Bedford, Drama and Variety to Bristol, until that got too dangerous, and Variety went off to languish rather glumly in the sedate town of Bangor in North

Wales. The remaining staff often could not get home at night so the BBC—not nicknamed Auntie for nothing—turned its Radio Theatre into a dormitory, with a curtain down the middle to keep the sexes apart. In October two bombs hit the building. Seven members of staff died as they tried to remove an unexploded one and the fire department rushed to the scene to keep the flames from spreading. The news reader for the nine o'clock news paused briefly as the building shook and then kept going, covered in soot and dust. By the next morning scaffolding had gone up around Broadcasting House and the rubble was being cleared. Think for a moment of the organization that was involved in that single episode, a tiny one in the overall history of the war. The German bombers, with their fighter escorts, were the products of Germany's war industry, which had mobilized resources from materials to labor and factories in order to get the planes made and into the air. Their crews had been chosen and trained. German intelligence and planners had done their best to select important targets. And the British response was equally organized. The Royal Air Force tracked the incoming planes and did its best to stop them, while on the ground crews manned barrage balloons and searchlights. The blackout over London and other key cities was complete and carefully monitored. The BBC had made contingency plans, the fire department came and the work of clearing up started at once.

War is perhaps the most organized of all human activities and in turn it has stimulated further organization of society. Even in peacetime, preparing for war—finding the necessary money and resources—demands that governments assume greater control over society. That has become increasingly true in the modern age because the demands of war have grown with our capacity to make it. In increasing the power of governments, war has also brought progress and change, much of which we would see as beneficial: an end to private armies, greater law and order, in modern times more democracy, social benefits, improved education, changes in the position of women or labor, advances in medicine, science and technology. As we have got better at killing, we have also become less willing to tolerate violence against each other. Murder rates are down in most parts of the globe, yet the twentieth century saw the greatest deaths in war in absolute figures in history. So there is yet another question: How do we reconcile killing on such a scale while simultaneously deploring violence? Most of us clearly would not choose to make war to get its benefits. Surely there is some other way of doing it. But have we yet found it?

There are many such paradoxes about war. We fear war but we are also fascinated by it. We may feel horror at the cruelty of war and its waste, but we can also admire the courage of the soldier and feel the dangerous power of war's glamour. Some of us even admire it as one of the noblest of human activities. War gives its participants license to kill fellow human beings, yet it also requires great altruism. After all, what can be more selfless than being willing to give up your life for another? We have a long tradition of seeing war as a tonic for societies, as bracing them up and bringing out their nobler sides. Before 1914 the German poet Stefan George dismissed his peaceful European world as "the cowardly years of trash and triviality" and Filippo Marinetti, founder of the Futurist movement and future fascist, proclaimed, "War is the sole hygiene of the world." Mao Zedong later said something very similar: "Revolutionary war is an antitoxin which not only eliminates the enemy's poison but also purges us of our own filth." But we have another, equally long tradition of seeing war as an evil, productive of nothing but misery, and a sign, perhaps, that we as a species are irredeemably flawed and doomed to play out our fate in violence to the end of history.

Svetlana Alexievich is right. War is a mystery, and a terrifying one. That is why we must keep trying to understand it.

WAR:
HOW CONFLICT
SHAPED US

CHAPTER I

HUMANITY, SOCIETY
AND WAR

—

"War is waged by men; not by beasts, or by gods.
It is a peculiarly human activity. To call it a crime
against mankind is to miss at least half its significance;
it is also the punishment of a crime."

—FREDERIC MANNING,
The Middle Parts of Fortune

IF YOU VISIT THE LOVELY ALPINE TOWN OF BOLSANO YOU will often see long queues outside the South Tyrol Museum of Archaeology. People wait patiently, many with their children, to see one of Bolsano's main attractions: the mummified body of a man who lived around 3300 B.C. Ötzi—the Iceman—died before the Pyramids or Stonehenge had been built yet the ice kept his body and possessions intact until he was found by two hikers in 1991. He wore a cloak made from woven grass and clothes, including leggings, boots and a cap, made from leather. His last meals, still in his stomach, were dried meat, roots, fruits and possibly bread. He was carrying wooden baskets and various tools, including an axe with a copper head, a knife, arrows and parts of a bow.

It was assumed at first that he had lost his path in a snowstorm and died alone, to be left undisturbed for the next five millennia. It was a sad story of an innocent farmer or shepherd. In the next decades, however, thanks to advances in medicine and science, it became possible to examine the body more closely, with CT scans,

X-rays and biochemical testing. Ötzi had an arrowhead embedded in one shoulder and his body was bruised and cut. His head had apparently been hit too. It is most likely that he died of the wounds he received from his attacker or attackers. And it is possible that he had at some point killed others, judging by the blood found on his knife and an arrowhead.

Ötzi is by no means the only piece of evidence we have that early humans, certainly by the time of the later Stone Age, made weapons, ganged up on each other and did their best to finish each other off. Graves dating back to Ötzi's time, and earlier, have been found across the globe, from the Middle East to the Americas and the Pacific, containing piles of skeletons which bear the marks of violent death. Although weapons made of wood and skins generally do not survive, archeologists have discovered stone blades, some still buried in the skeleton.

Violence seems to have been present even earlier, during much of the greatest part of our human story in fact, when our ancestors lived nomadic lives foraging for edible plants and killing other creatures for food. Much of what is known is naturally highly speculative. Collecting and reading evidence, especially the further into the past you go—and humans appeared on earth some 350,000 years ago—is extraordinarily difficult, but we are gradually accumulating more thanks to archeological discoveries and scientific advances such as the reading of ancient DNA. Until very recently in humanity's long history, we now know, we organized ourselves into small bands scattered across the more temperate parts of the globe. There was not much in the way of material goods to fight about and presumably if a band came under threat from others it could simply move away. For much of the twentieth century, those who studied the origins of human society tended to assume that the early nomadic bands lived a peaceful existence. Yet archeologists have also discovered skeletons from this long-distant period whose injuries suggest otherwise. Anthropologists have tried to get at what that world was like by looking at the few hunter and forager societies that survived until the modern age. It is a roundabout path with potential pitfalls: outsiders who observe such societies bring their own preconceptions and contact itself brings changes.

Having said that, there are some suggestive findings. In 1803, for example, a thirteen-year-old boy, William Buckley, escaped from an English penal colony in Australia and found refuge among the Aborigines for the next three decades. He later described a world where raids, ambushes, long-running feuds and sudden and violent death were part of the fabric of society. At the other end of the world, in the harsh Arctic landscape, the first explorers and anthropologists found that the local inhabitants, Inuit and Inupiat among them, made weapons including armor from bone and ivory and had a rich oral tradition of stories of past wars. In 1964 Napoleon Chagnon, a young American anthropology student, went to do fieldwork among the Yanomami people in the Brazilian rain forest. He expected that they would confirm the then prevailing view of hunter-foragers as essentially peaceable. He found that within each village the Yanomami lived for the most part in harmony and were gentle and kind with each other, but that it was a different matter when it came to dealing with other villages. Then differences were settled with clubs and spears, and one village would raid another to kill the men and children and abduct the women. In his thirty years of observations, he concluded that a quarter of Yanomami men died as a result of violence.

While there are heated exchanges—wars, indeed—of words and ideas between historians, anthropologists and sociobiologists, the evidence seems to be on the side of those who say that human beings, as far back as we can tell, have had a propensity to attack each other in organized ways—in other words, to make war. That challenges us to understand why it is that human beings are willing and able to kill each other. It is more than an intellectual puzzle: if we do not understand why we fight we have little hope of avoiding future conflicts. So far there are many theories but no agreed answers. Perhaps war is the result of greed or competition for dwindling resources—for food, territory, sexual partners or slaves. Or are we shaped by biological ties and shared culture to value our own groups, whether clans or nations, and fear others? Like our cousins the chimpanzees, do we instinctively lash out when we feel threatened? Is war something we cannot help doing or is it something we have constructed through ideas or culture? Since war and the fear of war are still very much with us in the twenty-first century, the answers to such questions matter.

War would not be possible without our willingness to kill, but that alone does not define it. We would not describe two men fighting in a bar or even a dozen or so gang members battling in a street or a park as making war. Violence leading to injury or death is part of war, but we tend to see that as a tool of war, not as an end in itself. The great German theorist Carl von Clausewitz, in one of his most famous observations, said, "War is an act of violence intended to compel our opponent to fulfill our will." War has a purpose whether it is offensive or defensive. As with individuals or gangs, fighting war can be about honor, survival or control, but it is distinguished from a bar fight by its scale and its organization. War involves dozens, hundreds, thousands, even millions rather than one or a few people committing violence on each other. It is a clash between two organized societies which command the adherence of their members and have existed over considerable time, usually in their own territory. As Hedley Bull, the English political theorist, put it, "Violence is not war unless it is carried out in the name of a political unit . . ." And, he went on, "Equally, violence carried out in the name of a political unit is not war unless it is directed against another political unit." Gangs are organized and their members can claim to share values and goals, but they are not stable political and social units. They might of course become so and grow in size and in time become clans, tribes, chiefdoms, baronies, kingdoms or nations which are capable of engaging in war.

One of the many paradoxes of war is that humans got good at it when they created organized societies. Indeed the two developments have evolved together. War—organized, purposeful violence between two political units—became more elaborate when we developed organized sedentary societies and it helped to make those societies more organized and powerful. It was only 10,000 years ago—an instant in the much longer human story—when some of us started to settle down and become farmers, that war became more systematic and started to need special training and a warrior class. Along with graves in different parts of the world, archeologists have found evidence of fortifications, in Turkey for example, which date back to at least 6000 B.C., and of clusters of dwellings which appear to have been burned down deliberately. With the advent of agriculture humans were more tied to one place and had more worth stealing, and worth defending. And to defend themselves they needed better organization and more resources, which in turn led to groups expanding their territory and growing their populations either peacefully or through conquest.

Among the many debates over the origins and evolution of war is whether humans have been getting more violent or less. Steven Pinker and others who think like him, such as the archeologist Ian Morris, are on the optimistic side and believe there is a clear trend away from violence. Most countries no longer have public executions; they have laws against cruelty to animals or children; and sports such as bear baiting or dog fighting are normally illegal. The optimists go further and attempt to tot up deaths from war in the past—not in itself an easy task—to argue that homicide rates in the past were far higher than they are today and that deaths in war, as a proportion of humans alive at the time, are fewer in the twentieth and twenty-first centuries, even allowing for the great bloodlettings of the two world wars, than in earlier wars. Others challenge the figures and also point out that war deaths in the twentieth century may amount to 75 percent of all war deaths in the last 5,000 years. And if you really want to be depressed about the prospects for humanity, studies using mathematical tools at the University of Florence and the University of Colorado claim to show that the trend is for fewer but more deadly wars. Their argument is that the more interconnected societies become the quicker a conflict can spread along the paths of the network—just as computer viruses or forest fires do. A small squabble in the Balkans in the summer of 1914 grew into the Great War because Europe's powers were so interlinked by treaties, understandings or plans that tensions spread upward and outward from the assassination of the Archduke Franz Ferdinand in Sarajevo until a general war exploded.

Even if Pinker is right—and the debate goes on—it somehow does not seem very reassuring. Those of us who have enjoyed the Long Peace since 1945 need to reflect that much of the world, including Indochina, Afghanistan, the Great Lakes district in Africa and large parts of the Middle East, has seen and still sees conflict. A long-running project at Uppsala University in Sweden estimates that between 1989 and 2017 over 2 million people died as a result of war. Since 1945 perhaps 52 million have been forced to flee because of conflict.

The prevalence of violence and war in the past and their persistence in the present raise the awkward question as to whether humans are genetically programmed to fight each other. One avenue of research has been to look at our closest relatives in the animal kingdom: the chimpanzees and the bonobos. Both live in organized groups, have ways of communicating with each other and make primitive tools. (In Northern Ireland, a pair of enterprising chimpanzees recently worked together to escape from Belfast Zoo by making a ladder out of a branch.) Chimpanzees and bonobos are so alike in appearance that until the 1920s it was assumed that they were the same species. In fact they have evolved to be quite different in the ways they live together and deal with strangers.

Jane Goodall studied chimpanzees in their natural habitat in Tanzania for over half a century. She and her teams of colleagues became so much part of the scenery that the chimpanzees grew to ignore their presence. The observers watched as the chimpanzees developed relationships, cared for their young, engaged in play— and killed each other. Male-dominated groups, each fiercely attached to its own territory, waged organized conflict against other chimpanzee groups, often without being provoked. They killed lone chimpanzees who strayed too far out of their own territory and they carried out raids, killing rival males as well as females and infants. In a particular long-running conflict one group exterminated another and occupied its territory. In her memoir Goodall said that at first she thought the chimpanzees in her study were "for the most part, rather nicer than human beings." Then, she went on, "suddenly we found that chimpanzees could be brutal—that they, like us, had a darker side to their nature."

Before we settle on human beings having an indelible dark stain on their natures, we should look at the counterexample of the bonobos, who do not fight or hunt each other. Bonobos seem as intelligent as their chimpanzee cousins but they have evolved very differently, possibly because they live on the south side of the Congo River, where foraging is easy and they do not have more powerful rivals, gorillas in particular, as the Tanzanian chimpanzees do. Among the bonobos, females rather than males form strong groups and they tend to dominate the males. When strange bonobos meet, their first instinct is not to attack but to tentatively gaze and then move slowly toward each other. They start to share food, groom each other and embrace indiscriminately, giving each other a variety of pleasures. (Videos of bonobos at play are very popular on the internet, even if some would think them not suitable for family viewing.) Whether the bonobo preference for making love and not war is the result of environment or evolution or a mix of the two is still being debated.

Which set of our cousins do humans most resemble? The answer seems to be both. We cannot deny the relationship: humans share some 99 percent of our DNA with chimpanzees and bonobos. Unlike them, however, we have developed language, elaborate technologies and an ability to think in abstract terms. We have built highly complex societies with social and political institutions, ideas, belief systems and values. We are certainly capable, like the chimpanzees, of reacting violently when we are fearful, but like the bonobos we have a highly developed capacity for friendly interaction, cooperation, trust and altruism. In his *The Goodness Paradox* the anthropologist Richard Wrangham argues that over the long course of human evolution we have learned to tame our aggressive side, partly by domesticating ourselves as we have domesticated wild animals. Think of how wolves eventually became our trusted pet dogs. He believes that humans working together gradually got rid of the more violent members of their groups by killing them. Perhaps, as other anthropologists have suggested, sexual preference played a role too as women and their parents looked for peaceable, cooperative mates. While this gradual domestication of our ancestors was happening, humans, Wrangham continues, were also building social and political institutions, including strong central governments, which had a monopoly on violence. So their subjects, unlike the chimpanzees, could no longer maim and kill at will. Yet that did not mean an end to violence; rather organized societies could now use it in an organized and purposive way. The paradox, as Professor Wrangham sees it, is that as humans became nicer, they also got better at killing and on an ever-larger scale.

We cannot deny, I think, the inheritance evolution has left us. We have impulses, feelings including fear, and needs and desires for things such as food and sex. Like most species, from birds to mammals, we have a strong attachment to territory. But we are also sentient beings and we have the capacity to make decisions, to listen to the better angels of our natures or the worse. We have created cultures which in turn shape who we are and help to determine what we think is important. So we do not fight just for survival—food, sex, shelter—but also for abstractions such as religions or nations which we think worth killing and dying for. Nor do we invariably fight, no matter how important the cause may be to us. We also look for peaceful solutions. Indeed humans have dreamed and still do of ridding the world of war altogether.

The jury is still out on how and why we evolved as we did—and how much it matters when it comes to war. Another equally heated and long-running discussion is whether society itself makes us better or worse, more peaceful or more warlike. Instead of contrasting chimpanzees and bonobos, this debate revolves around two eighteenth-century European thinkers: Thomas Hobbes and Jean-Jacques Rousseau. Both grappled with the relationship between human beings and their societies and whether war or peace was our normal condition. Both described humans in a state of nature before organized societies appeared on the scene. Unlike us, they had no evidence of how humans had lived in the distant past; rather they found it useful to imagine how humans might coexist with each other without rules or organization and then look at their own societies.

Rousseau argued that violence was not an integral part of being human. Human beings, he held, were naturally good until society made them corrupt. He described a pastoral idyll where hunter-foragers lived in harmony with each other and with nature. They had sufficient sustenance for their needs and had no need to fight, either to take food from others or to defend what they had. Evil crept in when humans settled down and started to farm. That led, Rousseau argued, to the development of private property and specialized trades, as some remained farmers while others became craftsmen, warriors or rulers. The successful accumulated more property so that society, which had once been egalitarian, became unequal and hierarchical. The weak were exploited by the strong and society came to be marked by greed, selfishness and violence. As society and states evolved and became more complex, with greater powers over their members, humans had less and less freedom. Since separate states tended to think only of their own interests, they were more likely to go to war with each other than not. Rousseau's solution, which he laid out in *The Social Contract*, was not to go back to his putative paradise, which he accepted would be impossible, but to create a new relationship between individuals and their social and political institutions. Humans need to live and work together, but they should be able to do so willingly, in a state that works for them and not the other way around, and one that guarantees them freedom. If humans can behave as though they have entered freely into a contract with each other, both individuals and society will become happier and more harmonious. Once that has been achieved states, by now enlightened, can work together to overcome the mutual fears, suspicions and greed which have so often led to war. At times Rousseau seems to have been imagining a federated states of Europe whose members would outlaw war and ensure peace.

Hobbes painted a very different picture. In his state of nature, humans lived precariously and struggled against each other to survive. Life, as he said, was "solitary, poor, nasty, brutish, and short." There was no time and there were no resources left over for making tools, cultivating crops, trade or learning. "No Knowledge of the face of the Earth; no account of Time; no Arts; no Letters; no Society; and which is worst of all, continual fear, and danger of violent death." Far from the growth of settled societies and large states leading to conflict, the opposite was more the case. The growth of a big and powerful polity—what Hobbes called Leviathan—offered the way to bring violence under control, at least within societies. International society remained much like the state of nature, with states jostling for advantage in an anarchical world. The strong ones bullied the weak and the weak capitulated or were subjugated by force. Unlike Rousseau, he had no expectations that societies and states could become more enlightened and learn to work with each other voluntarily.

Many of us still prefer the Rousseau version of the past and the assumption that humans are by nature innocent and peaceful.

The twentieth century was so awful in so many ways that it is not surprising that we keep searching for contemporary societies which are better and gentler than ours. If they are not hidden away on tropical islands or in rain forests or deserts perhaps they can be created based on the right sorts of principles. For a time in the 1920s and 1930s Western intellectuals thought they had found their Garden of Eden in the Soviet Union, until, at last, the evidence of mass starvation and organized murder inflicted by the state became too obvious for most to ignore. In the 1960s Mao's China became the great hope, partly because so little was known about it. The Cultural Revolution seemed benign at first, with the high-spirited young remaking society into an egalitarian paradise where everyone worked happily to build a new world. Again the rosy picture changed and grew much darker as we learned about the real brutality and the destructiveness of those years.

From the Garden of Eden in the Bible onward, literature and the arts have portrayed peaceful golden ages of the past or Utopias to come. Greek and Roman poets such as Hesiod or Seneca believed that humans had enjoyed a golden age in the distant past and that history was heading ever downward toward the bronze and the iron ages, when men acquired weapons and became greedy and warlike. Similar stories exist in Indian and Chinese traditions. Early explorers who encountered peoples in the Americas or the Pacific were struck by how peaceable many of them seemed to be. Their reports caught the imagination of a rapidly industrializing West. In the nineteenth century Western artists such as Henri Rousseau and Paul Gauguin painted dreamlike scenes of beautiful Africans or Pacific Islanders surrounded by fruit ready to fall from the tree. There was apparently no willingness to fight and no need.

When anthropology appeared as a serious field of research in the nineteenth and twentieth centuries, its findings largely appeared to confirm such a happy picture. The American Margaret Mead, who did her fieldwork in Samoa in the 1920s, painted a world where there was no guilt, greed or anger. And no war, the curse of other civilizations. No one in Samoa, she wrote, "suffers for his convictions or fights to the death for special ends." Young people easily followed their elders into loving open sexual relationships and families feasted together as a matter of course, sharing their plentiful food with each other. "Sometimes sleep will not descend upon the village until long past midnight; then at last there is only the mellow thunder of the reef and the whisper of lovers, as the village rests until dawn . . ." Her book *Coming of Age in Samoa* had a huge impact, especially in the 1960s, when it seemed to point the way to a world with no more Vietnams and unlimited and guilt-free love. More recently both her research and her conclusions have come into question. Mead's later critics pointed out that she did not speak the local language well, was only in Samoa for a few months and, perhaps most damning of all, was prepared to believe uncritically everything the locals told her. (A couple of them later said they had lied to her about Samoan teenagers' uncomplicated guilt-free sex lives.) Earlier visitors to Samoa such as missionaries and sailors had described Samoans rather as busily engaged in fighting each other. It was only with the coming of imperialism, in this case in the shape of the Americans and the Germans, then later the British, that peace came to Samoa. For a time we thought that Mayan civilization in Mesoamerica might provide a heartening example of how states could live in harmony with each other. Regrettably, the deciphering of the Mayan script after the Second World War shows that the surviving literature is largely about war.

So, the Rousseauian version of human history or the Hobbesian? The archeological and historical evidence points firmly toward Hobbes, with war as a long-standing and integral part of human experience. That does not mean that we should not hope for a future more like Rousseau's. In the meantime, perhaps it can be some consolation that war, surprisingly, has brought peace and progress for societies.

That brings me to a second paradox of war: that growing state power and the emergence of bigger states—what Hobbes called Leviathan—are often the result of war but that in turn can produce peace. The power of the state and its institutions is based on the perceived authority of the rulers, whether that comes from the gods or from the voters, and on the acquiescence of those who are ruled over, but somewhere, crucially, in the mix is war or the threat of the violence that the state can exert both over its own people and against its enemies. The emergence of state-run police forces in much of the Western world and parts of Asia in the nineteenth century gradually put an end to banditry and low-level violence. The power of feudal lords in Europe was broken when monarchs acquired sufficient force to destroy their private armies and level their castles. The emergence of the strong state went hand in hand with its increasing monopoly over the use of force and violence within its borders. If you refuse to pay taxes, set your neighbor's house on fire or ignore the summons to do military service, a strong state will lay hands on you and often your property as well and you will be punished and even, sometimes, executed. The peoples of Yugoslavia lived together peacefully if not always happily under Tito's firm rule because, as a Croat put it, "every hundred yards we had a policeman to make sure we loved each other very much." When Tito died and his Communist Party fell to pieces, the different ethnicities in Yugoslavia, urged on by unscrupulous demagogues, turned on each other. We may see the state as oppression incarnate, but we should think for a moment what it is like to live where there is no state power. The Samoans and the New Guinea highlanders once knew that and the unfortunate people of the failed states of Yemen, Somalia and Afghanistan know it today.

Success in war against external enemies has often been used to further legitimize and enhance the authority of the state as governments, whether democratically elected or dictatorships, point to great victories as signs of virtue and markers of their accomplishments. In his 2019 State of the Union address President Donald Trump talked about the American victory after the D-Day landings in Normandy (ignoring the presence of other Allied troops), which, he said, they did for America and "for us." And, he went on, "Everything that has come since—our triumph over communism, our giant leaps of science and discovery, our unrivaled progress toward equality and justice—all of it is possible thanks to the blood and tears and courage and vision of the Americans who came before." The Romans erected columns and victory arches to glorify the emperor and the state. Napoleon used writers and artists to laud his triumphs as he rose to power in France. When he made himself emperor, one of his obsequious senators called him "the incomparable Hero who has conquered them all, who has plucked everything out of chaos and created another universe for us." As long as he seemed invincible, Napoleon kept his hold over France and much of Europe. Hitler's string of victories won over even German conservatives who had doubted his fitness to rule.

Conversely, rulers who cannot defend their own peoples or suffer defeats abroad lose their support. In classical China, emperors who failed to deal with violent revolts within or attacks from outside were said to have lost the mandate of Heaven and were therefore no longer fit to rule. Napoleon III, nephew of the great Napoleon, led France to defeat in the Franco-Prussian War; his regime fell and he fled into exile. When Hitler invaded the Soviet Union in the summer of 1941, Stalin, so it is said, panicked and said, "Lenin founded our state and we've fucked it up." President Lyndon Johnson decided not to run in the 1968 election because of the failure of his government to bring the Vietnam War to an end.

States and empires have grown through wars of conquest or when weaker powers have capitulated to them rather than engage in a hopeless one-sided struggle. The Athenians used their navy and their land forces to bring their neighbors under their control.

Alexander the Great led his armies to build a vast empire. The Roman legions marched outward from Rome conquering as they went. China was once divided among some 150 small states which were gradually consolidated in a painful and bloody process. The Chinese still remember with horror their Warring States period from the fifth to the third century B.C., when the remaining handful of states fought an endless series of wars and the people were ground down and impoverished. The Qin Emperor who finally brought the different states under his control in 221 B.C. was a ruthless tyrant, but he has been remembered with gratitude as the ruler who brought peace and order to China. He was buried in Xi'an with ranks of terra-cotta soldiers, a fitting reminder of the role that military force had played in creating his state. Closer to our own times, Prussia, that patchwork collection of territories, used its army to accumulate more and more territory and ultimately to create modern Germany. The Soviet Empire in the Cold War was acquired and held down by the Red Army.

Great powers are not necessarily nice ones—why should they be?—but they do provide a minimum of security and stability for their own people. Those powers that last use military force to sustain themselves, but their longevity has rested on providing reasonably effective government which has helped to win the acquiescence and even loyalty of their peoples. The Romans understood very well that they had used war to create peace for themselves but that they had other tools worth using too. As Virgil has it in the *Aeneid*, "Remember, Roman, it is for you to rule the nations with your power (that will be your skill), to crown peace with law, to spare the conquered and subdue the proud." Power alone without some support from the people cannot ensure the survival of Leviathans. The Roman Empire lasted as long as it did because it replaced a collection of often-quarreling states and because, within its borders, peoples, foods and goods could travel freely along its well-built roads or across the Mediterranean, which had been cleared of pirates. Within the empire economic prosperity grew and people lived longer. Indeed foreigners moved into the Roman Empire rather than Romans moving away. Roman subjects were not held down by force, although that threat was always there. Most of the fighting Roman soldiers did was along Rome's frontiers. The better Leviathans have consistent laws, reasonable taxes and security of property, and sometimes even, as in the Roman Empire, a tolerance of different customs and religions.

Strong armed forces build strong states, but they can also undermine them when they get out of control. In the Roman Empire, unscrupulous generals led their loyal troops against the state or the soldiers themselves sold their loyalty to the highest bidder. When the Emperor Pertinax was assassinated in A.D. 193 after his three-month reign there was a disgraceful scene, according to the historian Dio Cassius: "For just as if it had been in some market or auction room, both the city and the entire empire were auctioned off." Over time Leviathans decay, their governments becoming less and less competent, unable to deal with armed revolt from within and enemies along the borders. The Vandals sacked a weakened Rome. The horse-borne Mongol warriors swept away old regimes in Persia, China, India and Russia. The Ming dynasty was founded in 1368 when rebel armies led by a peasant defeated the last forces of the Mongol Yuan dynasty. Two and a half centuries later the Manchu poured through a gap in the Great Wall to overthrow the Ming in turn.

Leviathans can also bring peace to their neighborhoods if they are powerful enough. In the nineteenth century the British Empire acted as the world's policeman, ensuring that the world's waterways were secure and conflicts, where possible, were dampened down. The British did this out of their own self-interest, to protect their trade and their empire, but the Pax Britannica, like the Roman one before it, made possible the flourishing of trade and commerce and vast movements of peoples around the globe. We may be living through the end of the hegemony of the American

Leviathan and we are starting to realize that the world needs someone or something to maintain order. A less stable substitute is a coalition of powers of roughly equal size and strength that agree to work together to keep the peace. This happened in Europe in the first half of the nineteenth century with the Concert of Europe and during a brief period with the democracies in the 1920s. It only takes one or two powers, however, such as Germany before the First World War and Germany, Japan and Italy before the Second, to decide to challenge the status quo and for peace to tip toward war. The world reverts surprisingly easily to Hobbes's state of anarchy where no power trusts another. Then the prospect is repeated conflict, just as it is within failed states.

After the fall of the Roman Empire in the West in the fifth century A.D., Europe gradually reverted to a lower level of development: trade fell off because the roads and waterways were too dangerous for travelers, and learning and the arts faded. Waves of invaders—Angles, Vandals, Huns, Goths—swept through, looting and pillaging, because there was no force to stop them. Local strongmen with their castles and their retainers exploited their subjects and waged war on each other. In the twelfth century a chronicler wrote of how one Robert of Vitot's will left "almost forty kinsmen, all proud of their knightly status, who were continually at war with one another." Europe has had far fewer periods of unity than China but it has moved by fits and starts from some 5,000 independent political units (mainly baronies and principalities) in the fifteenth century to 500 in the early seventeenth century, 200 at the time of Napoleon in the early nineteenth and fewer than thirty after 1945. That did not bring an end to war but it did limit the number of potential combatants and therefore the number of likely wars. The growth of European unity with European institutions was consciously conceived as an alternative to the European state system, with all its dangers for conflict; and war among its powers, so it is hoped, has become unthinkable.

The need to make war has gone hand in hand with the development of the state. The historian Charles Tilly goes so far as to say, "War made the state, and the state made war." Protecting yourself, from neighbors or raiding nomads, takes organization—to get the bodies to fight and then to provide leadership and the discipline and training to exact obedience. Governments need to know how many fighters they can muster and that leads to counting and to keeping records. The word "census" comes from ancient Rome; in the sixth century B.C. the authorities started to list male citizens both for collecting taxes and because they were expected to bear arms. While early soldiers often brought their own weapons and food, with larger and longer campaigns the government had to provide them and that meant more bureaucrats to count and find the supplies and the animals and the boats to transport them. For the famous Battle of Cannae against the Carthaginians in 216 B.C., it has been estimated that the Roman army of some 80,000 (figures are always tricky in the ancient world) would have required about 100 tons of wheat a day for their army. In the eighteenth century, the British navy was the single biggest industry by far in the whole of the British Isles. While you could build a cotton mill for £5,000, a large capital ship for the navy such as Nelson's *Victory* cost over £60,000. To build, staff and maintain the navy required shipyards, warehouses and bases both in the British Isles and overseas and a growing number of officials, administrators, suppliers and workers. The navy needed money, a great deal of it, as well as organization and management, and the British government developed the necessary tools and institutions, which then came in handy for managing other aspects of British society. The Treasury was founded in the second half of the seventeenth century to keep military expenditure under control but over time developed into a body which kept track of the spending of all government departments. In the 1690s, when Britain was at war with France and desperately needed funds, the government as an emergency measure founded the Bank of England, which could take money from subscribers and lend to the government at a fixed rate. Again, like the Treasury, the Bank grew into a key part of Britain's fiscal system. Because the government was able to guarantee regular interest payments thanks to its efficiency in collecting taxes, investors found government-issued annuities or bonds solid and desirable investments. The result was more funding available for such purposes as war.

Tacitus, the great Roman historian, said, "Money is the sinew of war." Centuries later the British diarist Samuel Pepys complained, "Want of money puts all things, and above all things the Navy, out of order." In the Peloponnesian War Athens managed to rebuild its fleet three times, but when the last one was destroyed in 405 B.C. it had run out of resources and was forced to surrender to Sparta and its allies. Wars sometimes pay for themselves if the defeated enemy has good pickings. Alexander the Great accumulated huge wealth from the Persians. In the sixteenth and seventeenth centuries the Spanish financed their European wars largely from the gold and silver they brought back from the defeated Aztec and Inca empires. The German Confederation made France pay a lump sum after the Franco-Prussian War of 1870–71. Germany forced Russia to hand over its gold and send natural resources westward in the 1918 Treaty of Brest-Litovsk and the Allies tried to extract reparations for war damage from Germany under the Treaty of Versailles.

Often, however, governments need to extract the necessary funds from their own people or borrow from willing lenders. Until the second half of the twentieth century war constituted by far the largest expenditure for the most powerful states of Europe. In the Nine Years War of 1688–97 between the France of Louis XIV and Britain, it is estimated that France was spending 74 percent of its revenue and Britain 75 percent. Although his armies won repeated victories, Louis was eventually obliged to make an unsatisfactory peace because he could no longer find anyone willing to lend him the money he needed. The British, it turned out, were much better at taxing as well as borrowing and managing their debt. Although France was the richest country in Europe, Louis XIV and his successors never managed to tap into that wealth and this eventually affected France's capacity to wage war. Government borrowing only drove the state toward bankruptcy. In 1789 Louis XIV's grandson Louis XVI was forced into taking what became the fatal step of calling an assembly of representatives of the main French classes in the hope that they would vote for taxes.

The British, it is true, found it easier to collect taxes because they could impose customs duties at their ports. More important, however, they had a parliament which was prepared when necessary to raise taxes and, by the eighteenth century, had what was probably the most efficient tax-collecting system in Europe. The public grumbled but paid up. By the end of the American Revolutionary War in 1783 the average Englishman was paying almost three times as much in annual taxes as his French counterpart. What is more, the taxes were collected by a government agency, not, as in France, by tax farmers who bought the rights to raise taxes on the understanding that they could keep whatever extra they raised as long as they gave the government a fixed amount. Dr. Johnson, in his dictionary, may have defined the important excise levied on domestic commodities as "a hateful tax" collected by "wretches," but it was key to Britain keeping its navy afloat and its armies abroad. As the British state became more organized, efficient and powerful, it was able to strengthen its control over British society, including the rebellious Scots and Irish. The excise commissioners amassed quantities of information, from the number of candle makers to the number of shops. The Excise Office gave licenses to thousands of brewers, publicans, tea and coffee dealers, and a host of other trades. Its inspectors were everywhere, with "ten thousand eyes," as people complained.

That secure annual revenue meant that if the government decided to borrow funds, its lenders could be assured that they would be repaid. Following the earlier Dutch example, the British government developed a system of cheap public credit, borrowing from its own citizens through issuing short-term and longer-term paper instruments which it systematically paid off. Government often used another new device, the sinking fund, where certain government revenues were assigned to paying off particular debts. Without that steady, reliable pipeline of funds, Britain would not have had the navy to make it a European and world economic and military power in the late seventeenth and eighteenth centuries. We remember Pepys for the wonderful human details in his diaries, his descriptions of London, his impatience with his wife and her friends or his roving eye, but he was also a serious, dedicated bureaucrat who over many years of painstaking work transformed the British navy from an inefficient and corrupt institution into a formidable fighting force. He studied shipbuilding, checked every contract and knew the price of everything that went into a ship, from the tar to the cannon. He found, he said, "great content in it, and hope to save the King money by this practice." He did much more than that; by the end of his thirty years of service the navy had double the number of ships and guns and it was being managed efficiently and honestly.

The growth of centralized state power in Europe by the eighteenth century, with armies and navies that were organized, controlled and paid for by the state, also meant that governments had at their disposal the means to crack down on the recalcitrant and rebellious, whether these were local magnates, riotous crowds or brigands. The state's need to maintain its monopoly on force at home and to defend itself from outside enemies has led to its having more control over society, its resources and the lives of its peoples. In the Middle Ages both the English and the Scottish governments ordered their subjects to engage in regular archery practice. The Scots were told to give up football as well. In the First and Second World Wars, the governments of countries involved determined what goods factories would produce and what would be rationed. Skilled workers in certain jobs—for example, munitions or mining—lost their freedom to change employment or volunteer for the armed forces. Fashion, food, amusements, travel, all were regulated for the sake of the war effort. And military discipline and regimentation creep in even during peacetime. Think of factories with strict times for clocking in and out, of the Amazon warehouses of today, or of the way public education in the nineteenth and early twentieth centuries put pupils in uniform and lined them up in orderly rows, and sometimes still does.

On the other hand, states have had to bring changes which have benefited parts or the whole of society in order to improve their military capacity. Consistent laws and efficient administration may be a necessary part of mobilizing a nation's resources for war but they can also enlarge the rights of subjects and the space in which they can operate. Entitlement to the rights of citizenship has repeatedly been tied to military service. In the classical worlds of Greece and Rome being a citizen meant the obligation to take up arms which in turn validated citizens' rights. Although citizenship was tied to property in most city-states, among sea powers such as Athens the need for rowers for galleys meant that free men who possessed little but strength could obtain citizenship by picking up an oar. In the early Roman Republic, when Rome was almost constantly at war with its Italian neighbors, the aristocratic leaders who monopolized power were obliged to call on the ordinary men—the plebeians—to fight. Legend has it that on one occasion the plebeians withdrew to a place outside Rome and elected their own representatives, the tribunes, and successfully demanded rights including a veto for their tribunes over certain decisions of the aristocratic magistrates and the Senate. Countries have often awarded citizenship to foreigners for service in wartime. Until 2018, immigrants to the United States who served in the military had their citizenship applications expedited.

In the nineteenth and twentieth centuries, as the capacity for nations to make war on a large scale grew thanks to the Industrial

Revolution, governments, even autocratic ones, found themselves making reforms in response to war or in anticipation of it and to keep public support. Governments encouraged railway building in part to be able to move troops easily about the country in case of domestic unrest or to the frontiers for war. Germany got a single time zone in place of the existing patchwork when the military demanded it so that they could move troop trains smoothly. Better education and better nutrition were needed to produce fitter soldiers and sailors. The British government and British public opinion were dismayed to discover that one out of three volunteers for the South African War of 1899–1902 had to be rejected as unfit. That spurred demands for improvements in public health and innovations such as free school meals for indigent children. After Russia's disastrous defeat in the Crimean War Tsar Alexander II abolished serfdom partly to reform the conscription system. He tried, with some success, to modernize his country's bureaucracy and justice and education systems. Later generations of Russian reformers advocated for representative institutions in part as a way of building the nation. As Prince Yevgeny Trubetskoy said before the First World War, "It is impossible to govern against the people when it is necessary to turn to it for the defense of Russia."

Between 1914 and 1917 the Russian government was to find itself doing just that, governing against the will of many of its own people. War has often opened the way to massive political and social changes when it weakens government and undermines its legitimacy. Victory can entrench a regime in power just as long-drawn-out wars of attrition can destroy it. Sometimes the change is political, one set of rulers replacing another, but it is often more fundamental. The First World War imposed heavy strains on all the powers engaged, but the stronger ones—Britain and France and to a certain extent Germany—weathered the storms. They underwent change but did not emerge after 1918 as fundamentally altered societies. (Germany, it is true, became a republic but its institutions, from the bureaucracy to the military, and its culture remained much the same.) The experience of Russia, before 1914 the most fragile of the great powers, was quite different. The tsarist regime proved incapable of managing the war and coping with the strains on society and by 1917 its power had drained away in the face of popular dissatisfaction, increasingly organized opposition and a growing unwillingness of many of its military to fight. And it was not just the competence of the regime that was being called into question but the very nature of Russian society. Before the war revolutionaries had been calling for an end to autocracy and the transformation of Russia into some form of socialist society, but they were deeply divided, small in number and harried by the authorities. The war increased their support and gave weight to their calls for radical, social and political change. Even then the regime might have hung on in some form but for the obduracy of the tsar and the failure of his successors in the Provisional Government to extract Russia from the war. That provided the opportunity for one of the most hard-line, ruthless and tactically brilliant of the revolutionaries to seize power. Yet if Lenin had remained in exile in Switzerland, where he was when the first, February, revolution broke out, he would today be a minor footnote in the history of the twentieth century. The German High Command, going for the short-term gain, as they did so often, launched him back to Russia across German territory in the famous sealed train. Lenin and his Bolsheviks carried out their coup in November 1917 and established a new order which was to alter the course of Russian and world history. We are still living with the consequences.

It is another uncomfortable truth about war that it brings both destruction and creation. So many of our advances in science and technology—the jet engine, transistors, computers—came about because they were needed in wartime. Penicillin, which has saved so many lives, was first discovered in 1928 by Sir Alexander Fleming but the funds to develop it were not available until the Second

World War. The Canadian doctor Norman Bethune pioneered blood transfusions on the battlefield. The practice of triage, now common in emergency rooms in hospitals, started in wars, possibly the Napoleonic. By the First World War French battlefield doctors were leading the way in the division of the wounded into those whom no treatment would help, those who might live if they were dealt with immediately and those who could wait. Surgery—for traumatic wounds or to rebuild shattered faces— made huge advances during the wars of the twentieth century in part because there were so many patients to practice on.

Women in many societies gained access to careers, education and rights as a result of their participation in war. Even before the end of the First World War the British government brought in the Representation of the People Act of 1918 to extend the vote to all those who did not own property—which meant the working classes—and women over thirty in recognition of their contributions to the war effort. At the end of the Second World War, the introduction of the welfare state was prompted by a similar sentiment. During the Cold War, American political leaders, including Presidents Eisenhower and Johnson, accepted that they must do something to provide civil rights for African Americans, not necessarily because they believed in the rightness of the cause. In the long struggle to show which society—the United States or the Soviet Union—was better, the Soviets had a handy weapon for propaganda in American racial discrimination.

Recently, prominent historians and economists, among them Walter Scheidel and Thomas Piketty, have argued persuasively that major wars can also act to narrow the gap between the rich and the poor and that the experience of the nations involved in the First and Second World Wars bears this out. Major wars stimulate employment; labor becomes more valuable so wages and benefits go up; and the rich pay higher taxes voluntarily, or find it harder to avoid doing so. At the end of destructive wars it is also easier to contemplate major programs of reconstruction and social benefits and gain support for them. As William Beveridge, whose report laid the foundations for the British welfare state, wrote, "Now, when the war is abolishing landmarks of every kind, is the opportunity for using experience in a clear field. A revolutionary moment in the world's history is a time for revolution, not for patching."

There is some evidence too that war brings social as well as economic leveling. Men and sometimes women are conscripted and thrown together with people unlike any they have ever met before. In the First World War, when young British officers, mostly educated in public schools, censored the letters their men were writing home, they were often surprised to find that ordinary soldiers expressed the same sorts of loves, fears and hopes as they themselves felt. George MacDonald Fraser, later to be famous for his Flashman novels, found himself in the Burma campaign in the Second World War in a regiment largely made up of tough, taciturn, working-class Cumbrians. As an educated middle-class boy he found them fascinating but alien. When his family sent him a couple of books, one a comic novel and the other *Henry V,* he expected—"intellectual snob," as he said of himself—that there would be no takers for borrowing the Shakespeare play. When his sergeant, who had left school in his early teens, took it away, Fraser assumed it would remain unread. To his considerable shame but also his enlightenment, when the sergeant brought the play back three days later he had clearly read it all and been moved by it. Shakespeare must have been in the army, he told Fraser, because he knew so much about what it was to be a soldier. A young middle-class woman in Britain during that war who joined the Women's Royal Naval Service because she thought it had more people of her type than the women's auxiliaries for the army or air force found herself on a mechanic's course with Scottish working-class women. "The war," she later admitted, "really did a lot of good to girls like me, who had been privately educated, it really did. It taught me that working-class people could have emotions, and that they could be bright, really bright, because my goodness some of those girls were clever. These were things I had simply never considered before."

To say that war brings benefits and can help to build stronger, even fairer, societies is not to defend it. Of course we would rather improve our world, help the weak and unfortunate, or have advances in science and technology in a state of peace. Yet finding the will and the resources to make great advances is harder in peacetime; it is all too easy to put off doing something about poverty, the opioid crisis or climate change until another day. War concentrates our attention and, like it or not, has done so throughout human history.

CHAPTER 2

REASONS FOR WAR

"No war is inevitable until it breaks out."

—A. J. P. TAYLOR,
*The Struggle for Mastery
in Europe, 1848–1918*

B ORED GODS DECIDE TO PLAY WITH HUMANS AND SET IN motion a train of events so that a man steals another man's wife; kings fall out over a piece of territory or succession to a throne; a British sea captain loses an ear; an emperor's representatives are pitched out of a window in Prague; an American battleship explodes in Havana harbor; monks fight in a shrine in Jerusalem; an archduke is killed in Sarajevo; or Japanese soldiers are fired on near an ancient bridge in Beijing, and so there is a war. Soldiers die, ships sink, cities and towns are sacked and civilians, always, suffer.

The causes of wars can seem absurd or inconsequential, but behind them usually lie greater quarrels and tensions. Sometimes it takes only one spark to set ablaze an already smoldering pile of timber. The Trojan War, so it was believed in the ancient world, occurred when Zeus, king of the gods, decided there were too many humans on earth and hit on the neat solution of encouraging them to fight and kill each other off. He allows the goddess Aphrodite to promise the long-lost son of the king of Troy that one day he, Paris, will marry the most beautiful woman in the world. Paris duly falls in love with Helen, who is already married to Menelaus, the king of Sparta. Helen fulfills her role by sailing off to Troy with Paris, taking with her a good deal of Menelaus's riches. Thus, according to the ancients, the Trojan War started. Greeks from Sparta and its many allies made their way to the shores of Asia Minor, many to die there, and in the end Troy was destroyed and its surviving peoples taken into captivity. Did it really happen? And, if not the fault of the gods, who started it? There is evidence of fighting around the ruins of Troy and those who came after Homer certainly believed there had been a long-drawn-out war. We know that the world then was an unstable and violent one in which small states fought for prizes: land, cattle, precious metals, women. Homer turned what was probably a real war, fought by rapacious thugs, into a great work of art.

We know more about dynastic wars in the Middle Ages and early modern Europe. Rulers regarded their land as their personal estates and saw nothing wrong in trying to expand their possessions. It was almost always possible to find a reason for war, whether an insult or an ancient claim to revive. The web of family connections which linked Europe's rulers meant that most successions could be disputed. In 1328 the king of France died without a son and heir. The question of who had the better claim, the cousin or the nephew—who also happened to be the king of England—led to the Hundred Years War between France and England. Five centuries later, another king died childless, this time in Spain, and three countries—England, the Dutch Republic and France—quarreled over the succession, triggering a war across Europe and around the globe that lasted for thirteen years from 1701 to 1714.

An affront to honor—the ruler's or the nation's—has often been the excuse for trying to settle a long-standing rivalry. In 1731 Captain Jenkins's ear was cut off, so he claimed, by Spanish sailors who suspected him of smuggling. He complained, in vain, to the British king. In 1738 Parliament chose to take notice after he displayed what he said was the grisly relic. The war that broke out the following year lasted until 1748 and the real reason was not Jenkins's ear but British ambitions to get a share of the lucrative trade, including in slaves, with the West Indies and Spanish America. The Spanish, understandably, were equally determined to preserve their monopoly.

Wars in the past may have been made by a single leader or elites but often they had some popular support. The citizens of the Greek city-states feared for their way of life and so came to-gether to fight the Persians. The quarreling Arab tribes of the Arabian Peninsula were welded together by religion and the Umayyad caliphs after the Prophet's death in A.D. 632 and swept through the Middle East, North Africa and parts of Europe. Re-ligion was behind what became known as the Defenestration of Prague in 1618. Protestants—and they were a strong force in Bohemia—saw the rights guaranteed by the Austrian emperor being violated by his representatives and so threw them out of a window of the great castle that still dominates Prague. Although the imperial officials survived, the episode set off a revolt and sub-sequent attempts by the Austrians to suppress it, which in turn drew Europe's major and minor powers into a long and compli-cated struggle that combined religious, social, national and dy-nastic wars.

Protecting co-religionists can be a most convenient excuse for war. In the middle of the nineteenth century the great powers were looking greedily at the declining Ottoman Empire. Britain and France, both of which had extensive interests in the eastern end of the Mediterranean, did not want Russia reaching out toward Constantinople, with its all-important command of the straits that led to the Mediterranean. When Orthodox and Cath-olic monks hit each other over the head with candlesticks and crucifixes in the Church of the Holy Sepulchre in Jerusalem, the tsar took it upon himself to defend the rights of the Orthodox Church in the Ottoman Empire, and Protestant Britain and anti-clerical France expressed their determination to protect both the Catholics and the Ottoman Empire.

At the end of the nineteenth century the United States was starting to exercise its growing power outside its borders, especially in its own neighborhood. Attempts to invade Canada or persuade its inhabitants that they would like to be annexed had failed (and taking on the British Empire was not a good idea), but the pickings looked better to the south. The Americans had already lopped off large parts of Mexico and they were increasingly interested in the Caribbean for both trade and security reasons. The idea of a canal joining the Pacific and the Atlantic across the Panamanian isthmus or possibly Nicaragua was already under consideration, which did much to focus American attention in the region. The main obstacle, apart from the British, was the moribund Spanish Empire, which controlled, among other possessions, the rich and strategically important island of Cuba. So when the American battleship *Maine* blew up and sank in Havana harbor in 1898, taking with it most of its crew, it was highly convenient for American expansionists. The influential Hearst press blamed the Spanish (it is just as likely that faulty design or seamanship had caused the tragedy), urging its readers to "Remember the *Maine*," and demanded vengeance. Congress obligingly joined in the chorus and pushed the president into the Spanish-American War, which left the United States dominant in the Caribbean and Central America and, almost accidentally, gave it the Philippines as well.

In June 1914 the heir to the Austrian throne made the singularly stupid mistake of going to Sarajevo, capital of Bosnia, which Serbian nationalists felt belonged with Serbia, and moreover on the 28th of the month, the great Serb national day, which commemorates the defeat of the Serbian Prince Lazar at the hands of the Ottomans at the Battle of Kosovo in 1389. The target was irresistible to a group of young fanatical nationalists and their shadowy supporters in Serbia and by sheer good luck one of them managed to kill the Archduke and his wife. Neither the Austrian imperial family nor the government mourned the deaths and gave the couple a mean and hasty funeral. The Archduke had not been popular and his wife was looked down upon as a mere countess. In death, however, they provided the perfect excuse for Austria to attempt to destroy Serbia, which, so it was felt in Vienna, had been stirring up trouble along the southern border for far too long. Germany decided to back Austria with the famous "blank check." Russia felt that it could not stand by and see its little client Serbia destroyed. German military plans called for attacking Russia's ally France through Belgium, and Britain decided to come to France's and Belgium's defense. In five weeks Europe moved from one of the most peaceful periods it had known since the Roman Empire into a general war.

The Second World War started in Asia with another convenient episode but it too had deeper roots. The Japanese militarists and nationalists were looking to build an empire in Asia to provide raw materials, markets, cheap labor and land for settlement. Japan had already taken the rich Chinese province of Manchuria in 1931 after a series of bombs had conveniently exploded on a Japanese-owned railway line. In 1937 Japanese soldiers were out on regular patrol in Beijing, a right established after a multinational force had defeated the anti-foreign Boxer Rebellion at the end of the nineteenth century. As the patrol neared an ancient bridge in Beijing, said to be the one the Venetian explorer Marco Polo had crossed on his way into the city centuries before, shots apparently rang out. The next day the Japanese produced a body in Japanese uniform. Although rumor in Beijing claimed that the Japanese had simply dressed up a dead Chinese beggar, the Marco Polo Bridge incident became Japan's justification for invading China south of the Great Wall and occupying a great swathe of the coast down to the border of Hong Kong. That invasion helped to turn American opinion away from isolationism to confrontation.

So there are apparently many different reasons for wars in different times and places. Abductions, romances, religion, dynastic struggles, conquest, imperialism, assassinations or fabrications.

Yet certain motives appear again and again: greed, self-defense, and emotions and ideas.

Greed for what others have, whether it is food for survival, women for servitude or procreation, precious minerals, trade or land, has always motivated war. Hobbes said that humans fight each other "to make themselves masters of other men's persons, wives, children and cattle." The Mongol horsemen were looking for loot but ended up destroying and creating empires. Cortés and Pizarro toppled the Aztec and Inca empires in the early sixteenth century in their search for gold. The rulers of Prussia, Austria and Russia divided up Poland at the end of the eighteenth century because they wanted to add to their possessions. Hitler took his war into the East because he believed that the German race needed more land and resources to survive. Saddam Hussein seized Kuwait in 1990 because he wanted its oil.

Thucydides said, "The strong do what they can and the weak suffer what they must." But the weak can decide to fight in their own defense rather than submit. Tiny Finland took on the giant Soviet Union in the Winter War of 1939–40 and, while the Finns eventually had to surrender and give up part of their territory, the country preserved its independence. The Poles fought in 1939 against both Nazi Germany and the Soviet Union because the alternative seemed worse. And it is hard to say they made the wrong choice when you consider the treatment of occupied Poland by both its enemies. Individuals and groups will fight out of fear—of an imminent threat, of what might happen in the future—even if they have not been attacked. And they fight to protect what they hold dear: possessions, homeland, families.

Although war has normally been seen as a sphere for men, women can be its excuse. The French, said the nineteenth-century German writer and nationalist Ernst Moritz Arndt, were "mean, lascivious, ravenous and cruel" and had defiled German women and dishonored their men. German men must fight to set right the shame. In the First World War, a popular English postcard showed a woman's face with the caption "The Star That Shines Above the Trenches at Night." Recruiting posters on both sides showed helpless women being menaced by bestial soldiers. Wartime propaganda directed against the enemy warned that his women were not being as faithful as they should. In the Second World War the Japanese broadcast warnings to Australian soldiers that their women were too familiar with the Americans stationed there. During the "Phony War" of 1939–40, when French soldiers stood on guard on their frontiers in anticipation of a German attack, the Germans put up huge billboards, visible from the French side, with messages such as "SOLDIERS OF THE NORTHERN PROVINCES, LICENTIOUS BRITISH SOLDIERY ARE SLEEPING WITH YOUR WIVES AND RAPING YOUR DAUGHTERS!" One French unit replied, "We don't give a bugger, we're from the south!" The Nazi propaganda machine also played on racial fears by describing French and British women being seduced by black soldiers from their empires or the United States.

Sometimes, it is argued, a preventive war, against a threat which is more anticipated than actual, is the best form of self-defense. The citizens of Sparta, according to Thucydides, voted for war "because they were afraid of the further growth of Athenian power, seeing, as they did, that already the greater part of Hellas was under the control of Athens." The Romans took on the more powerful Carthage in the First Punic War because, as Polybius said, "They were beginning, therefore, to be exceedingly anxious lest, if the Carthaginians became masters of Sicily also, they should find them very dangerous and formidable neighbors." Israel attacked its neighbors Egypt, Syria and Jordan first in 1967 because it feared, with reason, that they were planning a coordinated war. In the crisis of 1914 the German High Command argued that it had only three years left before a rapidly modernizing Russia became too strong for Germany to defeat, and that added to the momentum toward war. The Japanese military argued much the same in 1941 as they watched the United States ramp up its preparations for war. The attack on Pearl Harbor was a gamble intended to knock the United States out of the war and leave Japan in possession of all its gains and the ones to come. In the Cold War each side worried that the other might launch its nuclear warheads first to gain the advantage.

And another sort of fear can add to the pressures for war. In Europe before 1914 there was concern that too much peace was softening society, and a lot of talk about how a good conflict every so often toned up a nation's moral fiber and made tough patriots out of its young. In 1938 Hitler was horrified that Germans rejoiced when the Munich Agreement appeared to end the possibility of war. He told a meeting of German editors and journalists (all of course by now under Nazi domination) that they must educate the Germans so "the inner voice of the people itself slowly begins to cry out for the use of force."

Suspicions and fears of others, from rival gangs to countries, can create perceptions of threats even where they might not exist, just as they do for our cousins the chimpanzees. During the Cold War the mutual mistrust of the West and the Soviet bloc meant that each tended to interpret words and actions by the other, even accidents, in the most unfavorable light. A bear trying to climb a fence around an American missile was mistaken for enemy intruders, flocks of birds appeared on American and Canadian radar to be planes or missiles, or the sun glinting off clouds looked like an incoming attack to Soviet technicians, and the Third World War, briefly, came much closer. Once an American technician put a training tape into a computer at the North American Air Defense Command by mistake and suddenly command centers got warnings that Soviet missiles were heading in. Bomber crews went to their planes and American missiles were put on heightened alert. Fortunately the mistake was discovered in time. In 1983, after it had accidentally shot down the Korean airliner KAL007, the Soviet Union wove together unrelated coincidences—NATO training exercises, for example, and an increase in encrypted communications between Prime Minister Margaret Thatcher and President Ronald Reagan—to construct a scenario of an imminent nuclear attack.

Today in both Beijing and Washington there are those who say that a conflict between China and the United States is inevitable. If they look for signs of course they can find them. A project at Harvard University argues for something called the Thucydides Trap. Named after the author of the classic on the Peloponnesian War, it takes his famous line about the growth of Athens's power and the fear in Sparta leading to war and elevates it into a rule which, so it is argued, nearly always holds true: when a rising power threatens an established one, war is likely. Since that conclusion depends on a selective interpretation of examples from the past, it has and will continue to provide much scope for experts to disagree.

Humans also start wars because of what Hobbes called "trifles": "a word, a smile, a different opinion, and any other sign of undervalue, either direct in their persons or by reflection in their kindred, their friends, their nation, their profession, or their name." Honor and glory are abstract concepts yet they can matter more than life itself. Alexander the Great, it is said, modeled himself on the great warrior Achilles, who would not suffer insults, and slept with a copy of the *Iliad* under his pillow. Louis XIV, the Sun King, beggared France and inflicted years of war on Europe in a search for glory, not for his country but for himself. "I shall not attempt to justify myself," he said after starting a war with the Dutch. "Ambition and [the pursuit of] glory are always pardonable in a prince ..." Victory in battle, the acquisition of territory, the quest to put the king's relatives on other European thrones, even if the wars that followed did not benefit France, were for Louis's glory. Napoleon, who seems to have admired Louis's great antagonist the Duke of Marlborough more than the king, shared the hunger. His model above all was Alexander the Great. He invaded Egypt longing to build an empire in the East as Alexander had done. "I was full of dreams," Napoleon later wrote to a friend. "I saw myself founding a religion, marching into Asia, riding an elephant, a turban on my head and in my hand a new Koran that I would have composed to suit my need." In his own search for glory, Napoleon turned Europe upside down and destroyed hundreds of thousands of lives.

The fictional character Cyrano de Bergerac, who will fight a duel to the death if necessary rather than allow insults about his nose, has many counterparts in history. Maintaining honor or taking vengeance for insults and hurts, whether real or perceived, has started many wars. As Austria tried to decide how to respond to the assassination of its archduke in 1914, its leaders were sensitive to the empire's honor and prepared to face the threat of a war with Russia. "It will be a hopeless struggle," the chief of the Austrian general staff told his mistress, "but it must be pursued, because so old a Monarchy and so glorious an army cannot go down ingloriously." In the speech he made to the House of Commons on August 3, announcing that the government had decided to intervene in the unfolding struggle, the British Foreign Secretary, Sir Edward Grey, talked of Britain's "obligations of honor." Are the street gangs of today, whose members would rather die than be dissed (disrespected), different in their motivations?

Carthage, its aristocratic rulers above all, was humiliated by its defeat by Rome in the First Punic War in the third century B.C. It is said that the great Carthaginian general Hamilcar took his little son's hand and made him swear a sacred oath that he would never be friends with Rome. The child, Hannibal, grew up to be an even greater general who came close to destroying Rome in the Second Punic War. After France's stunning defeat by the German Confederation in 1871, the French draped black cloth over the statues in Paris, signifying their two lost provinces of Alsace and Lorraine. When war broke out in 1914 cheering crowds tore down the mourning. In its turn Germany longed for vengeance after its defeat in 1918. The Treaty of Versailles, the "Dictated," was widely seen by Germans of all political persuasions as vindictive and unjust and it was held to blame for much that went wrong in Germany in the 1920s. An English journalist met two elderly sisters who said they could no longer send their laundry out once a week, all because of the treaty. Hitler and the Nazis rose to power in large part because they promised to break its "chains." And break them Hitler did, declaring reparations payments at an end, openly breaching the disarmament clauses, moving troops into the demilitarized Rhineland and incorporating Austria into Germany.

His aim was always much greater than destroying the treaty or making Germany the most powerful nation on the Continent. It was to give the German people—the Aryan race, as he thought of them—a huge territory befitting their status as the master race and, ultimately, ensure them domination of the world. Ideologies, whether idealistic, messianic, wicked or simply crackpot, lie at the heart of some of the greatest conflicts in history. Nationalists—and that covers a wide range, from the racists at one extreme to the patriots who value a shared culture and history at the other—have fought and killed and still do today in the name of the nation. "I regret," said the American revolutionary soldier Nathan Hale, "that I have but one life to lose for my country."

Religion, and it can merge into nationalism as orthodoxy does with the Serbs and the Russians, offers both a cause worth dying for and the promise of eternal life. The Crusaders did not leave their homes all over Europe and make the long and dangerous journey to the Holy Land just to acquire loot and land. There was more and better to be had much closer to home. They were driven by what they thought was a divine mission, to retrieve the land where Christ had once lived for Christendom. Many Crusaders—kings such as Richard I of England, the Lionheart, and Philip II of France and great landed magnates—left behind properties, position and families and many never returned. Egged on by religious leaders such as Pope Gregory VII, who reminded the faithful of the passage from the Book of Jeremiah "Cursed be he that keepeth back his sword from blood," they killed indiscriminately those they thought of as infidels. In the massacres in Jerusalem in 1099 the streets were said to have run with blood, in some places up to the knees of the Crusaders' horses. "None of them were left alive; neither women nor children were spared," said a contemporary account.

Wars of ideology, whether religious or political, are often the cruelest of all because the kingdom of heaven or some form of earthly paradise justifies all that is done in its name, including removing human obstacles. Those who hold the wrong ideas or beliefs deserve to die much as diseases ought to be stamped out, or they are simply the necessary sacrifices on the way to achieving a dream which will benefit all of humanity. As Martin Luther, whose influence on Protestant thinking was enormous, once said, "The hand that wields the sword and kills with it is not man's hand but God's." Such attitudes fueled the internecine religious wars of his own century and contributed to the Thirty Years War in the following, as, in the twentieth century, did wars for revolutionary socialism, which saw itself as doing history's work rather than God's. Today of course we have religious wars again and the targets are again without limit until the final goal is achieved. Sadly even wars which are meant to be about ending war itself take on that limitless character. If the purpose is to remove forever the scourge of war, then whatever atrocities and cruelties are committed in its name will be justified because the sacrifice is surely worth it. In the lead-up to the Thirty Years War radical Calvinists, espousing an extreme form of Protestantism, came to believe that the Habsburg monarchy was the force of darkness which must be eradicated before the righteous could be saved. When the radicals in the French Revolution prepared to wage war on Europe it was for earthly salvation. As one revolutionary said in 1791, "It is because I want peace that I am asking for war."

The enemy, as in religious wars, becomes the enemy of humanity itself and must be utterly destroyed, not merely defeated.

Civil wars so often take on the character and cruelty of a crusade because they are about the nature of society itself. The other side is seen as having betrayed the community by refusing to agree to shared values and a common vision and so extremes of violence and cruelty become permissible, even necessary, to restore the damaged polity. When peoples who come from what has been the same family turn on each other, what was once love or at least tolerance becomes hatred, even to the extent of each wanting to annihilate the other. Each side in a civil war is struggling for legitimacy and dominance within a space that was once shared. An external enemy is a clear but understandable threat; a civil war is rather fueled by anger and hurt at the incomprehensible betrayal of the other side. The Romans, who first came up with the notion of a civil war, saw the very existence of strife within Rome as a serious moral failing which called into question Roman civilization itself.

We feel a particular horror at civil wars both because they rip apart the bonds that hold societies together and because they are so often marked by unrestrained violence toward the other side. The American Civil War probably had more casualties than all other American wars combined. Some 3 million men fought out of a total population of 30 million and at least 600,000 died and another 500,000 were injured. (The equivalent number of dead today with a much larger American population would be closer to 5 million.) Civilians, perhaps 150,000, died too, as a result of direct violence or starvation and disease. If anything, civil wars have been increasing since 1945 as wars between states become rarer. Greece, Nigeria, Sudan, Afghanistan, Yemen, Syria, Congo, Northern Ireland, Yugoslavia: the list is long and touches much of the world. Establishing the numbers of deaths in such conflicts is difficult if not impossible, partly because often there are no good records. And which deaths are the result of war? Do we count only the combatants or those who support them? Also the deaths as a result of starvation or disease as a result of war? So estimates run from 25 million dead in civil wars since 1945 to far lower but still horrifying figures, and we need also to take account of the millions of refugees fleeing the violence.

In a civil war the small grudges and enmities of peacetime are magnified and become lethal. During the Peloponnesian War a conflict broke out among the citizens of the city-state of Corcyra, ostensibly between enemies and supporters of democracy. In fact, said Thucydides, "men were often killed on grounds of personal hatred or else by their debtors because of the money they owed. There was death in every shape and form. And, as usually happens in such situations, people went to every extreme and beyond it. There were fathers who killed their sons; men were dragged from the temples or butchered on the very altars; some were actually walled up in the temple of Dionysius and died there."

Civil wars divide families and friends, often forever. Sir Ralph Hopton and Sir William Waller, seventeenth-century landowners in the West Country, were friends from childhood. They were both Puritans, on the same side of the great religious divide that ran through English society, both went to the same church and both became Members of Parliament. There they continued to agree on much. They both supported the Grand Remonstrance of 1641, which recorded Parliament's opposition to many of the policies of Charles I. In the end, though, Hopton felt that he must support the king against his opponents and, as England moved toward civil war, the old friends chose different sides. In 1643, as the Royalists and the Parliamentarians campaigned in the West Country, Hopton wrote to Waller to ask for a meeting. Waller's reply was heartfelt and heartbroken:

> Sir: the experience I have of your worth and the happiness I have enjoyed in your friendship are wounding considerations when I look at this present great distance

between us. Certainly my affection to you is so unchange-
able that hostility itself cannot violate my friendship, but I
must be true wherein the cause I serve. That great God,
which is the searcher of my heart, knows with what a sad
sense I go about this service, and with what a perfect hatred
I detest this war without an enemy; but I look upon it as an
Opus Domini [God's work] and that is enough to silence all
passion in me. The God of Peace in his good time will send
us peace. In the meantime, we are upon the stage and must
act those parts that are assigned us in this tragedy. Let us do
so in a way of honor and without personal animosities.

Whatever the outcome I will never willingly relinquish
the title of Your most affectionated friend.

They never met again. After the defeat of the Royalists Hopton
became an exile in Bruges, where he died in 1651. Waller ultimately grew disillusioned with the republic that was established
and worked for the restoration of the monarchy. He died in 1668.
There are many tragedies such as Hopton's and Waller's in civil
wars.

Civil wars are hard to forget, even when peace comes, because
they so often leave peoples living side by side who have very recently been enemies. Forgiveness is difficult and it is hard for the
losers to accept defeat and the victors to be magnanimous. The
Act of Pardon, Indemnity and Oblivion, for crimes committed in
and just after the Civil War, which the British Parliament passed
in 1660, is all too rare in history, although today we are seeing
more systematic attempts, in places such as Rwanda, Colombia,
Northern Ireland and South Africa, at peace and reconciliation.
More usual is what happened in Franco's Spain: "a long uncivil
peace," as one historian described it. Order of a sort returns, as it
did in Spain or Tito's Yugoslavia, but the bitter memories of the
savagery and atrocities on both sides simply go underground. The
Roman poet Horace warned of "fire / smoldering under ashes."

The arguments over the past can still divide the Spanish today, as the recent furor over the fate of the memorial to General Franco in the Valle de los Caídos shows. In the former Yugoslavia, where memories are much rawer, it is difficult even to discuss what happened in the 1990s. Over a century and a half later, the American Civil War still casts its shadow, in the arguments over the flying of the Confederate flag or the statues of Confederate generals or the tangled racial politics and the lingering resentments of Southern whites.

"Making peace is harder than waging war," the wise and cynical French prime minister Georges Clemenceau once said, and that is true of almost all wars. Too often nations start hostilities without thinking ahead to what they hope to achieve and what sort of peace they would like. Before 1914 the German military had an elaborate plan of attack which had taken many years, many hands and repeated exercises to create. The Schlieffen Plan was as good as the best general staff in Europe could make it, but it had fatal flaws. It assumed that Germany had to attack its neighbors France and Russia together and therefore ruled out all other options, including a one-front war or a defensive one, and it failed to take into account what the great Clausewitz called friction and the Americans call Murphy's Law—all those things that can go wrong in war and disrupt the best of plans carried out by the best of military. Most dangerous of all, it was the product of a leadership where the military focused on winning battles and the civilians had given little thought to what happened after that.

That limited vision is more common in war than one might think. The Germans in 1914 had not worked out their war aims or what they would do if France and Russia sued for peace. In September 1941, as Japan moved closer toward war with the United States, a high-level imperial war conference took place in the presence of the emperor, key civilian and military leaders and elder statesmen. The military, which by now dominated policymaking, produced a document of breathtaking vagueness on its goals in the coming war. "We cannot exclude the possibility," it said, "that the war may end because of a great change in American public opinion ... At any rate we should be able to establish an invincible position ... Meanwhile, we may hope that we will be able to influence the trend of affairs and bring the war to an end." The Japanese prime minister, Tojo Hideki (who was later tried for war crimes), shortly afterward compared the decision to jumping off a cliff with one's eyes closed. "There are times when we must have the courage to do extraordinary things." Asia, the Americans and the Japanese people paid a heavy price for that sort of courage.

Too often those making the decisions for war assume that, somehow, victory will magically sort out all problems. In 1998 the American military spent a lot of time developing plans to defeat Saddam Hussein and testing them in war games. General Anthony Zinni, head of the United States Central Command with responsibility for the Middle East, later said, "It struck me then that we had a plan to defeat Saddam's army, but we didn't have a plan to rebuild Iraq." He organized his own war game in 1999 and came to the conclusion that the invading forces would encounter considerable problems; the country was likely to fragment "along religious and/or ethnic lines," rival forces would battle for power and the Americans would face growing hostility. In 2002, as the United States moved toward war against Iraq, a final, huge war game tested American forces' ability to defeat an unnamed Middle Eastern power. The American side had a clear advantage in advanced electronics, tanks, planes and warships. The general in command of the much weaker "enemy" forces, however, rang rings around his opponents. He kept radio silence and used motorcycles to deliver messages and so made it difficult for his opponent's electronic surveillance to follow his moves. He had fleets of suicide bombers in speedboats knock out, on paper, sixteen American warships. The Pentagon suspended the game partway through and rewrote the rules. The warships were miraculously resurrected and the "enemy" general was ordered to turn off his air defenses and reveal the location of key units. He chose to quit in disgust.

His demonstration of asymmetric war, where a weaker power can disrupt and challenge much stronger forces through unconventional means, was a warning of what was going to happen to coalition forces in both Afghanistan and Iraq, where they were battered by hit-and-run attacks by guerrillas who communicated through secure channels and who used cheap improvised explosive devices, often shells or other containers packed with explosives and pieces of metal such as ordinary nails which can be set off with cheap, readily available technology such as the remote controls for children's toy cars or garage-door openers. Such devices have caused the majority of casualties for the occupying forces in both countries. Moreover, the occupations lacked clear goals after the initial ones of toppling the Taliban or Saddam Hussein. The military found themselves taking on nation-building, something they were not trained for and for which they were not given clear directives. Before the invasion and occupation of Iraq in March 2003 there was only one meeting in Washington—that February, far too late to be helpful—when representatives from all the different departments involved, including State, Defense, Treasury and the CIA, came together to discuss the postwar situation. Although the State Department had spent a year preparing a massive study, the Defense Department and the White House made it clear that they had no interest in its findings and did not want leading US Iraq experts anywhere near the planning for what happened after victory.

War, as the coalition was to discover in Iraq, takes on its own momentum and is often easier to start than to stop. Governments today may talk and hope for limited wars or "police actions," but once in they can find extricating themselves difficult. A decisive victory, in which the victor can impose peace on the loser, can be hideously expensive but negotiated settlements, in which neither

side gets everything it wants, can be hard to sell to elites as well as
to publics. And war aims tend to expand as the costs—in casualties and in gold—or the desire for revenge mount up. Political
leaders are tempted to promise outlandish rewards to their publics to forestall political and social unrest. When quick victory
eluded all sides in the First World War, governments, urged on by
their foreign offices, politicians and lobby groups, drew up shopping lists which got ever more elaborate and ambitious. Russia, it
thought, would take over the Black Sea and the straits into the
Mediterranean from the Ottoman Empire, while Britain and
France, for their part, intended to carve up Ottoman territories in
the Middle East. Germany's September Program, drawn up for
the Chancellor after the first bloody month of the war, envisaged
a huge German empire in Africa to include British and French
colonies and German economic dominance across the Continent
from the Channel to Ukraine and down into the Balkans. By 1918,
as the Treaty of Brest-Litovsk with the new Bolshevik government made clear, German war aims had expanded to include political hegemony. Russia lost huge swathes of territory in the west;
Poland, Finland, the three Baltic States and Ukraine were to become protectorates of Germany or its subservient ally Austria. In
2002 NATO forces went to Afghanistan, initially to remove the
Taliban government, but as they became bogged down in low-
level warfare their aims grew to encompass a wide range of no
doubt laudable objects, from nation-building to public health to
women's education.

The excuses for war are many and varied, but the underlying
reasons have not changed significantly over the centuries. The vocabulary may be different: where nations once talked of honor
they now tend to say prestige or credibility. Yet greed, self-defense
and emotions and ideas are still the midwives of war. And in its
fundamentals, strategy, meaning the broad goals of war, has not
changed. On land or sea, opponents seek to undermine each
other's capacity to wage war or destroy it forever. Strategic goals

can be defensive, letting the enemy exhaust itself, or offensive, taking the war to the enemy's military forces, besieging its towns and ports, or damaging its trade and production. Tactics, the ways wars are fought to achieve strategic goals, and logistics, ensuring that the military have the supplies they need, have changed over time, however, and in different parts of the world, because societies, their organization and values, evolve and change, and they have different resources and technologies available to them.

CHAPTER 3

WAYS AND MEANS

"The human heart is the starting point
in all questions of war."

—COLONEL LOUIS DE GRANDMAISON

"Three men and a machine gun can stop
a battalion of heroes."

—FRENCH GENERAL IN
THE FIRST WORLD WAR

IN THE LEONARD BERNSTEIN MUSICAL *West Side Story*, gang members boast that their loyalty to the group lasts until the day they die. In Shakespeare's *Coriolanus* the terrifying Volumnia lauds the return of her son from battle. She would, she tells Virgilia, Coriolanus's wife, have been as proud if he had died.

> Then his good report should have been my son; I therein would have found issue. Hear me profess sincerely: had I a dozen sons, each in my love alike and none less dear than thine and my good Marcius, I had rather had eleven die nobly for their country than one voluptuously surfeit out of action.

In such societies—and they have existed in all times and in many different places—young men, and they are almost invariably men, are brought up by their elders to value such qualities as discipline, bravery and a willingness to die. And the epics they hear, the books they read, the songs they sing or the paintings and sculpture they see, hold before them the examples of great warriors. In the *Iliad* Sarpedon, one of the Trojan allies, urges his fellows to take their place in the front lines of an attack on the Greeks so that no one in the future will say of them that they were cowards. The young British officers who went to the Western Front had been raised on the classics and hoped, until they encountered the reality of the trenches, to fight like the Greek and Roman heroes.

In Europe's Middle Ages the songs of the troubadours and the richly illustrated stories of heroes and their heroic deeds created a culture of chivalry for the feudal aristocracy. Legends such as those of King Arthur and the Quest for the Holy Grail inspired generations of young men to fight. Launcelot and Galahad were admired for their honor and virtue as much as for their ability to kill. Medieval women of the royal and upper classes had their own role to play in sustaining the myth of chivalric war, by bestowing their approval on their chosen knights and rewarding them for valor. Chivalry served, conveniently, to cast a sheen of glamour and nobility over the reality of bloody wars, often made for the most selfish of ends and fought with the utmost brutality. The tournaments, with their elaborate rituals and courtesies, were both a substitute for war and training for it. In 1241 eighty knights were said to have died at one tournament at Neuss on the Rhine alone. The chroniclers defended their violence. "He is not fit for battle," said one in the twelfth century, "who has never seen his own blood flow, who has not heard his teeth crunch under the blow of an opponent, or felt the full weight of his adversary upon him." Rugby coaches at British boarding schools said much the same thing in the nineteenth and twentieth centuries.

How societies fight wars and the weapons they use affect and are affected by their values, their beliefs and ideas, and their institutions, their culture in the broadest sense; and women, as much as men, serve to reinforce and transmit such cultures to the next generations. In oligarchic societies the upper classes dominate war-fighting, while in more democratic ones the obligations to fight are spread more widely. Styles of fighting vary greatly too. At the start of the Peloponnesian War, as Thucydides recounts, Corinth sent envoys to Sparta to warn it against Athens. You Spartans, said the Corinthians, are conservative; you hang back and wait until you are attacked. The Athenians, by contrast, are innovators and take risks. "If they win a victory, they follow up at once, and if they suffer a defeat, they scarcely fall back at all." Yet all Greek phalanxes preferred to fight on the plains than in the mountains and the fighting usually ended after one day when one side or the other had given way. The Aztecs had "flower wars," regulated by rules and fought in a predetermined place on a special day. Warriors wore special costumes and used only certain weapons. In their wars in the eighteenth century European generals set their forces out for battle in neat lines and tried to come up with proven formulas for victory, a reflection of the time's newfound faith in mathematics. One of the leading commanders of the time, Maurice de Saxe, wrote, "War can be made without leaving anything to chance. And this is the highest point of perfection and skill in a general." One of the things about Napoleon that so shocked and disoriented his opponents was that he did not follow the rules, marching his troops through the night, for example, and rushing them onto the battlefield in disorderly columns rather than the usual lines.

We talk of warrior societies, and they can be a state, a nation or something even smaller, like a New York gang. The most famous of all has become an adjective, so we talk of spartan accommodation, spartan races, spartan lives—things that involve courage, frugality or discipline. In nineteenth- and twentieth-century Britain the upper classes prided themselves on sending their sons to schools with spartan regimes—a mix of cold showers, hard beds, beatings, poor food and stories of past heroes—to toughen them up. Ancient Sparta was one of the most militarized societies in history. Unfit male infants were killed and those who survived were taken from their families for military training at age seven. They were allowed to marry but their primary loyalty was always to the state and its needs. Spartan men remained soldiers, if they survived, until they were sixty. Since it was shameful for a Spartan warrior to lose his shield in battle, Spartan mothers told their sons only to come home with their shields or carried, dead, on them. The Swiss mercenaries who fought under an elected leader in early modern Europe or the Sioux warriors who hurled themselves against American troops in the nineteenth century were distant in time and space, but they too had grown up to endure hardship and be unflinching in the face of death, and they too heard stories of great deeds in the past.

In the classical world the Romans had a culture of war in which fighting and facing death bravely were venerated and it also became a model for later generations. As Josephus, the first-century-A.D. Jewish historian, commented of the Romans, "They seem to have been born with weapons in their hands . . . " In the early Roman Republic male citizens were liable for sixteen years of military service and could not hold office until they had done at least ten. Even in imperial Rome, when more of the fighting was done by mercenaries or Rome's foreign allies, military symbols and language permeated Roman society. The civil service was run on military lines complete with uniforms. When they died, well-to-do Romans often chose sarcophagi with battle scenes. Rome would come to a standstill, often for several days, as victorious generals celebrated their triumphs. Crowds gathered for the spectacle—the marching soldiers, the trumpets blaring, the wagons groaning under the loot, the captured enemies and of course the triumphant general—and the free banquets. In the Forum marble panels showed the names of everyone who had ever earned a triumph, starting with the legendary Romulus, founder of Rome.

Prussia, the powerful German state that grew, improbably, out of a disjointed collection of territories, is often called the Sparta of the North. It survived and flourished because it had an efficient army and a militarized society. Prussia, said a wit, was not a country that happened to have an army but an army that had a country. And that army was sustained by the Junker class of landowners and their military culture. Junkers were meant to be brave, God-fearing and ready to serve the king. The most respectable career was that of soldier; state bureaucrat or jurist came some way behind. Junker children, girls as well, were brought up to be tough and bear pain uncomplainingly. One woman from such a family, who later became a distinguished journalist in Germany after the Second World War, remembers having a broken arm as a child that no one noticed for several weeks partly because it had not occurred to her to mention it. A friend of mine from university who grew up on their family estate in East Prussia during the Second World War once told me of how he and his little male cousins were taught by their grandmother to use their knives and forks in either hand because, as she said, they were going to be soldiers when they grew up and might well lose an arm. Yet they would still be expected to eat politely. The Anglo-Irish upper classes, as Molly Keane describes them so well in her novels, were similar, at least in their physical bravery and willingness to face death. The British army drew a disproportionate number of officers from among them.

By contrast, classical China produced many great generals, fought many wars and conquered many peoples but did not elevate military values above civilian. (It helped, perhaps, that the scholars rather than the military wrote the histories.) Fighting was not held up as something admirable but rather as the result of a breakdown in order and propriety. There is no equivalent of the *Iliad* in Chinese literature and the heroes held up for the young to emulate were the great bureaucrats and wise rulers who maintained the peace. Early on Chinese thinkers such as Confucius and the great strategist Sunzi (also known in the transliteration Sun Tzu) stressed that the state's authority rested on its virtue as well as on its ability to use force. And for Sunzi, the greatest general was the one who could win a war, through maneuver or trickery, without fighting a battle. Prestige in Chinese society came rather from being a scholar, poet or painter; and from the Tang dynasty onward the examination system to enter the imperial civil service was the favored path for fame and prestige. Successful generals were sometimes awarded a scholar's rank and gown as a mark of particular favor where many European societies would have given military decorations to meritorious civilians. Societies' values can change over time, of course. Swedish soldiers were once the terror of Europe when now we associate Sweden with the Nobel Peace Prize or international mediation. Steven Pinker has argued that much of the West has, at least since the eighteenth century, moved away from accepting violence as natural or desirable.

Cultures that admire war tend, not surprisingly, to disparage enemies who do not share the same values and virtues. Perhaps they also despise in their enemies the things they fear might be in themselves. The Romans, like the British when they had their empire, could admire the bravery of opponents but saw them as undisciplined and uncivilized and, for the Romans the mark of inferiority, not good at making war. When the Greeks fought the Persians and the Romans the Carthaginians, both dismissed their enemies as lazy and pleasure-loving, in part because they lived in hot, enervating climates. The Greeks found the Persians to be servile and overemotional as well. Africans, so the Romans believed, did not have much blood in their veins because of the heat and so were cowards, afraid of getting wounded. The Carthaginians, a particular bugbear, were greedy and liars; the men were unmanly because they wore loose robes and the women were amoral seductresses. The British developed similar stereotypes in India. They saw the Bengalis, in a telling choice of words, as effeminate. By contrast the British admired the "martial races";

peoples such as the Gurkhas, Pathans or Coorgs who lived in
cooler climates and were said to have the right military qualities
as a result. By the time of the First World War, the descendants
of the British who had settled in Australia, Canada or New Zealand were held to be tougher and more brutal than their cousins
in Britain, thanks to their geography. When the "less civilized"
and therefore the less adept at war won victories, these had to be
written off as mistakes. When a Maori force defeated a British
one in the wars in New Zealand in the mid-nineteenth century,
The Times of London was quick with an explanation: "just as at
chess a bad and reckless player is sometimes more formidable
than a master of the game."

How groups of humans contemplate and plan for wars is also
affected by their culture, including geography. Island nations or
those with long coasts have understood and invested heavily in
sea power. In the case of Britain, its navy—tellingly called the
Senior Service—has absorbed more resources and had much
greater prestige over the centuries than its army. While paintings,
poems, films and histories memorialize the great naval battles—
Salamis, Lepanto, Trafalgar, Midway—when one navy destroyed
another, the main strategic purpose of navies is to control the seas,
and the highways that crisscross them, and prevent their enemies
from doing so. Even today land communications are vulnerable to
disruption, either man-made or natural; how much more so in the
past before surfaced roads and railways? Ever since humans began
to build floating craft, water has been the most reliable way of
moving people and material. Navies exist to protect their nations,
their coasts, people and shipping, and to project their power
abroad. By landing troops on enemy coasts, acting as floating gun
and aircraft platforms in more recent times to bring firepower to
bear on land targets, or destroying enemy capacity to wage war,
whether by sinking or seizing enemy and sometimes neutral shipping or blockading ports so that needed resources, including soldiers, cannot move in or out, a powerful navy can make it difficult,

even impossible, for its enemy to wage war on land or at sea. "We destroy the national life afloat," said the leading British naval theorist Julian Corbett, who taught generations of officers before the First World War, "and therefore check the vitality of that life ashore, as far as one is dependent on the other."

Athens's great advantage over Sparta in the fifth century B.C. was that it controlled virtually every port in the Aegean and its fleet was strong and large enough to prevent enemy ships traversing the seas. The Spartans recognized this and turned to the Persians for support in building their navy, but it was only when the Athenians wasted many of their ships and men in their expedition to Sicily between 415 and 413 B.C. that the advantage at sea and in the war started to shift to the Spartans. Napoleon was supreme on the Continent but he never managed to defeat the British navy. As a result the British were able to send supplies and reinforcements to their allies and damage the French economy by sinking French shipping and blockading French ports. In the First World War the British navy successfully enforced a naval blockade on Germany which included interdicting goods which the British deemed necessary for the German war effort even if these were carried on neutral ships. While the impact of the blockade is still debated, senior German officers blamed it for their defeat. "We were in the end defeated by sea power," said Erich Raeder, who headed the German navy from 1928 to 1943, "which deprived us of our food and raw materials, and slowly throttled by the blockade."

The United States is not an island but for much of its history it was protected on either side by two great oceans and had as neighbors the much weaker Canada and Mexico. As a result detachment, even isolation, from the rest of the world and limited land forces made sense. German military planning in the twentieth century, by contrast, was fixated on the possibility of a two-front war opened up by having a hostile France in the west and Russia, later the Soviet Union, in the east. Israel too for much of its short history has lived with the fear of being surrounded by enemies. In the lead-up to the Second World War Britain could invest heavily in long-range bombers to be launched against Germany's infrastructure and cities from the relative safety of its islands, but the Germans had to think of how to support their ground troops against their opponents. As a result Germany favored short-range planes capable of bombing and strafing the enemy forces rather than longer-range ones, something that stood it in good stead in the rapid, blitzkrieg opening stages of the Second World War.

The experience of previous wars can shape attitudes as well as planning. The horrors of the Thirty Years War of the seventeenth century may have influenced the Europeans in the eighteenth to wage war more sparingly and treat civilians more gently. Religion, which had produced such cruelties earlier, no longer had the same motivating power. In addition, the cost of training a soldier was now considerable, so generals were more careful about risking their men. After the First World War the French decided that they could not afford another such bloodletting (France lost the highest proportion of men of military age of any belligerent except Serbia) and so France developed a defensive strategy expressed in the great engineering works of the Maginot Line. And in both France and Britain a strong desire to avoid casualties fed into their appeasement of the dictators in the 1930s.

With the examples of the Greek defeats of the Persians or the Battle of Cannae in the Punic Wars in mind, much but not all of Western strategy over the centuries has revolved around the search for the decisive military victory which will oblige the enemy to surrender. Cannae when Hannibal defeated the Romans is a favorite example—but it is easy to misread its significance. Yes, Hannibal won the battle in a dazzling encircling maneuver, but Carthage lost the war because in the end Rome outlasted it. And the price Carthage paid was heavy indeed: the Romans leveled its cities and sowed its fields with salt. Memories of the Battle of Trafalgar, when Nelson destroyed the combined French and Spanish fleets in 1805, haunted British naval strategy for decades, and the idea that the proper role of a navy was to seek out and destroy the enemy fleet was a key part of the influential naval doctrines of the American theorist Admiral Alfred Mahan. When the Japanese drew the United States into the Battle of Midway in 1942—which Japan lost at great cost—they were trying to replicate their great victory over the Russians in the Straits of Tsushima in 1905.

Napoleon continued to search for the decisive battle which would confirm his hold over Europe until he was finally defeated at Waterloo. Even if Napoleon had won on that battlefield, he could not have sustained the war because the allies had worn France down. In 1914 the Germany military devised their Schlieffen Plan to defeat French forces in a series of battles and encircle Paris within forty days. At that point—and the German civilian leadership went meekly along with the plans—France was supposed to capitulate even though that had not happened in 1870, when the French had fought on even after the great German victory at Sedan. One of the few German generals to criticize the Schlieffen Plan said, "You cannot carry away the armed strength of a Great Power like a cat in a bag."

In the sixth century B.C. Sunzi argued that it was better to conquer others with a minimum of bloodshed: "Preserving their army is best, destroying their army second best." And successive dynasties in China successfully kept the nomadic peoples along their northern borders at bay through a combination of walls and bribes, with armed force as a last resort. After their stunning defeat in the First Afghan War in the nineteenth century the British found a similar approach worked well with Afghanistan. Moreover, war has often been won through attrition, cutting enemy supplies as the British have done repeatedly with their navy, harassing enemy forces while avoiding battle as the Spanish irregular forces did when Napoleon invaded Spain, or denying invaders sustenance through a scorched-earth policy as the Russians did in the Napoleonic Wars and again in the twentieth century in the face of Germany's invasions. In the First World War military planners on both sides counted on decisive battles; what they got instead was a long slog as each side tried to grind down the other to the point of collapse.

For all its fascination with decisive battles, the West also has a strong tradition and experience of defensive wars and of using natural obstacles—the Swiss mountains or the waterways in the Netherlands—walls such as Hadrian's or castles and fortresses to exhaust and defeat their enemies. The Roman general Fabius Maximus was sent to challenge Hannibal in the Second Punic War but chose to avoid battle and rather wear the Carthaginian forces down through picking off isolated parties of their soldiers and attacking their supply lines. In the eighteenth century the great commander Maurice de Saxe was famous for avoiding battle as much as for fighting: for example, in 1741 he captured Prague at night before the garrison was aware of what was happening. One of Napoleon's greatest and cheapest victories came when he outmaneuvered and captured an entire Austrian army of some 50,000 to 60,000 soldiers at Ulm in 1805 with tiny French losses.

His campaigns have been studied, as he studied those before him, in an attempt to find the formula for success in war. War is such an important business, its consequences potentially so momentous, that some of the greatest thinkers in different cultures have devoted themselves to trying to work out infallible prescriptions for success. The Romans studied the Greek wars and Renaissance Europe rediscovered both the Greeks and the Romans, just as military colleges today still study the great battles of the past. The manual by the fifth-century-A.D. Roman bureaucrat Vegetius, which drew on earlier work by great Roman generals such as Julius Caesar and was full of advice about such things as leadership, drill and tactics, is now largely forgotten, but it was the most widely read military treatise in the West until Clausewitz's

On War displaced it in the nineteenth century. Machiavelli, who studied Vegetius with care and who himself wrote at length on war, approved of consulting past examples: "The prince should read history, studying the actions of eminent men to see how they conducted themselves during war and to discover the reasons for their victories or defeats, so that he can avoid the latter and imitate the former." Ransacking the past in search of the key rules that determine success or failure in war has produced useful advice and less useful lists. In the last part of the nineteenth century French experts spent time and energy disagreeing over whether there were twenty-four or forty-one rules.

In the famous Chinese treatise *The Art of War*, Sunzi laid down precepts which succeeding generations studied carefully, among them the famous "Know the enemy and know yourself, and you can fight a hundred battles with no danger of defeat" and "He will win who knows when to fight and when not to fight." He also had specific advice, with lists of key factors, situations or types of actions, on the various phases of war, from making the plans to choosing the right terrain to fight. From the Qin Emperor to Mao Zedong, *The Art of War* has provided leaders throughout China and Asia with guidelines for how to win a war. General Vo Nguyen Giap, the architect of Vietnam's victories against the French in the 1950s and the Americans a decade later, was an admirer, as are the Western businesspeople who have flocked to buy *The Complete Sun Tzu for Business Success: Use the Classic Rules of The Art of War to Win the Battle for Customers and Conquer the Competition* or *The Art of War for Women: Sun Tzu's Ancient Strategies and Wisdom for Winning at Work*. Perhaps they like his assertion that "All warfare is based on deception" or enjoy his passages on the importance of the strong leader for victory, and it must help that *The Art of War* itself is short and consists of pithy maxims.

Even the strongest and most skilled of leaders can only work with the tools and resources they are given, and what those are

depends on their societies and their culture. Social and technological change are so intertwined that it is impossible to say which
drives the other, but some societies encourage invention and innovation while others adopt new weapons or techniques slowly or
not at all. The scientific and technological revolutions in early
modern Europe helped to give it, and later the larger West, an
advantage over much of the rest of the world which is only just
ebbing. India, China and the Ottoman Empire were all as rich as
Europe in the sixteenth century and possessed advanced technologies, from printing to gunpowder. Yet they were not able to
build on what they already knew. Historians continue to argue
about why this is so but agree that its growing technological edge
made it possible for Europe to reach out and conquer much of the
rest of the world.

How much of a difference technology makes depends on how
it is used—or whether it is used at all. The British first tried out
the tanks they had developed during the First World War as a
sort of moving gun platform supporting the infantry attacks. It
took them a while to realize that tanks could go ahead of soldiers
to punch holes in the enemy lines. A Greek invented a steam
turbine in the first century A.D. It made an amusing toy but its use
never went further. Why bother to build steam-powered machines when there was lots of cheap labor, including slaves? Some
inventions were used for a time then abandoned. Greek fire, a
terrifying early precursor of napalm which was squirted out of a
tube and burned on the surface of water, was first used by the
Byzantine Empire in the seventh century A.D. but it had disappeared by the thirteenth century, its secret apparently so well
guarded that it had eventually been lost.

Technology in war has been and still is a race between the new
devices or inventions and ways of dealing with them. Armor developed in the ancient world as a riposte to metal-tipped spears,
swords and arrows. Societies—notably the Greeks and the Romans in Europe—gradually developed foot soldiers and fortifica-

tions as a response to horse-borne warriors, but the pendulum was to swing back and forth between cavalry and infantry until the nineteenth century. For a time warriors in chariots carried all before them until armies worked out how to use archers and foot soldiers against them. The machine gun and the repeating rifle forced the world's armies on to the defensive at the start of the twentieth century until new technologies—the tank, the airplane, poison gas—and new tactics gave the edge to the offensive again. Today states are scrambling to find ways to deal with developing threats such as cyberwar.

One generation can forget what an earlier one learned through painful experience in order to counter new technology and has to reinvent counter-technologies and tactics. Mounted warriors armed with spears or bows overwhelmed those on foot when they first appeared, but gradually peoples such as the ancient Greeks learned to deal with them with phalanxes of well-disciplined infantry which, packed several rows deep and bristling with spears, formed lethal obstacles against which horses and riders dashed themselves in vain. Many centuries later European armies had to learn all over again how to use similar formations of foot soldiers and archers against knights in armor. The Romans were masters at building roads, some 55,000 miles of them around the Mediterranean (many of which are still there today). Their successors in Europe and Asia Minor continued to use them even as they slowly crumbled and weeds grew in the cracks, but they lost for centuries the knowledge and ability to build for themselves. Archimedes, the great Greek mathematician, devised a super-catapult which threw 1,800-pound boulders at Roman galleys, but it had no imitators in the following centuries. The Romans also built, and knocked down, fortresses. Europeans had to learn for themselves how to do this in the Middle Ages. After their unhappy experience in Vietnam the American military decided that it would never fight wars of counterinsurgency again. The army dropped the study of guerrilla war and countermeasures from its curriculum and the standard book on the subject went out of print. With Afghanistan and Iraq the Americans had to start all over again.

Until recently changes in technology and war moved slowly and in fits and starts. On land, armor, swords, spears and bows and arrows remained the key weapons until the early modern age, although tactics changed from time to time and from society to society. Alexander the Great wore a suit of armor that was reputed to date to the Trojan Wars centuries before, and the weapons the Greeks and the Romans used would have been familiar to soldiers in Europe's Middle Ages or in classical India and China. For centuries, from the Greeks to the Venetians, sea power depended on galleys powered by rowers.

In the history of war and society we single out three main innovations to describe significant changes before 1800: the introduction of metal, when humans abandoned stone weapons for ones made from bronze and iron; the domestication of the horse, which gave warriors greater mobility and speed; and the introduction of gunpowder, which transformed war on land and at sea. (Since other parts of the world, such as the Americas, did not have horses until the Europeans brought them in the sixteenth century and some parts of the world, such as Australia, never developed metal weapons, not all human societies have experienced change at the same time.) In each case, of course, many other things were happening both to technology and to society. Metal weapons were only a part of the story: societies had to develop the soldiers and the infrastructures to make use of them. Horses were more formidable when the wheel enabled them to pull chariots or later on when they could carry armed warriors. The introduction of gunpowder too was accompanied by other important developments: in metallurgy, for example, so that guns did not explode when they were fired, or in the design and navigation of ships, so that they could make use of the new cannon.

The earliest weapons, which changed very little over the first millennia of human history, were spears, knives, and bows and arrows tipped with hard flint that were used for hunting animals as well as fellow humans. Gradually humans began making implements whose only purpose was to kill each other. While different societies introduced refinements in design, making specialized spears for stabbing, for example, and others for throwing, the basic designs remained very much the same from era to era and place to place. The materials, however, gradually changed and war entered a new and more lethal stage. At some point, perhaps as early as the second millennium B.C., some societies worked out how to make composite bows rather than simple wooden ones. Archers could now fire their arrows with more force and farther. While it happened at different times in different societies—and in some not at all—an even more significant step forward in the lethality of war came with the appearance of metal weapons. The first ones, in bronze, appeared sometime in the Middle East in the fourth millennium B.C. (and somewhat later in India and China and Europe). Bronze, which was becoming scarce, eventually gave way to the tougher iron in the second millennium B.C. In time it was replaced by the even more effective steel.

The horse was as important for war and human society as the introduction of metal and has remained so up until nearly the present. (The last cavalry charge may have been in Afghanistan in 2001.) Horses made possible new means of communication and of moving goods and peoples about—and of making war, whether with war chariots or with mounted archers and swordsmen—and so the horse increased the reach and power of armies and governments. By the second millennium B.C. small domesticated horses capable of pulling carts were spreading westward from Central Asia. The new technology of the horse-drawn chariot carrying its warriors armed with metal weapons and composite bows proved to give such an advantage to whoever had them that states were obliged to invest in them or go under, as many did. Assyria and Egypt were able to put thousands of chariots into the field.

Horses, or rather their effective use, made possible the emergence of strong states with professional warrior classes, which in the hands of strong rulers led to the further expansion of their empires.

Quite suddenly, around 1200 B.C., chariots lost their edge as tools of war, perhaps, as some historians speculate, because foot soldiers now had new, more formidable iron weapons or possibly because mounted fighters from the steppes to the north and east could outmaneuver the chariots. Over the next centuries, to the fall of Rome in the West, war and society, at least in Eurasia, was marked by the dominance of foot soldiers, with cavalry in a supporting role. The Greeks and the Romans won their great victories using foot soldiers, but when Rome began to fall apart in the fourth century A.D. its disciplined legions slowly vanished and the man on horseback, whether raiders from outside such as the Huns or local strongmen, grew in power. A small but crucial innovation—the stirrup attached to the saddle, which allowed riders to rest their legs—greatly enhanced the power of the mounted warrior. Try sitting bareback on a horse without stirrups, as the early warriors did (or on a high stool without rungs), and you will know how tired your legs get. And there is a limit to how much weight including armor you can carry. The development of the stirrup made it possible, first in India and China and then in Europe by the eighth century A.D., to have the mounted knights in their elaborate suits of armor so familiar to us from paintings, novels and films. Yet they too were to pass from the scene as infantry regained its power.

Culture, technology and war are so interdependent that it is hard to say which drives which. War pushes ahead the development of technology but it also adapts what is already there. The ancient world used levers for their wine and olive presses; the Romans adapted those to hurl stones against enemy soldiers, ships and fortifications. In the Middle Ages craftsmen learned how to make high-quality metal for casting church bells and that then helped in the making of better guns. In the nineteenth century the Swedish chemist and businessman Alfred Nobel invented dynamite for use in mining; it was rapidly adapted to produce a whole range of increasingly effective guns. Farmers in America used barbed wire to pen in their cattle; strung out in front of the trenches in the First World War, it contributed greatly to the power of the defense. The tank incorporated the caterpillar treads which had been developed for tractors. Albert Einstein and his fellow physicists had worked out the theory of how to split the atom, proving on paper that doing so would release a huge surge of energy, but no way of finally testing that hypothesis existed until the Second World War. In their search for victory in the monumental struggle against their enemies, the British and, in particular, the Americans found the resources to refine the necessary uranium and to build and test the first successful bomb. The Manhattan Project, it is estimated, cost over $20 billion in today's dollars, not far short of what the United States spent on all its small arms over the duration of the war.

How technology is used depends in part on the values and organization of society, which themselves change over time. Our distant hunter-forager ancestors, as far as we can tell from the scanty historical record and by using evidence from direct observations of similar societies, lived and fought as equals without much organization. The stronger and more elaborate social and political organization which came with agriculture brought a more disciplined form of war, with specialized equipment, training, a hierarchy of leaders and fortifications. By the eighth millennium b.c. the first known defensive walls had been built at Jericho. By the third millennium b.c. soldiers in early civilizations such as Sumer and Ur were fighting with bronze-tipped weapons in highly organized formations.

The strong state which centralizes authority in a single pair or a few pairs of hands and then uses that to acquire more power, territory and loot goes back deep into the past. At its height in the seventh century B.C. the Assyrian empire stretched from present-day Sudan into Turkey and from the Mediterranean to Iran. Its rulers claimed their power came from the gods because of their success in war. Byron was not being fanciful when he wrote, "The Assyrian came down like the wolf on the fold." The Assyrian state organized and was organized around fighting. Its standing armies had specialized units, from infantry to archers to cavalry. They could move quickly thanks to a network of roads and were sustained by a series of depots established throughout the empire. That took another army of bureaucrats to make sure that the state armories produced the necessary equipment, the depots were stocked and the men and their animals were fed. The Romans are remembered for their roads and ports, but those underpinned the superb logistics which got their troops with their equipment to where they needed to be. At the siege of Masada in A.D. 73 the Romans kept some 15,000 men in a waterless desert for weeks.

In such hierarchical societies war was and still is the responsibility and prerogative of the upper classes or a single ruler such as Louis XIV or Augustus Caesar. In Shakespeare's *Henry V* the common soldiers talking before the Battle of Agincourt know that the war is the king's business; "for we know enough," says one, "if we know we are the king's subjects: if his cause be wrong, our obedience to the king wipes the crime of it out of us." There is another equally ancient model, however, for societies to decide on war. In the Greek city-states the citizens voted on whether or not to go to war and in the Roman Republic the Senate made the decision. It was not what we would understand as a democratic decision but it did involve at least some citizen participation. Conversely, citizens were meant to come to the defense of their state. In classical Greece, from the sixth century B.C. onward, well-to-do farmers or artisans belonging to one of the highly organized city-states were, as men of means, obliged to fight in its defense and indeed they expected to. Thessaly, which lagged behind the rest of Greece in political development, was the exception: there politics was dominated by a feudal aristocracy which preferred to fight on horseback rather than foot. The typical city-state in the rest of Greece, the *polis,* was a community, at least for free men, which inspired passionate loyalty. For at least three centuries Greek warfare mainly involved two bodies of men, in bronze armor, armed with spears and swords, marching toward each other in a tight formation, the phalanx. The Greeks could not have achieved that level of coordination without much practice and training (something the Persians dismissed contemptuously as dancing and gymnastics) but, equally important, without the discipline and social bonds that bound the men together. The soldiers, the hoplites, fought for their neighbors as much as for themselves. In the line each man's shield, carried on his left arm, protected his neighbor. "Men wear their helmets and breastplates for their own needs," went the saying, "but they carry their shields for the men of the line." When opposing Greek forces finally clashed, they entangled themselves in a struggling mass. The side that broke usually took heavier casualties as those fleeing were cut down. Mardonius, the Persian general who led massive invasions of Greece in the fifth century B.C., is said to have complained to his king, Xerxes, that the Greeks fought each other in "the foolish way through sheer perversity and doltishness." The Persians were to learn in the most costly manner just what that Greek way of war could do to an enemy. At the crucial Battle of Marathon in 490 B.C., where the Greeks fought a Persian force of perhaps twice their number, the hoplites outlasted Persian attacks attempting to break their enemy's lines. Herodotus claimed that 6,400 Persians lay dead on the field while the Greeks lost 203 men.

Centuries later knights on horseback were to learn a similar lesson in fighting from the massed infantry of Swiss soldiers who, like the Greek hoplites before them, fought with and for each other as equals. We now think of the Swiss Guards who stand on duty at the Vatican in their multicolored Renaissance uniforms as a charming detail and Switzerland as peaceful and bucolic, home to good chocolate, discreet banks and, as the character Harry Lime in *The Third Man* unkindly says, the cuckoo clock. For 200 years, until a square was finally broken in 1515, the Swiss formations, bristling with pikes and sheltering archers with their deadly crossbows, were the terror of Europe and the key to victory, at least for anyone who could afford to hire them. *"Pas d'argent, pas de Suisse,"* as the saying went.

When strong central government collapses, as it did in the Thirty Years War in Europe in the seventeenth century, Yugoslavia in the 1990s or in Iraq today, power flows downward as well, to those who are strong and ruthless enough to attract followers and maintain themselves by extorting resources. The collapse of the Roman Empire in the West by the fourth century A.D. left a Europe where power increasingly devolved to local strongmen whose wealth and status depended on land and their ability to defend it with armed retainers against their neighbors or invading peoples. Many such private armies increasingly fought on horseback and used armor for both the warrior and the horse. The cost of equipping a mounted knight and the problems of logistics after the collapse of much of the Roman road system kept the forces relatively small. It has been estimated that it took a large prosperous farm of between 300 and 450 acres to equip and sustain a knight. Over time the armor, for both man and horse, became more elaborate and heavier to the point that they rendered both less mobile and so more vulnerable to the new weapons and tactics of the infantry. And like turtles flipped onto their backs, the riders struggled to move if they were thrown to the ground. Some historians have compared medieval knights to the massive battleships of the last century or the aircraft carriers of today; they absorb a lot of resources yet can be destroyed by much cheaper technology.

To keep the loyalty of their forces and to defray the costs, European rulers, whether modest nobles or kings, rewarded them with land, which provided a strong incentive for continued fighting. Charles the Great, Charlemagne, managed to found a large kingdom and dynasty in the seventh century A.D. through a string of victories. He attempted to systematize military service and centralize power in the crown. His richest lords were expected to come with their arms and their retinues when called in return for their land, and at the other end of the scale small landowners were allowed to club together to provide the resources to send one of them to fight. His empire barely survived one generation and broke into pieces, while military and political power continued to lie with the landed aristocracy. In time another turn toward the power of foot soldiers was to doom them as a class.

The emergence of strong city-states, dominated by merchants, from the twelfth century onward and the growth of centralized royal power, both developments that depended in part on military strength, challenged the knights politically. Equally important, more disciplined infantry appeared, such as the Swiss mercenaries, to challenge them militarily. The Swiss, said the Emperor Charles V, were "ill-conditioned, rough and bad peasant-folk, in whom there is found no virtue, no noble blood, and no moderation." They were also deadly for two centuries. If you want to see what their weapons looked like, go to the Tower of London and, while you admire the Yeomen of the Guard in their wonderful scarlet and gold uniforms, take a closer look at their elegant long halberds, which seem to be a curious mix of spear, axe and hook. Wielded in battle, the halberd's point rammed into knights and their horses, the axe could smash heads in and the hooks dragged riders from their horses to make finishing them off on the ground easier.

Even before gunpowder and guns appeared in Europe new and improved weapons and tactics were starting to nullify the advantages of armor, on both men and horses. Many earlier cultures—China and India, ancient Greece and possibly Rome—had developed crossbows which could be drawn ahead of time and were easy to aim and fire. (Their disadvantage was that they took time to reload, leaving the side that fired first vulnerable.) Europeans had rediscovered crossbows by the twelfth century and kept improving them for the next 200 years. The Italians, who also hired themselves out as mercenaries, became famous for their accuracy.

Although time was running out for horse-borne warriors, they remained formidable in the right circumstances. In the thirteenth century Genghis Khan welded quarreling Mongol tribes together into a highly centralized state which proved, for a time, to be an unstoppable military force, sweeping away regimes in China and Persia. Mongol warriors were highly mobile and, when they were challenged by forces from more settled empires, withdrew into the vast spaces of Central Asia. One of the secrets of their success may have been another simple piece of technology like the stirrup. Mongol warriors wore silk undershirts, so that if they were hit by an arrow the silk wrapped around its head. It was not only easier to get the arrow out; the risk of infection, until the modern age a greater killer of soldiers than death in battle, was much less. Under Genghis's successors his warriors stormed westward through Central Asia and Russia to the shores of the Black Sea, carrying all before them and leaving a trail of death and ruin. No force could stand against them and by 1241 they were probing into Hungary, Poland and present-day Romania and Austria. It looked as though much of what was a weak and divided Europe would become part of their empire—and think what a different history it would have had—when the Mongols suddenly stopped and withdrew in 1242. It may be because word had come that, thousands of miles to the east, the Great Khan had died, but historians have recently speculated that poor weather had turned the ground marshy and ruined the fodder for the Mongol horses.

On the other edge of Europe, in the countryside of Wales, another formidable weapon against men and horses was being perfected. The English kings began to appreciate the possibilities of the Welsh longbow in their twelfth-century wars in Wales when Welsh archers with six-foot bows, taller than they were, fired arrows that could go through layers of chain mail, wooden saddles and flesh. In 1346, during the Hundred Years War between the French and the English, Edward III brought his Welsh archers to France. At Crécy a much weaker English force turned to fight the pursuing French. The French had three times as many mounted soldiers, considered the finest cavalry in Europe, 6,000 Genoese crossbowmen and 20,000 foot soldiers against 5,000. The English, however, had 11,000 archers armed with longbows. The Genoese fired first but did not inflict much damage on the English army. As the Genoese scrambled to reload, French knights, impatient for glory, started to trample them from behind, while the English archers launched a devastating fire. As one witness said, "Every arrow told on horse or man, piercing head, or arm, or leg among the riders and sending the horses mad." The French knights charged again and again, while the Welsh archers steadily reloaded and fired. By nightfall the ground was covered with dead and dying horses and men. The French lost over 1,500 knights and 10,000 who were "not of gentle blood." The English losses were two knights, forty "others" and some "few dozen" Welsh. The unchallenged dominance of knights on the battlefield started to die there too.

Further nails in their coffin were already appearing with the early infantry guns and the siege cannon, which could blast holes in the tall, slender walls of feudal fortresses. As powerful rulers built up their own armies, armed with the new weapons, the private armies and domains of the knights disappeared, to be succeeded by the central absolutist state. Once governments had a monopoly on force and workable institutions, they could extract more resources from society, whether men or the means to arm and keep them. And, in an early arms race, the growth of your neighbors' armed forces meant that you had to keep up or risk being conquered. Armies were going to increase dramatically in size, ten times between 1500 and 1700 alone. That was a reflection of and also a spur to an increase in the powers of government and its control over society.

The three centuries after Crécy saw in Europe a transformation in both war and society and in the relationship between them so great that some historians talk of a "military revolution." Gunpowder, originally developed in China by alchemists looking for the secret of eternal life, was central to this, much as metal or the horse had been to earlier changes in war. The advances in European science helped to improve the efficacy and reliability of gunpowder and the guns that used it. The medieval forts fell like so many sandcastles before the new cannon until, eventually, Europeans learned to build forts with thick, low walls and crisscrossing fields of fire to hold off attacking forces. Improvements in metallurgy and design brought better and lighter guns; the cumbersome arquebus gave way to the lighter musket.

Initially muskets were nearly as dangerous for the soldier, and anyone near him, as they were for the enemy, because the piece of smoldering cord he carried to light the small gunpowder charge often blew up his whole supply. The early musket was also highly unreliable and could only get off one shot per minute, as soldiers painstakingly loaded and fired. Someone, it is not recorded who, got the clever idea of adapting firelighting flints, which caused sparks when they were struck against steel, to muskets. By the second half of the seventeenth century most European armies were going over to the new improved musket. In another one of those simple discoveries that can make a huge difference, a Swedish ironmaster in the seventeenth century found that he could halve the length of a cannon's barrel without making it less effective. So smaller, lighter cannon mounted on horse-drawn carriages brought artillery to the battlefields.

There was much more to the changes in European war than that. It took decades for soldiers and their officers to accept and learn how to use the new technology (and their governments to want to pay for it), and without changes in attitudes and organization the gunpowder revolution in warfare might not have occurred or been so far-reaching in its consequences. At first armies rejected the new lighter cannon, partly because the early versions had an unfortunate propensity to explode but also because they were not useful for siege warfare, which, until the later part of the eighteenth century, was seen as the proper target for artillery. Using muskets brought the challenge of creating soldiers who could stand their ground while the enemy came into range. Firing too soon—before you could see "the whites of their eyes," as the saying had it—meant that the shot, which at best could hit a target about fifty yards away, did little harm. As the side that had fired prematurely scrambled to reload (it took nearly fifty separate motions to load and fire), the men, who had to stand up in the process, became an easy target for shots or cavalry attack from the other side.

The Dutch, who produced so much in their golden age of the seventeenth century, from Rembrandt to microscopes, also were innovators in war. Maurice of Nassau, who became their head of state in 1585, freed the northern Dutch provinces from Spanish rule in part because he built such an effective fighting force. He organized his forces on the battlefield in ranks, up to ten of them, and pioneered an elaborate form of battlefield movement where, as the first rank fired, it wheeled to the back, allowing the next ones to fire and wheel in sequence. The rate of fire was much greater if, and it was a major if, the troops could stand firm when ordered and move in unison on command. Without discipline, often savage discipline, and repeated drills so that movement and following orders became second nature even in battle, soldiers could not have used the new weapons effectively. The old-style armies, where the ruler hired mercenaries or got their local magnates to raise forces which then tended to disperse at the end of a campaign, were not the right sort of material for the new training and tactics. It was a strong incentive for governments to have their own armies, and, of course, in time that increased their power.

Louis XIV was passionate about drill, which he saw as the key to winning battles, and he took a personal interest in military training and maneuvers. In his spare time he often occupied himself by drilling soldiers. "I continue to drill carefully," he said, "the troops which are close to my person in order that, by my example, the other individual military chiefs will learn to take the same care with those that are under their command." It took, one expert at the time estimated, five or six years to make a good regiment of trained infantry. The great Swedish military leader Gustavus Adolphus, who built on Maurice's work, introduced what came to be known as Swedish discipline: compulsory prayers, executions for serious offenses such as plundering, or decimation for regiments that ran away in battle. Thanks to the introduction of printing, illustrated drill manuals spread the new practices across Europe. And in yet another example of how war affects the civilian world, movements in dancing, also spread through illustrated manuals, became both more economical and more stylized. Military historians have argued that it was the tight and effective organization of the European armies as much as their weapons that made them so deadly in their wars with the peoples of Asia or Africa. And with their new sailing ships the Europeans had the means to reach out around the globe.

War at sea was also changing dramatically as wind power replaced human power. The Battle of Lepanto in 1571 between the Holy League, a coalition of Christian states, and the Ottoman Empire was the last major sea battle fought with galleys. The early sailing ships were primitive and difficult to maneuver, but the new technology of a sternpost rudder made steering easier. The compass, which came from China sometime in the thirteenth century, and much later the sextant and the maritime chronometer, which made it possible for navigators to know exactly where they were and where they were headed, not only made navigation much easier and more reliable but extended the reach of Europe's navies. Finally, an adaptation from trading vessels, the watertight port which could be closed for sailing and opened for such purposes as loading cargo, made it possible to put cannon lower in the vessel. (The danger in putting cannon well above the waterline had always been that the ships could easily turn turtle and sometimes did.) The result was that where navies had once maneuvered as close as possible to ram and grapple with each other they now waged battle with their cannon from a distance.

The outlines of much of what we now think of as standard military organization and practice were set in Europe between the sixteenth and eighteenth centuries, whether it was the division of land forces into cavalry, infantry and artillery or the establishment of special schools for officers, both military and naval. The military were becoming more professional. Soldiers lived in barracks and wore uniforms and, since they were financed by the crown, soldiers and sailors were seen as employees of the monarch or the state, not the private property of their officers, as in the past. At sea the privateers—bandits licensed by governments—disappeared as state navies took their place, while mercenaries dwindled in importance although they have never entirely disappeared. In return governments took on more responsibility for their military, feeding and housing them and, crucially, paying them regularly. In 1676 the French government completed a hospital, Les Invalides, for its soldiers and in 1690 the British followed with the Royal Hospital in Chelsea.

The eighteenth century saw its share of wars in Europe, but these were markedly less violent and unrestrained than the wars of the previous century, where the toxic admixture of religion and social revolution had produced slaughter on the battlefields and atrocities against innocent civilians. In the Age of Enlightenment, as superstition and religion appeared to be giving way before science and reason, Europeans had a brief spell of hope that humanity, or at least the European part of it, was getting more peaceable and learning to control its passions. Observers believed that war was getting less cruel; Emeric de Vattel, one of the influential early theorists of international law, remarked that "the Nations of Europe almost always carry on war with great forbearance and generosity." War, or so it was hoped, was becoming civilized, fought between professionals and with proper respect for the rules of war. By contrast with what was to come or had happened during the wars of religion, eighteenth-century wars were "cabinet" ones, undertaken for clear and limited goals, relatively easy to stop and neatly concluded with an agreement or treaty.

Which technologies are adopted and when, will also depend on a number of things: the need for the technology, the transmission of knowledge and the openness of a particular society to change. The Chinese developed gunpowder and guns early on, before Europe, and until the fifteenth century were in the lead. After that they fell behind, probably because they were largely fighting along their northern frontiers and guns, which were slow to load and, in the case of cannon, hard to move, were not much help against mounted warriors. Peoples will usually adopt new technologies when they see an advantage in them. Genghis Khan depended on his mounted warriors but he also learned how to use gunpowder and siege engines as he moved to attack cities. In the Meiji Restoration, which started in 1868, the Japanese used and improved upon Western techniques to transform their country into a modern industrial and military power. When horses were introduced into the Americas by the Spanish in the sixteenth century, they were adopted so enthusiastically by the indigenous peoples that we now invariably picture the peoples of the Plains, such as the Blackfoot, the Sioux or the Comanche, as hunting and fighting on horseback and using that other new device, the gun.

Societies or some of their members can also resist new technology out of distaste, inertia, nostalgia for the old ways or ethical objections. The air force pilots of today who lament that they are no longer needed in the cockpit have a forerunner in the Spartan leader who witnessed a stone hurled by a catapult bowl over a man and exclaimed, "O Hercules, the valor of man is at an end!" European armies clung to the cavalry long after it became clear that horse and rider could not maneuver on the modern battlefield in the face of withering long-range fire. To officers from the landed classes who had grown up on horseback, the horse had a glamour that the tank or armored car could never have. Machine guns were initially deeply unpopular with many officers when they became standard in armies. According to the first commandant of the British machine-gun school in France, the usual response of British battalion commanders at the start of the First World War to the new weapon was "Take the damn things to a flank and hide them!" When the first ironclads were mooted for the British navy in the first half of the nineteenth century, many naval officers were skeptical as to their value. In 1828, in the early days of steam power, an Admiralty memorandum said, "Their Lordships feel it is their bounden duty to discourage to the utmost of their ability the employment of steam vessels, as they consider that introduction of steam is calculated to strike a fatal blow at the naval supremacy of the Empire." Sail continued to have its defenders against steam power for decades.

The crossbow, said Pope Innocent II, was "hateful to God and unfit for Christians." Later the Church decided that it was all right to use the crossbow against infidels, who were damned in any case. The cumbersome early infantry guns, the arquebus or the musket, were seen as devilish inventions, probably the work of infidels. Inventors of new weapons themselves have sometimes felt shame or dismay at what they have done. The great scholar Roger Bacon may have discovered the secret, already known to the Chinese and the Arabs, of making gunpowder in the middle of the thirteenth century but, if so, he took it to the grave with him. Leonardo da Vinci said of his design for a submarine that he would not reveal the whole, "on account of the evil nature of men, who would practice assassinations at the bottom of the seas by breaking the ships in their lowest parts and sinking them together with the crews who are in them."

The ruling classes in Japan, who at first welcomed guns when Portuguese travelers brought the earliest examples in 1543, turned against the new devices in the following century. Not only had Japan learned how to manufacture guns but it was making improvements to the technology. Yet somehow by the middle of the seventeenth century the Japanese appear to have decided against any further development. Was this a heartening example, relevant still today, of a people voluntarily giving up new and more deadly weapons? Sadly it seems not. From the point of view of the powerful warrior class, the samurai, who had perfected elaborate ways of fighting with high-quality steel swords, guns made their skills useless and so they had little incentive to adopt them. Equally important, however, the government had established order after a period of civil war and guns were simply not needed to maintain peace. Unfortunately for Japan, that meant it had little hope of fighting back when the American commodore William Perry rudely broke its isolation in 1853 with demands that the country open itself to American trade.

The West's use of what was its temporary edge in technology, including guns, armor and steel, enabled it to take over much of the rest of the world before the subjugated peoples learned how to fight back. It also helped, in the case of the Americas, that the Europeans brought new diseases with them. The Spanish adventurers Cortés and Pizarro overthrew great empires in Mexico and Peru, which had millions of subjects and huge armies, with mere handfuls of men. The odds were fantastic but the Spanish had the advantage of the germs they carried, which were already spreading inland, going ahead of them to lay waste the local populations, which had no immunity to such things as smallpox or measles. In addition, the Spanish rode horses against foot soldiers, wore steel armor and carried steel and guns against men armed with bronze and wood and armored with quilted cotton. In his book *Guns, Germs, and Steel,* Jared Diamond has woven together eyewitness accounts of what happened to the Inca when Pizarro, known as the governor, and his 168 Spaniards surprised the emperor and his thousands of supporters:

> The governor then gave the signal to Candia, who began to fire off the guns. At the same time the trumpets were sounded, and the armored Spanish troops, both cavalry and infantry, sallied forth out of their hiding places straight into the mass of unarmed Indians crowding the square, giving the Spanish battle cry, "Santiago!" We had placed rattles on the horses to terrify the Indians. The booming of the guns, the blowing of the trumpets, and the rattles on the horses threw the Indians into panicked confusion. The Spaniards fell upon them and began to cut them to pieces. The Indians were so filled with fear that they climbed on top of one another, formed mounds, and suffocated each other. Since they were unarmed, they were attacked without danger to any Christian. The cavalry rode them down, killing and wounding, and following in pursuit. The infantry made so good an assault on those that remained that in a short time most of them were put to the sword.

The Spanish victory came not just because of their horses and weapons but because they seized the emperor, not only violating the sacred rules of Inca society, but in a rigidly hierarchical order leaving the subjects adrift and leaderless.

It was part of China's tragedy in the First Opium War of 1839–42 that it faced a similar technological and organizational gap. The Chinese sent sailing junks, of designs and with cannon it had used successfully for centuries, against more advanced British sailing ships and weapons and one of the earliest armed steamships, appropriately enough named the *Nemesis.* And that was only at the start of a transformation which was going to underpin a new, more encompassing and more terrible form of war. The nineteenth century's Industrial Revolution, shorthand for far-reaching economic, technological and scientific changes, was making it possible for Western societies and those like the Japanese who, after the old order was overthrown in the Meiji Restoration of 1868, were prepared to learn from their example to produce more and better weapons and to wage war on a much greater scale.

The pace of change and the growing lethality of weapons have gone on accelerating ever since. Think of the flimsy, single-engined, unarmed planes which took to the skies in 1914 at the start of the First World War and compare them to the faster and more powerful ones that had emerged by 1918, capable of firing machine guns and dropping heavy bombs on the enemy. By the end of the Second World War aircraft were flying higher, faster, farther and carrying much greater loads, and the jet engine was starting to replace propellers. When the American bombs fell on Hiroshima and Nagasaki in August 1945, the new and terrifying nuclear age was inaugurated. Today new weapons, from fighter planes to aircraft carriers, are often obsolete by the time they are in service. The world's arsenals are immense: it is estimated that there are over a billion small arms alone in the world and, at the other extreme, nuclear weapons capable of destroying humanity several times over. And serious disarmament measures remain more distant than ever. Yet so many of us, our leaders included, still talk of war as a reasonable and manageable tool.

CHAPTER 4

MODERN WAR

"From this place, and from this day forth,
begins a new era in the history of the world, and you
can all say that you were present at its birth."

—GOETHE

B Y 1792, IN THE THIRD YEAR OF THE FRENCH REVOLUTION,
France was at war with Austria and Prussia, two of Europe's leading conservative powers. The odds did not look at all good for the
French: many of the officers from the old army had fled abroad
and what armed forces remained were in as chaotic a state as
French politics. True, revolutionaries were filling up the ranks, but
they lacked experience, training and discipline, unlike the old-
style armies marching toward them. Late that summer, the Prussian army entered northeast France, seizing several strongholds
and meeting with little resistance. As the Prussians were heading
for Paris, the revolutionaries turned on each other: in their panic,
the government and its supporters in the streets started a search
for traitors at home. The guillotine, invented to provide humane
executions, now came into its own as a tool of oppression. Rather
more sensibly, the government also called for volunteers to defend
France and its revolution.

On September 20, near the village of Valmy, just west of Verdun, the ill-equipped, poorly organized French came face to face
with the enemy. The Prussians were still formidable but they had
already lost some thousands of men to dysentery. Cold rain had

fallen through the night and the fields, as they would be again in the First World War, were sodden and muddy. As day broke the two sides started an exchange of intensive and sustained artillery fire; the Prussians made a couple of forays against the French lines, which held their ground; as dusk was falling the Prussians decided to retreat, which they did in good order. They had suffered around 180 casualties out of some 34,000 soldiers and the French 300 out of 32,000. It was neither a glorious victory nor a defeat.

So why did the poet Goethe, who was with the Prussians, apparently say, "From this place, and from this day forth, begins a new era in the history of the world, and you can all say that you were present at its birth"? Part of the significance of Valmy is that the French, out of necessity, were starting to discover new tactics that alarmed and unsettled their enemies. The French soldiers did not behave like those in other armies; they sang revolutionary songs in the middle of battle, took unnecessary risks and did not seem to know when they were beaten. (At a battle the following year between French revolutionary forces and those of the growing coalition against France, an observer complained about the French style of fighting: "Fifty thousand savage beasts, foaming at the mouth like cannibals, hurl themselves at top speed.") Valmy is important for its symbolism: the defeat of the old-style eighteenth-century professional army by a new citizens' one, whose members were motivated not by fear of their officers but by passionate love for their cause.

Nationalism—the identification of people as part of something called the nation—had erupted into history. In the course of the nineteenth century two further huge changes would join this first one and together make war more violent, deadly and destructive. The Industrial Revolution, which brought enormous changes in the means of production, in science and technology and in the economic potential of societies, was going to transform first Europe and then much of the rest of the world in the century after the Napoleonic Wars. And then, dependent on and influencing the other two, were the broader social, political and intellectual changes, from urbanization to new ideas about human nature. Nationalism was fostered by ideas, by the works of intellectuals, novelists, ethnographers and historians, but it extended its impact downward into society and across Europe and then the rest of the world thanks to mass literacy, cheap books and rapid communications. The Industrial Revolution brought innovation and mass production and also stimulated social change. The middle and working classes grew in size and eventually in power, while the old landed elites saw the sources of their wealth and their influence attenuate. The widening of the franchise and the move toward constitutional government brought the masses into a different relationship with the foreign and military policies of their countries. Where once war and peace had been the business of the few, now these were questions for the many. Nationalism provided the passion for war, the Industrial Revolution the tools and the changes in society the bodies to fight, as well as support from civilians for the war efforts.

Modern war was going to last longer, cost more and demand much of society. In the First World War nearly 70 million men were mobilized into the armed forces of both sides, 40 percent of the male population in France and Germany alone. Think what that meant for their societies; almost everyone would have known someone who had gone to war and mourned those who did not come back. Daily life changed in so many ways, big and small, as consumer goods disappeared from the shops and food and fuel ran short. Taxes increased and factories worked round the clock to provide the tons of food, the millions of boots, the miles of fabric, the mountains of shells, or the lakes of oil. In the Second World War, according to the Stanford historian Walter Scheidel, "the main belligerents manufactured 286,000 tanks, 557,000 combat aircraft, 11,000 major naval vessels, and more than 40 million rifles, among many other armaments." A new term, total war, had to be coined for the two huge global wars of the twentieth century.

In 1812, when Napoleon invaded Russia, he led an army of some 600,000 men; in 1870, when the German Confederation went to war against France, its forces were double that size; in 1914 Germany mobilized over 3 million men against its enemies; and in 1944 Stalin threw 6.5 million men against the Axis powers on the Eastern Front. Modern war was industrial war, producing armies and navies and eventually air forces on a mass scale. While ground forces were still using horses and mules for transportation in the two world wars, it was the train, the steamship and the internal combustion engine that made their scale and reach possible. And while some weapons—for example, bayonets and knives—harked back to an earlier age, the vastly improved guns or the completely new airplanes, submarines, armored vehicles and nuclear weapons represented another epoch in war, just as the introduction of metal weapons, horses or gunpowder had done in their time.

As in the past, technological and tactical advances stimulated a search for their antidote. The range of the standard infantry weapon increased tenfold in the nineteenth century alone and it could be fired more often and faster. Field artillery in 1800 was effective up to about a mile and a half on the battlefield; by the First World War the range was at least eight times that. The Germans built a massive cannon which dropped shells on Paris from sixty-eight miles away. So in response the world's armies developed better fortifications, battlefields strung with barbed wire and ever more elaborate trenches. Wire cutters and shovels became standard infantry equipment. When General Sherman's troops marched through Georgia to force its capitulation in the American Civil War, they threw away their bayonets but kept their shovels. Uniforms changed too. In the battles of the eighteenth and early nineteenth centuries, when the black powder used in the guns created a thick fog over the battlefield, bright uniforms with bold markings made sense for identifying friend or foe. With smokeless gunpowder, adopted by most armies by the last quarter of the nineteenth century, the beautiful red or blue or green coats, the shining buttons and the gold braid, made wonderful targets for the much more accurate and longer-range rifles. And breech-loading meant that soldiers could load and reload lying down, making them much harder to spot. The British learned the lesson the hard way when they marched their redcoats across the dusty South African veldt in the 1899–1902 Boer War (known more today as the South African War). Afrikaner farmers, who tended to be excellent shots, lay on the ground in their dusty-colored work clothes and picked the British off. After the Battle of Colenso in 1899, during the "Black Week" when the British army suffered three severe defeats, one of their generals complained, "I never saw a Boer all day till the battle was over and it was our men who were the victims." The British authorities finally put their troops into khaki. In 1914 the French infantry marched off to the front in their dramatic red trousers. *"Le pantalon rouge, c'est la France!"* cried a war minister and much of the military, while the casualty lists lengthened and lengthened again.

For much of the nineteenth and early twentieth centuries technology gave the defense an edge as improved firepower extended the size of the killing zone through which attacking soldiers had to move. Imagine, as happened in the First World War, climbing out of the trenches, loaded with a heavy pack, trying to charge through often glutinous mud, across churned-up terrain crisscrossed with shell craters and tangles of barbed wire, knowing all the while that the unseen enemy could pick you off from 1,000 yards or more away. The American Civil War of 1861–65, the Franco-Prussian War of 1870–71, the Russo-Turkish War of 1877–78, the Russo-Japanese War of 1904–05, the Balkan wars of 1912 and 1913, all gave warnings of the direction war was turning by demonstrating that soldiers in well-defended positions could hold off much larger forces, which would suffer dreadful losses.

Near the start of the Franco-Prussian War, 48,000 Germans held a line twenty-two miles long against 131,000 French attackers. In 1877, during the Russo-Turkish War, at the Battle of Plevna, the Russians outnumbered the Turks by three to one but were unable to overwhelm their enemy. (The Russians finally won when the Turks ran out of supplies, an indication of how important logistics were becoming.) If more proof were needed the First World War provided it at the cost of millions of lives.

Yet in one of those turns that have marked warfare, the power of the defense was already ebbing by the end of the First World War as the opposing sides came up with new and innovative ways to break through: poison gas, flamethrowers, field mortars, tanks and aircraft. By the Second World War the advantage had swung back toward the offense. The German blitzkrieg, with dive bombers and fighters supporting ground troops who were equipped with tanks, armored vehicles and the humble motorcycle, swept through, around or over defensive positions. Other armies were quick to learn the lessons even as the new weapons and methods brought their own countermeasures such as anti-aircraft and anti-tank guns or land and sea mines. War moved as well into new dimensions, in the air above and into the seas beneath the surface. What was different from the past was the speed of the changes.

War also expanded in scope, because the energies of societies had to be harnessed to the war effort. Where once the military and civilian leaders had assumed that the supplies on hand at the start of hostilities would be adequate until the war's conclusion, the modern wars, like so many Molochs, demanded constant feeding, of bodies but also of resources. In 1914, in the first phase of the fighting in the First World War, the armies on both sides found to their surprise and dismay that they were running through critical supplies that were meant to last until the hostilities had reached a conclusion. The French used up half their ammunition stockpile in less than a month. Germany's artillery had fired all the shells it had at the start of the war within six weeks.

If belligerent nations could not harness their economies to the war effort, they could not fight on. As a result the line between legitimate and illegitimate targets in war blurred until it was nearly erased altogether. Bombing or shelling such things as railway lines, fuel depots, munitions factories and dams were after all ways of undermining the enemy's capacity to fight in the field. And gradually so too were attempts to destroy civilian morale by flattening their homes, churches, hospitals and schools and by killing the civilians themselves indiscriminately. The world got better at it in the twentieth century but it was already happening in the nineteenth. In the Franco-Prussian War, German forces deliberately shelled civilian areas in Paris to force France's surrender. As the Prussian Crown Prince wrote in his diary, "All that is in question is to punish that section of the population whose wickedness was the guilty cause of the war." Another new term was to enter the language by the time of the First World War: the home front. Whether or not they chose, civilians were now part of the battlefield.

One of the great tragedies of modern war was that the very strengths of societies—in organization, industry, science or resources—could turn them into such effective killing machines. Nations could sustain much longer battles, for months or years rather than days, and kill much larger numbers of the enemy. It is notoriously difficult to get accurate figures of casualties—dead, wounded, missing or taken captive—and, as authors such as Steven Pinker warn, we should always consider the numbers in proportion to the overall population. So, for example, if the Mongols had done their work in the twentieth century instead of the thirteenth, instead of 40 million dead there would have been 278 million. Yet however we try to understand the human costs of war, the casualty figures—and their sharp increases—in the period from the Napoleonic Wars, at the beginning of the nineteenth century, to 1945, the end of the Second World War, are chilling. At the single biggest battle of the Napoleonic Wars, at Leipzig in 1813, well before the great advances in weaponry, of the 500,000 soldiers on both sides who fought, some 150,000 were casualties. Leipzig was fought over four days; in 1916, the Battle of the Somme lasted for four and a half months and there were over 1 million casualties. The 1904–05 Russo-Japanese war gave warning of what was to come when between 130,000 and 170,000 combatants from both sides died. In the First World War the final death toll for those who fought is around 9 million and in the Second World War the figure is at least double that. Civilian casualties were going up even more thanks to the greater capacity of belligerents to reach each other's homelands with their weapons of destruction. In the Second World War as many as 50 million civilians may have died as a result of mass murder, bombing or famine and disease caused by the war. A single atomic bomb at Hiroshima killed between 60,000 and 80,000 people instantly and many more thousands died afterward as a result of radioactive poisoning. It is no wonder that someone has invented the term "hemoclysm" (the flood of blood) to describe the past century. Yet the race between technology and its countermeasures in the same period also produced responses such as better civil defense and better medical care. In wars before the nineteenth century soldiers died on the battlefields, but far more died of disease and their wounds. Now the wounded military survived, often to fight again.

During the Napoleonic Wars, the Vicomte de Chateaubriand lamented the new gigantic, all-encompassing shape of war. The old style of civilized warfare, he said, "leaves peoples in place while a small number of soldiers do their duty." The new type of war brought the mass mobilization of peoples by the emerging forces of nationalism. Although the French Revolution is often credited with introducing the idea that nations were organic bodies which had existed throughout time and which could demand the loyalty of their members, the roots can be found in the work of philosophers such as Rousseau, with his talk of the Social Contract and the rights of people to associate freely with each other, and in political events such as the American Revolution of 1775. "Every citizen should be a soldier by duty," wrote Rousseau, "none by profession." The American Declaration of Independence declared that men were endowed with "unalienable Rights" and that governments "deriving their just powers from the consent of the governed" existed to protect those rights. When governments did not fulfill the wishes and needs of the governed, the latter had the right to remove them. In other words, people were starting to be seen as citizens with a say in their own states rather than subjects of an unelected ruler. What was implied, however, was that citizens, usually assumed to be men, had a corresponding duty to come to the defense of their state. That was to be made explicit in the course of the French Revolution a few years later.

In 1792, as France's conservative enemies gathered against it, the new Legislative Assembly called on all French men to defend their nation. The following year the government decreed the *levée en masse,* a mass mobilization unlike anything seen in the previous century. And this time women were included in the appeal as well:

> From this moment until the enemy is driven from the territory of the Republic, all the French people are permanently requisitioned for the armies. The young men will go to the front, married men will forge arms and carry supplies, women will make tents and clothing, children will divide old linen into bandages, old men will be carried into the squares to rouse the courage of the soldiers, to teach hatred of kings and the unity of the Republic.

The wars that started then and merged into the Napoleonic Wars were about defending the French nation and its revolution, but they became something much more. The French spread out across Europe with missionary fervor, seeing their sacred mission as toppling unjust and authoritarian regimes and freeing their fellow

Europeans. Such goals not only justified war, at least to the French, but gave free license to how it should be waged and that meant without limits. Since France's enemies were standing in the way of a better world they should be attacked, said Robespierre, "not as ordinary enemies but as assassins and rebel brigands." The indiscriminate slaughter of men, women and children in the Vendée when the Republic put down a Royalist and Catholic rebellion in 1793 was an indication of what that could mean.

Their fervor made the revolutionary armies cruel but it also brought them victory after victory, and when a military genius, Napoleon, took charge, France proved, for a time, invincible. French soldiers may not have marched in perfect unison like their enemies, but they did not have to be forced into battle. Their skirmishers could be trusted to run toward the enemy lines ahead of the main attack. When French armies time and time again surprised the enemy by arriving much sooner than expected, it was because they could march at night. The old-style armies had to encamp with guards to keep their soldiers from deserting. The Comte Jacques de Guibert had written presciently in 1772:

> But suppose that there should arise in Europe a people vigorous in its genius, its resources and its government; a people in whom austere virtues and a national militia were joined to a settled policy of aggrandizement; one which did not lose sight of its purpose, which knew how to make war cheaply and to subsist on its victories, and was not reduced to laying down its arms through financial need. We would see such a people subjugate its neighbors and overthrow their feeble constitutions as the north wind shakes the tender reeds.

In the end the French were to be defeated in part because they had aroused the very emotions in others that had carried them to power. The Spanish, the Prussians and the Russians who experienced French invasions were not grateful to be offered their liberty on the point of a French sword and so the French found themselves confronting awakening, different nationalisms and wars of national resistance.

In the century after the Napoleonic Wars came to an end, old and new nationalisms welded together peoples who had never been accustomed to thinking of themselves as members of a "nation," sharing such characteristics as culture, language, history, religion, customs and, on the edge where racial theories flourished, biology. Education and improved communications helped to spread the uses of a national language. Where in the eighteenth century the majority of people within France's borders spoke languages such as Breton or Languedoc or local dialects, by the end of the nineteenth most spoke French. National histories—and they were the ones taught in all European schools—created national stories and myths, with moments of glory or of humiliation. Nationalisms dressed themselves too in the language and iconography of religion. The Polish or Serbian nations would rise again as Christ had after his crucifixion and sacrifices in the present would bring kingdoms of heaven on earth in the future. And organized religion—the Polish Catholic hierarchy or Serbian Orthodox Church, for example—supported the nation enthusiastically in return. In the First World War all sides and all the religions involved, from Christianity to Islam, called on their gods to aid them. "Kill Germans," was the Bishop of London's message in 1914. "To kill them not for the sake of killing, but to save the world, to kill the good as well as the bad, to kill the young men as well as the old . . ."

War was more often than not seen as an integral and necessary part of the emergence of the nation, as sanctifying it even, and the military wore a particular halo as its defenders and saviors. As a member of the Frankfurt Parliament said in 1848, a year marked by nationalist uprisings across Europe, "Mere existence does not entitle a nation to political independence: only the force to assert

itself as a state among others." The German historian Heinrich
von Treitschke, whose public lectures and writings were highly
popular before the First World War, argued that war not only cre-
ates the state but the nation too by welding people together in a
common cause (even if the people would rather not be welded
like so many bits of scrap metal). Authoritarian governments have
often used war as a way to unite their people against a common
external enemy. They have also found it a handy excuse to crack
down on dissent and those they see as dangerous revolutionaries.
Conservatives including Kaiser Wilhelm II himself had longed
before 1914 to dissolve the Reichstag, where to their alarm the
Socialist Party was steadily gaining seats, and get rid of the con-
stitution altogether. In 1914, as Germany went to war, the Chancellor had to intervene to prevent Wilhelm and his supporters
banning the socialists. It was a wise decision: not only did the
socialist deputies, who made up the largest single party, vote for
war credits, but Germany entered the war united as the working
classes rushed to support the war effort.

For many nationalists war was midwife to the nation and gave
it vitality and life. Mussolini declared that war "brings to its highest tension all human energy and puts the stamp of nobility upon
the peoples who have the courage to meet it." Indeed, so it was
argued, a people that was not prepared to fight for its existence
probably did not deserve to survive. "Is not war," asked an article
in a leading British military journal before the First World War,
"the grand scheme of nature by which degenerate, weak or otherwise harmful states are eliminated from the concerted action of
civilized nations, and assimilated to those who are strong, vital,
and beneficial in their influences?" So often in the nineteenth
century—and it still happens today—defeat in war was described
in the language of castration or emasculation. The assumption
that the French revolutionaries made with their *levée en masse*
that citizens had an obligation to the state and the nation reached
its ghastly apogee in 1945 in Germany when the top Nazi leader-

ship refused to take any measures that might have saved German lives. When the International Committee of the Red Cross suggested safe zones in Berlin where civilians could gather and be spared the coming battle, the Chief of Staff of the German Armed Forces spurned the offer with contempt. It was only an attempt to test the will to resist of the German people. "Agreement would be the first step toward becoming soft." Hundreds of thousands more Germans, military and civilians, died as a result. Hitler in his bunker went to his death, raving that the German nation had failed him. The state no longer belonged to the citizen but the opposite.

Nationalism served to inspire wars and it also, as in the Vendée, led to a demonization of the enemy, whether the military or civilians, who were seen as an existential threat to a just cause and as impediments standing in the way of the fulfillment of the nation. When General Sherman cut his swathe of destruction on his march to the sea in 1864 he said, "We are not fighting hostile armies but a hostile people and must make old and young, rich and poor, feel the hard hand of war, as well as their organized armies." In the Franco-Prussian War, any French civilians who took up weapons against the invasion were treated by the Germans as having no rights. More, whole communities could be punished. As the Prussian chief of the general staff General von Moltke, often known as the Elder to distinguish him from his less effective nephew, ordered, "The most effective way of dealing with this situation is to destroy the premises concerned—or, where participation has been more general, the entire village." As French resistance continued in the winter of 1870–71, a German officer was horrified at the mutual hatreds between the French and the Germans and their effect on his own troops. "Atrocious attacks are avenged by atrocities which remind one of the Thirty Years War." At von Moltke's headquarters, the American general Philip Sheridan, who had laid waste to the Shenandoah valley in the Civil War, gave his advice that, once the enemy army was finished off, it was necessary to inflict so much pain on the civilians that they would beg their government to make peace: "The people must be left with nothing but their eyes to weep with over the war."

Civilians were often even more vehement than the military. The wife of the great Prussian Chancellor Otto von Bismarck, who was otherwise a sedate German housewife, exclaimed that the French should be "shot and stabbed to death, down to the little babies." Years later, in one of his last public speeches, von Moltke was to warn about the new sorts of wars that he had helped to unleash. The age, he said, of "cabinet" wars—that is, wars determined by rulers for limited ends—was over: "All we have now is people's war, and any prudent government will hesitate to bring about a war of this nature, with all its incalculable consequences." The great powers, he went on, would find it difficult to bring such wars to an end or admit defeat: "Gentlemen, it may be a war of seven years' or of thirty years' duration—and woe to him who sets Europe alight, who puts the first fuse to the powder keg!"

Nationalism provided the motivation in the powder keg and the Industrial Revolution the means. Populations were growing, thanks to better living conditions, which meant that there were many more potential soldiers, and the new factories could turn out millions of what they needed, from boots to bayonets. Weapons production had formerly been limited because they were made by hand by skilled craftsmen. Now the introduction of standardized, machine-made interchangeable parts and assembly lines made guns available on a mass scale, much as it did the cheap pianos which decorated the living rooms of the growing middle classes. Holger Herwig, a military historian, has calculated that it would have taken the artisans of one of the biggest Prussian arms manufacturers in the first half of the nineteenth century thirty years to make enough guns for the 320,000 men of the Prussian army at the time but by 1860 one French arms manufacturer was able to produce 1 million guns in only four years.

In 1860, in the quiet open spaces of Wimbledon Common, Queen Victoria pulled a cord to fire the new Whitworth rifle and inaugurate the National Rifle Association. She hit the bull's-eye on a target 400 yards away. Rifled barrels made guns, both small arms and artillery, more accurate, and improved metallurgy meant they could contain far more powerful explosives capable of sending deadly balls and shells over much greater distances with greater force. As cartridges, bullets and shells replaced the separate projectiles, powder and wadding used for centuries, rifles and field artillery could be loaded quicker and fired more often by soldiers who needed much less training to do so. By the end of the 1860s the French army was equipped with the *chassepot* (not some archaic hunting term but the name of the inventor), which could be sighted up to 1,600 yards and, even when it was loaded with single bullets, could get off six shots per minute. Magazines, preloaded with bullets, increased the rate of fire still more. In the American Civil War a reasonably efficient soldier with a rifle and magazines could fire sixteen shots per minute. By the end of the nineteenth century the machine gun, which could fire hundreds of bullets a minute, had made its appearance. As a French general reportedly said after the long-drawn-out Battle of Verdun in the Great War, "Three men and a machine gun can stop a battalion of heroes." Today the famous Kalashnikov rifle can fire 600 rounds a minute to a distance of well over half a mile.

Another of the great changes in war in the nineteenth century was that where once armies had marched, they now had mechanized transport. (They still had to march once they had disembarked at railheads from their trains or if lorries were not available.) Before the Industrial Revolution, armies were like locusts: once they had eaten everything in sight, they had to move on. The size of Napoleon's armies, like those of Alexander or Frederick the Great, had been limited by the supplies, from food to ammunition, that they could carry or forage. Napoleon lost most of his great army in Russia when his soldiers starved or froze to death. Now, with trains or steamships, armies could be moved great distances more quickly and kept in the field much longer as fresh supplies kept coming in.

The changes to war were equally great at sea. Although the British navy kept sails on its first steam-powered ships, just in case, steam and the new turbines made ships more reliable, maneuverable and fast. Coal, and coaling stations around the world, and later oil now became important strategic assets and targets. The new technology made it possible for the ships to carry armor, which was initially installed over the wood, and much heavier guns. The invention of the gun turret which could swivel 360 degrees meant that ships no longer had to fire broadsides—which left their whole length exposed to counterfire—but could fire over their bows and sterns as well. Although some naval officers were convinced that ships made entirely of metal would sink, by the end of the nineteenth century all the world's navies were building steel ships. In 1906, before a crowd of 50,000 gathered at Portsmouth dockyard, Edward VII of Britain launched HMS *Dreadnought,* the largest warship ever seen on the seas. The "great mass of metal," said the *Daily Mail*'s correspondent, "glided into the sea so smoothly, noiselessly, and at such an even speed that it made one think of some graceful bird descending into its natural element." The *Dreadnought* was heavier and faster than anything in any other navy, including the German, which was very much the point of it. (Such was the integration of Europe's economy, however, that it was made of the best steel the German firm of Krupp's could provide.) It carried 5,000 tons of armor and ten twelve-inch guns (the measurement refers to the muzzle, which meant that they were firing very big shells indeed) as well as batteries of smaller guns. It immediately rendered the battleships of other navies obsolete and so, reluctantly, the other powers were obliged to follow suit and build their own versions. The growing range of the naval guns, from around ten miles in the First World War up to eighteen miles by the Second World War, meant that navies could engage without ever seeing each other. Inevitably navies scrambled to find countermeasures as well, from fast destroyers and torpedo boats designed to hunt out the heavier, slower vessels to mines. War at sea, as on land, also moved into new dimensions. With submarines, naval war was increasingly fought under the oceans and directed as much against shipping as enemy ships. By the end of the First World War theorists were embracing the aircraft as a way to both find and sink enemy ships and the first aircraft carriers were built in the 1920s.

The changes brought about by the Industrial Revolution did not happen overnight and there were many disasters along the way as the military and their societies learned to use and organize the new resources at their disposal. In 1859 Napoleon III, the nephew of the great man, sent a large force by train to Italy to fight Austria. The men arrived but without blankets, food or ammunition. It was, he admitted, "the opposite of what we should have done." Russia experienced the same difficulties in its war with Japan in 1904–05 when poor planning left the Trans-Siberian railway in chaos, with crucial supplies left to go to waste on railway sidings.

In the summer of 1914, however, Germany was able to move 2 million men, 1,189,000 horses and all their equipment on 20,000 trains, into Belgium and northern France on the Western Front with very few hitches. In the first two weeks of August, German trains, each of fifty-four cars, were moving toward the French frontier across the Rhine on the crucial Hohenzollern Bridge at Cologne every ten minutes. The Prussian government and then the German one after 1871 followed the wishes of the military in building its railway network so that troops and supplies could be moved quickly to the frontiers. The Germans were also among the first to realize that the new railways could only be useful if they were organized properly. Germany pioneered the general staff, the necessary brain to move the behemoth of the new mass armies about. A nineteenth-century joke had it that there were five perfect things in Europe: the Curia of the Catholic Church, the British Parliament, the Russian ballet, the French opera—and the German general staff. Manned with bright and ambitious officers, it had grown from a small experiment as Prussia scrambled to deal with Napoleon, to a professional and cohesive body 800-strong by 1905. The key railway section had a staff of eighty. General Groener, its chief in 1914, was so devoted to railway lines and junctions that he had spent his honeymoon plotting railway timetables with his new wife. The general staff's function was to gather intelligence about the enemy and above all to make plans to achieve victory. Staff officers studied everything from forts, to understand their strengths and weaknesses, to American circuses, to learn ways of moving quantities of people, animals and equipment across great distances. The plans that emerged were tested, modified and tested again year after year.

Modern war obliged societies as a whole to become more organized and mobilize their resources better or risk defeat. Perhaps the key factor that brought down the tsarist regime in 1917 was its inability to supply the troops at the front and feed the cities at home. Samuel Pepys in the seventeenth century was a harbinger of the growing bureaucracies of the modern age. Even in peacetime governments steadily extended their control over society with preparations for war in mind.

Growing bureaucracies amassed statistics and kept better records because governments needed to know how to find the money, the resources and the men they needed, and they also needed the means to extract them. Censuses, and most states were adopting them in the nineteenth century, provide all sorts of useful demographic information, not least the number of men of military age. We take citizenship and citizenship papers for granted today, but in the nineteenth century governments often had little idea of how many citizens they had and who, therefore, had an obligation to fight for the country. As a result new laws and regulations defined who counted and who did not. After 1842 Prussian men of military age could not emigrate without permission. In French villages, where conscription was regarded as unfairly removing valuable labor, the names of young men often did not make it onto the official returns. So an official had to come to count heads. If conscripts failed to report, as also happened, someone had to find the missing men. And much of the drive to improve public health, diet, living conditions and education came from the need for fit and healthy recruits.

When I was a student in Britain in the 1960s I never understood why all pubs closed for the afternoon. The authorities had introduced those hours in 1915 to ensure that factory workers did not drink too much or miss an afternoon's work and the British lived with the effects until the late 1980s, when the licensing laws were finally amended. Modern war, when it came, speeded up and extended the degree of government control over society. Factories were requisitioned, raw materials directed to where they were most needed and skilled labor in crucial industries such as mining could not move jobs or enlist without permission. Scientists have long been important in war—think of the work of Archimedes or Leonardo da Vinci—but increasingly governments have harnessed science to war by setting up special research centers, subsidizing industry or offering research grants to universities. One of Hitler's many mistakes was to underestimate the value of science, a field in which Germany had once led the world. The Nazi regime neglected basic research and allowed some of its best scientists to join up so that they wasted their expertise and often ended their lives on the battlefields. The Nazis also drove out Jewish scientists, among them Albert Einstein, with the result that the exiles were able to offer their talents to Germany's opponents. Without the work of the refugee scientists it is unlikely that the Allies could have developed the atomic bomb so quickly. Or, as a chilling alternative possibility, Hitler might have had it in his hands except for his own racial policies. The Manhattan Project to develop the bomb was the single greatest example of science being directed to military ends, but the war stimulated research into a vast range of new weapons and technologies. The British and the Americans in particular brought together hundreds of scientists in projects that ranged from the development of radar to rockets. For the first time what came to be known as operational research was used to calculate the efficacy, costs and benefits of particular devices or strategies.

At first glance the invention of a device by the British Ministry of Food to spray-dry eggs seems trivial beside powerful new weapons. And the daring exploits of a British engineer in the First World War who blew up Romanian oil wells and so denied their output to the Central Powers make an interesting footnote to the history of the war. Yet both point to another important part of modern war: the provision of resources, for sustenance of the population or the war effort of one's own side, and the denial of them to the others through sabotage, direct attack or blockade. "The first essential condition for an army to be able to stand the strain of battle," said the German general Erwin Rommel, "is an adequate stock of weapons, petrol and ammunition. In fact, the battle is fought and decided by quartermasters before the shooting begins." Napoleon tried to stop trade between the British Isles and the Continent to force the British to end hostilities; the British responded with their favored strategy of a naval blockade. They tried it again against Germany in the First World War. The German economy became increasingly unable to sustain the war effort without vital products such as foods or natural phosphates, crucial in making fertilizer. Germany responded, as it did again in the Second World War, with unrestricted submarine warfare directed against British and neutral shipping using British ports. Although Germany made up some of the shortfall in what it needed by plundering occupied Belgium and then, in 1918, by its peace with Russia, which gave it access to the wheat and minerals of Ukraine, it could never match the Allied powers for resources. Before the Pacific War broke out in 1941, the Americans embargoed exports of metal and oil to Japan, which relied largely on such imports. Although the Japanese opted for war and for a time swept all resistance before them, in the long run they too ran out of resources as American bombers, destroyers and submarines sank Japanese shipping at a much faster rate than it could be replaced.

Food has always been a critical front in the struggle over resources. Besieging armies have counted on the help of hunger to force garrisons to surrender. Armies, as Napoleon said, march on their stomachs and denying them food has long been a tactic in war. Just as the Roman general Fabius Maximus weakened Hannibal's armies by disrupting their supply lines, the Russians have countered invaders from Napoleon to Hitler by scorched-earth policies where they have destroyed their own crops and live-stock. As war became more encompassing, feeding the home front became crucial to maintaining the war effort. By the end of the First World War many Germans, especially the poorer classes in the cities, were starving, and desperate housewives marched banging their empty pots and pans. This was later characterized by the German High Command as part of the "stab in the back" which had made it impossible for German troops to fight on. The food shortages were partly caused by the British blockade but were also the result of the German government's inefficient planning and ineffective rationing. In both world wars Britain managed with much greater success to increase its food production and ensure a fairer distribution. During the Second World War the British doubled their arable land by plowing up pastures and parks. By focusing on crops such as wheat and potatoes at the expense of animal husbandry, they increased the proportion of home-grown food in the British diet. Stringent government controls meant that scarce shipping was used for high-calorie foods such as meat and cheese rather than sugar, nuts or fresh fruit. When my father, who was in the Canadian navy, docked in Britain for the first time and prepared to meet his new British in-laws he brought with him as a present a giant stalk of bananas which he had picked up as his ship came through the Panama Canal. His fellow train passengers looked at the sight with awe and asked only to be able to sniff the fruit. Yet if most British never saw a banana or an orange from one end of the war to the other, could have only minuscule amounts of sugar or butter, and ate some strange dishes, their diets were enough to keep them fed and healthy.

War, particularly large-scale prolonged war, makes many demands and it is hideously, often ruinously, expensive. Indeed when the First World War broke out most of the world, including the European belligerents themselves, assumed that it would have to end after a short time as money and resources ran out. Instead states rapidly learned how to manage and expropriate societies' wealth on a much greater scale than they had imagined possible. Walter Scheidel has estimated that in the First World War the state in belligerent powers such as France, Germany or Great Britain increased its share of GDP from four to eight times. By the middle of the Second World War, Germany was using the equivalent of 73 percent of its GNP for the war effort. When peace came, governments did not relinquish all the levers of power they had amassed or unlearn the lessons about extracting resources from society. Taxes certainly did not go back to prewar levels. Indeed, in the case of Russia after 1917, as it became the Soviet Union, Lenin and his successor Stalin organized and ran a "command" economy, allocating resources and directing labor, as if they were at war.

Because industry, technology and better organization of society made the mobilization of their resources possible even in peacetime, European countries found themselves obliged to create bigger armed forces, or be left behind their neighbors. By the end of the nineteenth century all the great powers, with the exception of Britain, which relied on the seas and its navy, the most powerful in the world, to protect it, had adopted peacetime conscription, which obliged young men of military age to do military service for a stated period and then remain in the reserves for another number of years. This meant that nations had large armies in existence and much larger ones that could be summoned up in a crisis. Nevertheless, conservatives saw conscription as potentially dangerous. Training men from the lower classes might be putting weapons into the hands of revolutionaries. And men from the cities, it was widely assumed, must be feebler and less able to endure hardships and discipline than sturdy peasants from the countryside. Another problem was that bigger armies needed more officers, which meant that the pool of recruits had to be expanded beyond the landed gentry and aristocracy, who had dominated the officer class for centuries. Middle-class men, used to comfortable bourgeois lives, perhaps with artistic or intellectual tastes, and certainly not toughened by country sports, could not be expected, so old-style officers said, to share their values or their willingness to serve their king and country and die in their service. In fact many such fears turned out to be groundless. Where the French authorities had expected that some 20 percent of their reserves would not come when called back to service, in 1914 less than 1 percent failed to report for duty. Middle-class men, far from infecting the officer corps with their values, rather took on aristocratic ones and military service tended to make ordinary soldiers more patriotic if anything. A German general speaking before the First World War urged his officers to ensure that they made their men into loyal subjects. Socialist ideas, he said, were a sickness which a good dose of military training would cure. He might not have been amused if he'd known that the revolutionary Leon Trotsky, later the creator of the Bolsheviks' Red Army, agreed on the value of military training. The army, he said, "is that school where the party can instill moral hardness, self-sacrifice and discipline."

Change is never easy for hierarchical organizations and the military through time has treated innovations such as conscription with suspicion. The British army clung to the practice of allowing young men to buy commands long after most Continental armies had abandoned it as inefficient. It was a convenient way for the government to raise funds and for the army to ensure that it got the "right sort" of men. (The Royal Navy, understandably, had never seen the point of putting rich, untrained ninnies in charge of expensive ships.) The practice was finally abolished in 1871, when disasters caused by incompetent officers, most notably the futile and bloody Charge of the Light Brigade during the Crimean War, had caused too much public furor to be ignored. New weapons were often greeted with equal suspicion. Just as knights in armor had tried to ignore the fact that the crossbow, the longbow and the gun had made them obsolete, many in the officer classes in the nineteenth century initially downplayed new weapons and tactics and refused to contemplate countermeasures. Field Marshal Sir Garnet Wolseley, a formidable Anglo-Irishman who served in conflicts all over the empire and was commander-in-chief of British forces from 1895 to 1901, opposed trenches on the grounds that they would make troops less willing to climb out and attack. In 1903 a young Colonel Ferdinand Foch, then an instructor at France's War College, presented neat mathematical proofs that two attacking battalions against one on the defensive could fire twice as many bullets and so all that was needed for victory was twice as many attackers as defenders. As Supreme Allied Commander in the First World War, he was to dismiss airplanes: *"Tout ça c'est du sport."*

Before that war (and sometimes long after) many in the military continued to see cavalry as a major component in fighting. "It must be accepted as a principle," said the 1907 British cavalry manual, "that the rifle, effective as it is, cannot replace the effect produced by the speed of the horse, the magnetism of the charge, and the terror of cold steel." Britain's Inspector General of Cavalry in the 1890s argued that smokeless gunpowder, contrary to what pessimists believed, gave an advantage to charging cavalry. True, the new gunpowder helped to conceal the enemy soldiers, whose weapons no longer gave away a telltale puff of smoke, but since the battlefields were now free from the fogs that had once covered them, the sight of the men on horseback bearing down was bound to demoralize the defenders. Cavalry officers, who came overwhelmingly from the landowning upper classes, also despised those they saw as mere technicians. In Austria's armies the cavalry dismissed officers in the artillery as the "powder Jews" and even among artillery officers themselves riding was considered to be more important than technical expertise. Many men and many horses were to die before the cavalry abandoned their horses for the despised new tanks and armored vehicles.

It did not help that anti-intellectualism was a matter of pride in many military circles. The British army staff college was established in the mid-nineteenth century over the objections of the senior military and in its early years only educated a handful of officers a year. When an officer in a fashionable British regiment thought of applying to it one of his fellow officers said, "Well, I will give one piece of advice, and that is to say nothing about it to your brother officers, or you will get yourself jolly well disliked." Horace Smith-Dorrien, who became one of the more effective British generals in the First World War, remembered his time at the staff college as rather pleasant: "I enjoyed every minute of my two years there. I do not think we were taught as much as we might have been, but there was plenty of sport and not too much work." He never managed to find the library but was still able to pass his final examination.

For all their bluster, however, Europe's military were uneasily aware that warfare and the world around them were changing. They could see the new power of the defense for themselves because they sent observers to major conflicts both in Europe and around the world. If they resisted new technology they were more open to ideas from the developing science of psychology, in part as a solution to the challenges posed by the hardware and in part because they were getting new sorts of recruits, with a degree of education, who had to be handled differently from illiterate peasants. The question of how to motivate soldiers goes back as far as war itself of course, but its study has become more systematic in the past two centuries. The military have brought in psychologists to help them find the best recruits, to test them in training and in battle and to try to understand how humans behave under pressure. Unfortunately, before the First World War psychology and motivation were seen too often as the antidote to increased firepower on the battlefield. As Colonel Louis de Grandmaison, one of the leading French military theorists of the period, said in his classic work on infantry training, "We are rightly told that psychological factors are paramount in combat. But this is not all: properly speaking, there are no other factors, for all others—weaponry, maneuverability—influence only indirectly by provoking moral reactions . . . the human heart is the starting point in all questions of war." Soldiers were trained how to use bayonets in combat on the grounds that it would make them properly determined in the face of the enemy. Against machine guns and poison gas on the killing fields of the First World War, determination and courage on their own were never enough.

Much as they might have preferred to remain a caste apart, the modern military were also forced to take account of the broader social and political changes in their societies. War or preparations for it have made ever greater demands and forced changes on societies, but this has never been a one-way process. People are not inert lumps waiting for some powerful hand to shape them; they have ideas and values, and these have also shaped the development of the military and its relationship to society. In the nineteenth and twentieth centuries, as we have seen, nationalism fueled wars and obligated citizens to come to the aid of their country, but, at the same time, citizens started to take a greater interest in the policies and decisions of their governments and assert a right to shape or change these.

The steady expansion of the franchise, first for men—Germany had universal male suffrage from the time it became a country in 1871—and after the First World War for most women, encouraged voters to take notice of what their governments were up to. Free public education, growing literacy and the emergence of cheap newspapers with huge circulations meant that the public had much greater access to news even far beyond the country's borders. And the advent of the telegraph, which by 1914 had bound the world together much as the internet does today, meant that the home audiences were following events such as wars and international crises virtually as they were happening. In the Crimean War of 1853–56 a new type of journalist, the war correspondent, appeared. William Howard Russell's dispatches for *The Times* in particular simultaneously enthralled and horrified the British public. For the first time, the British realized just how incompetent their own military could be and how badly their soldiers were treated. The subsequent public outcry brought much-needed changes to the army and paved the way for the work of Florence Nightingale and her colleagues in improving military hospitals and the general health of the soldiers.

Newspapers and publishers realized that war was good for sales. In the Franco-Prussian War, for example, the circulation of London's *Daily News* tripled. At the turn of the century an ambitious twenty-four-year-old Winston Churchill found fame and earned a fortune reporting on the South African War. War correspondents and photographers—Ernest Hemingway, Edward R. Murrow, Robert Capa, Michael Herr, Marie Colvin—have become modern heroes. Seeing the horrors of war can have significant impact at home, and television, film and now social media have vastly expanded our opportunities to do so. The American government lost the battle for public opinion during the Vietnam War because the networks' evening news and print reporting persuaded large sections of the public that the war was both unjust and disgraceful. After the war ended, Colonel Harry Summers, a leading American military thinker, visited Hanoi. In a conversation with a North Vietnamese colonel, he remarked, "You know you never defeated us on the battlefield." After a moment, the North Vietnamese replied, "That may be so, but it is also irrelevant." Democracies, where leaders are always conscious of the next election, have a particularly hard time sustaining unpopular wars, as the French had discovered in their own war in Indochina, but even the authoritarian Soviet Union paid a high political cost for its unsuccessful and unpopular war in Afghanistan in the 1980s.

Public opinion can also work the other way, pushing governments into stances and wars they do not want. Navy and army leagues, veterans' associations and defense industries have shown great skill in whipping up public demands for more spending on the military. In a farewell speech in 1961 President Eisenhower, who as a general knew what he was talking about, warned, "In the councils of government, we must guard against the acquisition of unwarranted influence, whether sought or unsought, by the military industrial complex." In the 1890s Britain and Germany found themselves in a confrontation over the Samoan Islands in the South Pacific because of public opinion even though diplomats and political leaders were willing to broker a deal. "For even though the great majority of our pothouse politicians did not know whether Samoa was a fish or a fowl or a foreign queen," a German diplomat complained, "they shouted all the more loudly that, whatever else it was, it was German and must remain forever German." General Charles Gordon was sent by the British government to Khartoum in 1884 to rescue Egyptian forces trapped there by a revolt against Egyptian misrule by the local Sudanese led by the Mahdi. The prime minister, William Gladstone, had been reluctant to intervene at all, but his government was pressured by public opinion, which had embraced the strange, half-mad Gordon as a hero. Although Gordon had strict instructions to leave as soon as he had fulfilled his mission, he disobeyed them and chose to stay, in a vain attempt to put down the Sudanese. The result was that he and his tiny force were besieged in Khartoum. Gordon, with his ostentatious piety, his apparent simplicity, his conviction that he had been sent by God to save the Sudan, whether from misrule or Islam or both, skillfully swayed public opinion in his favor from Khartoum, thanks to the dispatches he sent by telegraph (at least until the Mahdi's forces cut the lines). Gladstone, who was furious with Gordon, procrastinated over sending an expensive relief force, but when vicars across the country offered prayers for Gordon, when the press talked about Britain's shame and asked "Gordon or Gladstone" and when even Queen Victoria weighed in ("General Gordon is in danger; you are bound to try to save him," she told the Secretary of State for War), Gladstone was forced to give way. He sent an expedition, which arrived two days after Gordon had died. In 1896 a Conservative government sent an expedition to avenge Gordon; thousands of Sudanese died in the ensuing conflict, and Britain ended up with responsibility for the Sudan.

Governments and their military have learned to play the game of manipulating public opinion too. In the First and Second World Wars all sides controlled war correspondents carefully lest too realistic a picture of the fighting weaken public morale. Although the US military allowed reporters extraordinary access in Vietnam, it drew the conclusion that it must never make that mistake again. In both wars with Iraq the media were tightly controlled and managed. The Americans may have learned from the British in the 1982 Falklands War, when the Ministry of Defense went to great lengths to prevent publication of news from the South Atlantic, even the most anodyne.

Naval reviews, troop march-pasts, military bands playing and fighter planes in dazzling aerobatics have all entertained the public over the years and, so it is hoped, made them proud of their armed forces and willing to provide the funds for them. If most democracies show off their military less today, countries such as Russia, China or Iran still show off their military force and encourage public support. When Admiral Tirpitz set out to build

Germany's great fleet before 1914, one of the first steps he took
was to establish a special office for News and Parliamentary Affairs. Over the next decades it lobbied members of the Reichstag,
organized dozens of public lectures, distributed thousands of
pamphlets and made sure that each new battleship was launched
with great public fanfare. When the British responded to the
German naval challenge by building its dreadnoughts, the Royal
Navy played its own role in getting public support for the necessary funding. In 1909, during a crisis over increased naval and
social spending, it brought ships up the Thames to London for a
week-long show with fireworks, mock fights and special children's
programs which drew 4 million people.

Today the absurd spectacle of the high-stepping soldiers from
India and Pakistan who nightly strut their robotic lowering and
folding of flags, with their high kicks, stamps and twirls, at a border crossing on the Old Trunk Road between their two countries,
draws increasingly large cheering crowds from each side and is a
YouTube favorite. It is surely a bit of harmless fun. Or is it? Both
countries have nuclear weapons and a long history of conflict and
mutual suspicion. And militarism, whether that means elevating
the military to a position as the noblest and best of their societies
or the leaching of military values, such as discipline and obedience into the civilian world, can lead to trouble for democratic
societies. In Pakistan, in particular, the military are seen as the
bulwark and protector of the nation and are largely free from civilian control and scrutiny. The infamous Inter-Services Intelligence Directorate has backed and funded terrorist groups in
India, the disputed territory of Kashmir, Afghanistan and Central
Asia, not for the good of those countries or of Pakistan itself. It is
widely accepted that some of Pakistan's generals have sold nuclear
technology to North Korea. Civilian leaders who have tried to
rein in the military have rapidly found themselves out of office
and, if they are lucky, in exile. In both India and Pakistan civilian
politics have taken on a military tinge, with some political parties

sponsoring paramilitary organizations whose members wear uniforms, march in formation with flags and carry sticks to menace their opponents. Or in the case of India's Bharatiya Janata Party (BJP) it looks more as though the paramilitary Rashtriya Swayamsevak Sangh (RSS) sponsors it.

The First World War had a deep impact on European society, not least in the persistence of wartime values and organizations long after the war itself had ended. Former soldiers formed paramilitary groups and in some cases, such as the German Freikorps in the Baltics or the Black and Tans in Ireland, carried on fighting in the small wars that plagued Europe until the mid-1920s. Right-wing politics in Germany were imbued with nostalgia for the "spirit of 1914," when, so it was believed, the German nation had sunk all its differences in a common cause. Veterans turned out in their uniforms to march, and the new fascist and communist movements had their own uniforms and formations, obeyed their leaders unquestioningly and went out on expeditions to beat up their enemies. "For us," an Italian fascist said, "the war has never come to an end. We simply replaced external enemies with internal ones."

Wars can leave the marks of militarism, in both senses of the word, on society but militarism can also lead to war. Nineteenth-century Europe provides a warning of what can happen during a long peace when the military come to see themselves as superior to society, the best and bravest part of it with a special, even divine, mission to protect the nation, and when military values trump civilian ones. In Germany, Wilhelm Voigt, an enterprising petty crook, inadvertently exposed the impact of militarism on German society and held it up to ridicule. Dressed in odds and ends of uniform, he assumed command of a group of soldiers in Berlin and took them off to the nearby town of Köpenick, where he had a wonderful time arresting city officials and taking possession of a large sum of money. Although he was eventually found out and sent to jail, the Captain of Köpenick became a folk hero among the many Germans who were anti-militaristic and among Germany's enemies, and made a tidy living lecturing about his experiences.

Yet his story underscores the particular place the German military occupied. It answered only to the Kaiser and both its officers and he resented any questioning from the Reichstag. Although the army's Schlieffen Plan committed Germany to a two-front war against France and Russia and the invasion of Belgium (whose neutrality Germany had undertaken to respect), the Chancellor, Theobald von Bethmann Hollweg, did not learn about it until 1912 and then his only reaction was that if the military deemed the strategy necessary, he would do what he could to help diplomatically. His reverence for the military was such that when he had gone to the Reichstag for the first time as Chancellor, he wore his colonel's uniform. But then all over Europe crowned heads and their heirs appeared more often than not in uniform. Kaiser Wilhelm reveled in his collection and took, curiously enough, particular pride in the uniform of a British admiral. Little boys in most countries wore military-style uniforms to school and learned to march in the cadets, while little girls often wore pinafores modeled on seamen's uniforms. As they grew older they could join organizations such as the British Boy Scouts, the aim of which was to prepare boys to serve their king and country, or, in the case of girls, something like the Girl Guides, which would make them good wives, mothers and nurses.

The military took the cue that it had considerable latitude to go its own way. The British army, more subject to civilian oversight and control than most, nevertheless came close to committing and perhaps did commit itself in a series of talks with the French to coming to France's aid should it go to war with Germany. In the Dreyfus Affair, when the only Jewish captain on the general staff was wrongly convicted of selling France's secrets to Germany, the army resisted reopening the case for a decade. When German soldiers broke the law and behaved badly toward civilians in the Alsatian town of Zabern in 1913, the army's high command, with the full support of the Kaiser, refused to admit that anything wrong had happened. In the end Bethmann Holl-weg, in spite of his knowledge of the true state of affairs, went before the Reichstag and defended the military. Although duel-ing had gone out of fashion in Britain by the middle of the nine-teenth century, on the Continent, even in republican France, the military authorities defended it and refused to move against the practice on the grounds that it encouraged a good fighting spirit among the officers. On the eve of the First World War the Prus-sian Minister of War, General von Falkenhayn, protested to the Chancellor, "The roots of the duel are embedded and grow in our code of honor. This code of honor is a valuable, and for the Officer Corps, an irreplaceable treasure."

War was often seen as a duel on a grand scale and the language of honor and shame was transposed to the nation. Fighting was honorable, surrender was a disgrace that could only be expunged through another war. The idea that war is not only natural but es-sential to society, a test of humans and their state, has a long his-tory. The Romans, for example, thought a common enemy was good for them. As the Roman historian Sallust said about Rome's struggle with Carthage, "There was no strife among the citizens either for glory or for power: fear of the enemy preserved the good morals of the state." In the Rome of today we still find such attitudes. "War is terrible," President George W. Bush said in a 2006 interview, "but it brings out, you know, in some ways it touches the core of Americans who volunteer to go into combat to protect their souls." The nineteenth century brought in science as well to explain the good that war can do, in particular that ad-aptation of Darwin's theory of evolution. Social Darwinism, as it was called, asserted that human societies evolved just as though they were so many separate species and war was an important if not essential part of the process. It was a misreading of Darwin and in fact unscientific, but the idea that something called the survival of the fittest governed the fate of human societies or that each was likely to have a natural predator or enemy was enormously influential and continued to influence people, including of course Hitler and his Nazis, and continues to influence a radical fringe today.

Popular culture, from collectible cigarette cards with pictures of great military heroes to boys' magazines, served to reinforce the special aura and place of war and the armed forces, and the importance of military values for a strong society. In 1913 the editor of the new British *Boy's Journal* proudly described it as "essentially a man-making paper for the manly lad." The work of its writers, he said, "is naturally imbued with lofty ideals—love of home and of the homeland; a strong sense of the greatness of our Empire; patriotism and good comradeship; purity of mind and body; moral as well as physical courage; and contempt for anything that is untruthful, petty, base or brutal." Team games inculcated the right sorts of manly and team values. Robert Baden-Powell, the founder of the Boy Scouts, believed that they also provided the ability to lead and to make quick decisions. (He might have agreed with the American high school coach during the Vietnam War who told a student that he needed to take gym class seriously: "This training you get here is gonna give you an edge on them gooks in Vietnam.") Indeed for the Victorians war was often seen as a particularly elevated form of sport. In his poem "Vitaï Lampada" the influential editor and Edwardian man of letters Sir Henry Newbolt starts with a cricket game where the young batsman is being urged to play his best to win victory for his team and ends with blood on the sands of the Sudan as the boy, now an officer, rallies the men with "Play up! play up! and play the game!"

Where soldiers had once been banned, along with dogs and beggars, from inns, they were now regarded, at least much of the time, with reverence. Rudyard Kipling, who caught the voice of ordinary British soldiers so well, was skeptical about how deep the changes went in Great Britain, which had never prized its army highly:

I went into a public 'ouse to get a pint o' beer,
The publican 'e up an' sez, "We serve no red-coats here."
The girls be'ind the bar they laughed an' giggled fit
to die,
I outs into the street again an' to myself sez I:
O it's Tommy this, an' Tommy that, an' "Tommy,
go away";
But it's "Thank you, Mister Atkins," when the band
begins to play
The band begins to play, my boys, the band begins to
play,
O it's "Thank you, Mister Atkins," when the band
begins to play.

In Britain, it was the navy, the country's shield, that was revered. Another of Newbolt's best-known poems was about the great Elizabethan sea captain Sir Frances Drake, who would, so it was popularly believed, come again to save Britain in its hour of need, as this last verse promises:

Drake he's in his hammock till the great Armadas come,
(Capten, art tha sleepin' there below?),
Slung atween the round shot, listenin' for the drum,
An' dreamin arl the time o' Plymouth Hoe.
Call him on the deep sea, call him up the Sound,
Call him when ye sail to meet the foe;
Where the old trade's plyin' an' the old flag flyin'
They shall find him ware an' wakin', as they found him
long ago!

Somewhere amidst the chest-beating and the appeals to patriotism was a fear, which has certainly been there in other times, that if the test of war came society might not be able to meet it. Developed countries in the late nineteenth century worried, as some do today, that the modern human was weaker, morally and physically, than his or her ancestors. When the British asked for volunteers to go to the South African War, the authorities and much of the British public were shocked at what they saw as their low quality. Whether it was urbanization, too much comfort—or too little decent food or fresh air—or the wrong sort of education, were modern nations producing the warriors to defend them? William Balck, author of the leading German handbook on tactics, declared that it was quite clear that modern man was losing his physical and spiritual powers: "The steadily improving standards of living tend to increase the instinct of self-preservation and to diminish the spirit of self-sacrifice." In 1905 Elliott Evans Mills, a young Conservative, published an alarmist pamphlet entitled "The Decline and Fall of the British Empire." His topics included "The Prevalence of Town over Country Life, and its disastrous effect upon the faith and health of the British people," "Excessive Taxation and Municipal Extravagance" and "Inability of the British to defend themselves and their Empire." He made frequent reference to the decline and fall of the Roman Empire. (The Japanese bought a special edition for their schools.) Field Marshal Wolseley disliked the changes in British society as much as he did trenches; he found it a bad sign that ballet dancers and opera singers were now valued so highly. Men appeared to be getting less manly and women less womanly. In France there was widespread concern over declining fertility. A leading German intellectual said tactlessly to a French journalist, "A people whose men don't want to be soldiers, and whose women refuse to have children, is a people benumbed in their vitality; it is fated to be dominated by a younger and fresher race." One of the reasons the military planned for short, decisive wars before 1914 is that both they and many civilian leaders feared that modern societies would fall apart during a long war.

In fact such fears were largely misplaced. One of the main puzzles of the First World War is how both the soldiers and the civilians endured for so long. Russia, the most vulnerable of the powers, held together until 1917 and the rest staggered on until 1918. True, there were mutinies and individual acts of resistance, but again Europe's armies and navies held together. One explanation may be that the slow permeation of civilian society by military values had prepared many Europeans psychologically for the war. More, there was a hope, tragically wrong in retrospect, that war would be the great decider of issues, perhaps leading to calmer days ahead. The impending storm—the heaviness in the air, then the sudden flash of lightning, the crack of thunder and a short, sharp rain—would be followed by fresh air and blue skies.

CHAPTER 5

MAKING THE
WARRIOR

―――

"But the man who most truly can be accounted brave
is he who best knows the meaning of what is sweet in
life and of what is terrible, and then goes out undeterred to meet what is to come."

—PERICLES

TWO DIFFERENT BATTLES. THEY ARE DIVIDED BY SPACE—
one was in Europe and the other in America—and by time, some
400 years' worth. There are few if any guns of any size in the first
but in the second the soldiers have their own guns and there is
field artillery. In both battles the soldiers have swords and knives,
and in both there are mounted warriors. Both are parts of civil
wars and in each case their outcome makes a difference to history.
And both set a record for bloodshed. We wonder how the different sides got to this point of open conflict. And we wonder how
those fighting—they are almost always men—can do it. How
they can stand there hour after hour facing death. Or dole out
death to others, sometimes from a distance with arrows or guns,
but so often in close, hand-to-hand combat.

On March 29, 1461, Palm Sunday, two armies met in a snowstorm outside the tiny village of Towton, some ten miles southeast of the old city of York. The battle was one in a series in that
complicated dynastic and political struggle known as the Wars of
the Roses. It was about which royal house, York or Lancaster,

would rule England, but, as wars usually are, about much else besides, including the grievances of the ordinary English and divisions over what sort of government the country should have. Some 50,000 archers, foot soldiers and knights on horseback fought that day until, so reports had it, the rivers ran red with blood. Finally, as reinforcements arrived for the Yorkists, the Lancastrians broke and fled. Many were cut down by the triumphant Yorkists on what came to be known as the Bloody Meadow; others trampled their own comrades to death in their panic; and yet more drowned in a nearby river.

In one of his history plays, Shakespeare has the losing king, Henry VI, compare the battle to the changing fortunes of nature:

> *This battle fares like to the morning's war,*
> *When dying clouds contend with growing light,*
> *What time the shepherd, blowing of his nails,*
> *Can neither call it perfect day nor night.*
> *Now sways it this way, like a mighty sea*
> *Forced by the tide to combat with the wind;*
> *Now sways it that way, like the selfsame sea*
> *Forced to retire by fury of the wind:*
> *Sometime the flood prevails, and then the wind;*
> *Now one the better, then another best;*
> *Both tugging to be victors, breast to breast,*
> *Yet neither conqueror nor conquered:*
> *So is the equal poise of this fell war.*

Henry fled the country for France and the victorious Edward IV took the throne until another change in the fortunes of war brought Henry back again—temporarily—in 1470. While the details of the Wars of the Roses are obscure to most people today, Towton stands out as the bloodiest and biggest battle ever fought in England. It has been estimated that as many as 28,000 may have died there and many more were wounded or executed after the battle. Given that the population of England was probably around 2 million and is now around 56 million, a similar proportion of dead today would be around 784,000.

Four centuries later, on September 17, 1862, and a continent away from Towton, another 50,000 soldiers fought near the Antietam Creek in western Maryland on a warm autumn day. The Confederate armies had been on the attack since August, moving into Virginia and winning a series of victories. The Union forces were on the defensive, their leaders apparently incapable of protecting their territories. In a typically bold and daring move General Robert E. Lee led his Confederate forces north into Maryland at the beginning of September, so that he was able to threaten Washington to the southeast and Pennsylvania to the north. As the Union armies slowly moved to challenge him in the lovely Maryland countryside, with its rolling hills, its forests and its rivers, Lee was outnumbered, by some 38,000 to his 12,000 men, but certainly not outgeneraled. He came close to winning in part thanks to the caution and mistakes of his opponents.

The fighting, on a wide front stretching north to south, started at sunup and, unlike at Towton, we have eyewitness accounts of the day. A major in the 6th Wisconsin Volunteer Infantry Regiment described the first encounter, in a cornfield, with the Confederates: "We jumped over the fence, and pushed on, loading, firing, and shouting as we advanced. There was, on the part of the men, great hysterical excitement, eagerness to go forward, and a reckless disregard of life, of every thing but victory." The Rebels, as he called them, fled for their lives. "Great numbers of them are shot while climbing over the high post and rail fences along the turnpike." Elsewhere Confederate soldiers hung on for four hours in a sunken lane while Union soldiers poured fire on them. By the end, so the survivors said, "Bloody Lane" was carpeted with the dead and the blood flowed like a river. At Burnside Bridge a small body of sharpshooters from Georgia held off a much larger Union force until they ran out of ammunition and the Union soldiers charged with bayonets. The Union general chose prudence over daring and kept his reserves back, with the result that Lee and his forces were able to withdraw by the end of the day in good order.

He left behind some 1,500 to 2,700 of his men dead and it is estimated that there were also between 7,700 and 9,000 Confederate wounded. The Union suffered around 2,000 dead and nearly 10,000 wounded. The Union general Joseph Hooker described the scene in a cornfield after the fighting stopped: "In the time I am writing, every stalk of corn in the northern and greater part of the field was cut as closely as with a knife." The dead, he went on, "lay in rows precisely as they had stood in their ranks a few minutes before. It was never my fortune to witness a more bloody, dismal battlefield." Antietam was the single bloodiest day in the Civil War and indeed in all the wars the United States has fought. Although it was not a clear-cut victory for the Union, it served to end the South's attempt to take Maryland and possibly Washington itself. In its aftermath, President Lincoln issued his Emancipation Proclamation and its outcome may also have influenced Great Britain not to recognize the Confederacy.

Yet although the mood throughout the South was despondent after Antietam—its president, Jefferson Davis, said its "maximum strength has been mobilized, while the enemy is just beginning to put forth his might"—the Confederacy nevertheless fought on for two and a half more years. That earlier civil war in England lasted another twenty-four years.

What is it that will draw men, and less frequently women, into a conflict and keep them fighting even when the battle or the cause seems lost? And why is it that fighting can bring out the noblest and the basest sides of human nature? As we are both fascinated and repulsed by war, so too are we by those who fight, the warriors. We at once admire and fear them. And we wonder if we could do what they do. We puzzle over what it is that makes the warrior brave. As a Japanese soldier in China in the Second World War said, "Even when I gaze at the Chinese dead—forcing myself to look at them until I feel I can no longer stand it—no 'awakening' [satori] comes of it. I still cannot untangle the problem of where in one's heart practical bravery comes from." Men can be brave out of ignorance, said Pericles in his great funeral oration to the Athenians who had died in the Peloponnesian War, "and when they stop to think, they begin to fear. But the man who most truly can be accounted brave is he who best knows the meaning of what is sweet in life and of what is terrible, and then goes out undeterred to meet what is to come." One of war's many ironies is that the things worth living for can also be worth dying for.

The reasons why individuals fight, bravely or not, fall into the same rough categories that those for groups including nations do: for gain, to defend themselves or because of ideas and emotions. We can break them down still more. It is by no means an exhaustive list but here are some reasons people have given for fighting: because they have no choice; to protect their loved ones or their nation; out of a sense of honor; for fear of their officers; to win the approval of those they respect; to show off; to test themselves; to rape, pillage and loot; for glory; for a cause; for their comrades; or to get ahead in the world. In peacetime volunteers who join the military may not think of fighting at all but rather of seeing the world or learning a useful trade. The British military once came under heavy criticism for recruiting posters that showed tropical beaches, ski slopes or classrooms without a hint that those who signed up might be called upon to risk their lives in combat. Canada recently had an American deserter claiming refugee status because, he said, he had not understood that being in the military could involve going to a war.

Powerful states—and they have become that way at least partly through military force—often simply assume that their subjects belong to them and any attempt to avoid that obligation is equivalent to treason. Frederick the Great's father, the Prussian king Frederick William I, sent out scavenging parties to find tall soldiers for his beloved Potsdam Giants regiment. In many societies, slaves or those captured in war were forced into service. (Sparta, where only free men could serve in the army, never trusted its enslaved helots. In the Peloponnesian War it once asked its helots to volunteer for military service in return for their freedom; all those who did so were promptly executed to get rid of such dangerous initiative.) Christian slaves rowed the great fleets of the Ottoman Empire in the sixteenth century and Christian boys seized from their families and forcibly converted to Islam filled the ranks of the elite Ottoman Janissaries. Like the legions of Rome before them, the Janissaries ended by becoming the makers and breakers of rulers until finally in 1826 the Sultan, with the help of a new, more modern army and guns, destroyed them.

Before the advent of modern war, which drew in whole societies and required soldiers with education, European powers preferred to use the most expendable members of society to fill up the ranks of their armies. Shakespeare's great rogue Falstaff, who has newly been made a captain by Prince Hal, parades his motley recruits. The Prince is appalled: "I did never see such pitiful rascals." Falstaff is unrepentant: "Tut, tut; good enough to toss; food for powder, food for powder; they'll fill a pit as well as better: tush, man, mortal men, mortal men." In eighteenth-century Europe criminals, even murderers, were often given a choice, which was scarcely a real one at all: execution or join the military. Poor, friendless individuals were simply rounded up by press gangs to serve in the army or the navy. Or sometimes, as the Farquhar play *The Recruiting Officer* shows, young men were plied with drink until they signed on. There is a legend, which may even be true, that English pubs had glass-bottomed tankards so that the drinker could make sure that no one had slipped in a coin. Accepting the "king's shilling" was effectively signing a contract to join the military.

Good farmers or skilled artisans were much more valuable to their rulers at home. Frederick the Great said that his ordinary soldiers were the dregs of society, "sluggards, rakes, debauchees, rioters, undutiful sons and the like ..." The Duke of Wellington called his soldiers, who even after the French Revolution were recruited in the old way, "the scum of the earth." And to the earth they returned, their graves unmarked. When the peace came, many British proudly wore dentures made of "Waterloo teeth," taken by scavengers from the dead on the battlefield. In 1822 a London newspaper carried an item about how the battlefields from the Napoleonic Wars had been scoured for their bones, men's and animals' alike. Millions of bushels had been shipped to Hull and then sent on to bone grinders in Yorkshire, where powerful steam-powered machines had reduced them to powder. "In this condition they are sold to farmers to manure their lands."

Even the worst of wars can nevertheless also be an escape. The French Foreign Legion has always been known for not insisting on the real names or inquiring into the pasts of those who applied to join it. After the Second World War it recruited a number of men with French names who spoke with German or Italian accents and seemed to have a good understanding of military matters. Poverty was and still is an inducement to join the military. Today the American military recruits heavily in the poorer rural and urban areas. It is no accident that so many mercenaries in early modern Europe came from its poorest parts, such as Scotland, Switzerland or Ireland. Military service gave them more or less regular pay and food and the opportunity to help themselves to whatever they could, from money to women, as they marched along. For the exceptionally determined and lucky, war has provided an opportunity to rise socially. One of the most notorious figures of the seventeenth century's Thirty Years War was Ernst von Mansfeld, who was the illegitimate son of a German count. He first distinguished himself in fighting for the Habsburgs and their Holy Roman Empire and was rewarded when the emperor made him legitimate. Although he remained a Catholic, he switched to the Protestant cause, partly, it seems, because he felt that the Habsburgs had not treated him well, but also because he was likely to do better in terms of money and land. A century later Samuel Greig of Fife started out as an ordinary seaman and ended up as one of Catherine the Great's favorite admirals thanks to his bravery and success in naval battles. His elaborate tomb in Tallinn Cathedral was commissioned especially by the empress.

There is another sort of escape too that war offers and that is from the mundane and the boring. In Renaissance Europe upper-class young men offered their services to one army or another for the fun of it. "I have at all times," said one young Englishman proudly, "served as an adventurer at mine own charges ..." He had never accepted command of a company or taken pay because he wanted to be at liberty to come and go as he pleased. Benjamin Harris, who fought for the British in the Napoleonic Wars as a rifleman, an ordinary soldier, ended his days as a shopkeeper in London. "For my own part," he wrote in his memoirs, "I can only say that I enjoyed life more whilst on active service than I have ever done since; and as I sit at work in my shop in Richmond Street, Soho, I look back on that portion of my time spent in the fields of the Peninsula as the only part worthy of remembrance."

Before the First World War, a leading British Liberal, G. P. Gooch, wrote, "Long immunity from the realities of warfare has blunted our imaginations. We love excitement not a whit less than the Latin races; our lives are dull; a victory is a thing the meanest of us can understand." Many young men across Europe felt the tug of that excitement. Ernest Psichari, a young French-man who was already a hero for his adventures in French colonial Africa, loathed pacifism, which he felt was weakening France. In a book, *Call to Arms,* published just before the war, when the tensions were already rising in Europe, he looked forward eagerly to what he described as "the great harvest of Force, toward which a sort of inexpressible grace precipitates us and ravishes us ..." He was killed the following August. Rupert Brooke, the promising young English poet, said he longed for "some sort of upheaval."

When the war broke out he rushed to enlist and in one of his last poems before he died in 1915 he exulted:

> *Now, God be thanked Who has matched us with*
> *His hour,*
> *And caught our youth, and wakened us from sleeping,*
> *With hand made sure, clear eye, and sharpened power,*
> *To turn, as swimmers into cleanness leaping,*
> *Glad from a world grown old and cold and weary,*
> *Leave the sick hearts that honor could not move,*
> *And half-men, and their dirty songs and dreary,*
> *And all the little emptiness of love!*

Even in peacetime the military offers the enticing prospect of a secure world, where the rules are clear and decisions, at least for those in the lower ranks, are made by others. And, like a traveling circus or theatrical troupe, it has its own values, which are often pleasingly at odds with those of ordinary society. The great Renaissance philosopher Erasmus condemned the "wicked life of the soldier" and in his *Colloquies* imagined a monk talking to a soldier. The former remonstrates with the man for abandoning his family to become a soldier and butchering other Christians. And why, asks the monk, are you so poor? "You ask why?" says the soldier. "Whatever I got by way of pay, booty, sacrilege, theft and pillage was spent on wine, whoring and dice." Renaissance soldiers—and it is possible to think of parallels today, in the civil wars in Africa, for example—highlighted their differences from civilians by growing their beards and hair, wearing outlandish hats and garish clothes, and sporting outsize codpieces. When a man becomes a soldier, Machiavelli commented, not only does he change "his clothing, but he adopts attitudes, manners, ways of speaking and bearing himself, quite at odds with those of civilian life." During the American War of Independence, the inhabitants of New York complained to the British authorities about what happened when their Hessian mercenaries were paid: "For three days they are given up to intoxication, and we have trying and grievous scenes to go through; fighting brawls, drumming and fifing, and dancing the night long, card and dice playing, and every abomination going on under our very roofs."

The need to escape, whether from poverty or punishment, can force people into the military, while others are encouraged and sustained even in combat by their own cultures. Values and ideologies, including religion and nationalism, motivate individuals just as they do nations. Religions promise immortality or rewards in the afterlife for those who die in battle. Thousands of Iranian volunteers marched across mine-strewn battlefields in the long war between Iran and Iraq in the 1980s, believing that they would go directly to heaven when they died because the ayatollahs had told them so. Some carried keys they had been given which were supposed to speed their entry. The Soviet women interviewed by the great Belarussian writer Svetlana Alexievich all said they had no choice but to volunteer during the Second World War because their homeland had been invaded. Sermons, books, pamphlets, plays and paintings, then later radio, cinema and television can work powerfully on people to urge them into war. Revolutionary France was permeated with images and pageants showing heroism in war. Between 1789 and 1799 more than 3,000 revolutionary songs appeared. In the First and Second World Wars mass-produced posters—"Your Country Needs You" or "I want YOU for the US Army"—urged men to enlist and civilians to support the war effort.

For men war offers a chance to test themselves, against their peers but also their elders. In Germany before 1914 young men heard repeated stories from the older generation about how they had suffered and sacrificed to build the nation in its wars of unification, and they longed, or so they often said, for the chance to do the same; while in Germany's enemies, Britain and France, young men dreamed of heroically defending their homelands and, in the case of France, getting revenge for the defeat of 1870–71. It has almost always been the young men who volunteer or are taken first for war. They are physically fitter and more resilient than their elders and, as well, they have not yet developed the ties of family and community which might make them less willing to risk their lives.

The assumption that it is the men who should be warriors seems to be almost universal through time and across cultures and, while there are examples of women warriors, the overwhelming majority of those who have fought are men. And when rules of war have developed in different societies, women, along with old people, children and, sometimes, priests have been classified as noncombatants. The reasons why men have largely done the fighting and women have not are as much debated as the origins of war itself, and again the explanations range from the biological to the cultural. If gender differences are averaged, men come out higher on the scale of strength and size and possibly aggression, but there are many big strong women who can match and surpass men. The fact that men have more testosterone than women may make them more prone to being aggressive—although scientists are far from reaching a consensus—but there are many men who are gentle by nature and do not want to fight. Militaristic societies such as Sparta or the military through the ages would not have spent so much time on training which inculcates the "right" attitudes if the great majority of men were natural-born killers. Women, when they choose or are obliged to fight, can be as fierce as men.

The Chinese have a story of how Sunzi went to give advice on war to the king of Wu. The king had read Sunzi's writings and asked whether he could make the royal concubines into soldiers. The sage said he could and taught the women the words for drill. So he divided them into companies, gave them spears and set them to marching. When he ordered them to turn, they giggled. Sunzi was patient and said that the general is at fault if his commands are not clear. He went over the drill several times, and again the women marched. Sunzi ordered the drums to sound the signal to turn and yet again the women failed to obey and giggled. Finally, after several tries, Sunzi said that the general's commands had been clear and when soldiers disobey it is the fault of their officers. He ordered that the concubines who were in charge of the companies should be beheaded. These were the favorites of the king and he protested. Sunzi was implacable: he had undertaken to train the troops and he could not accept the order to spare the women. The two died and new officers were appointed. The women drilled perfectly and in silence.

Perhaps the existence in different cultures of war-making goddesses—Astarte, Athena, Kali, the Valkyrie—or the legends surrounding warrior queens such as Zenobia of Palmyra is a recognition of women's potential. It is also a way of limiting it to divine or perhaps unnatural women. From Boudicca, the British queen of the first century A.D., who is often portrayed in her war chariot, to the Rani of Jhansi, who led her troops against the British in the Indian Mutiny of 1857, many cultures have stories, some legend and some based on fact, of individual women warriors. Some have fought as women but many disguised themselves as men, including Deborah Sampson, who was in the American War of Independence, and Lizzie Compton and Frances Hook in the American Civil War, who kept reenlisting when their identities were discovered. Just like the women warriors in films such as *Crouching Tiger, Hidden Dragon, Wonder Woman* and *Kill Bill*, however, they are exceptions, seen as outside the normal order of things where war is the male sphere.

We used to assume that the Amazons were legendary despite accounts by the ancient Greeks which placed them somewhere in Asia Minor. The Greeks were fascinated and horrified by the stories of such unnatural women, who were reputed to cut off their breasts in order to pull their bows better and to cripple their own male children. The Amazons were said to have fought successfully in battle against men until the right order was at last restored and they were defeated. Recent archeological evidence suggests that the Amazons were not a fable believed by the ancient Greeks. Since it is now possible for archeologists to determine the sex of skeletons, a lot of what had been assumed to be male warriors have had to be reclassified as women. Among the nomadic horse-riding warrior peoples from the steppes whom the Greeks called Scythians women appear to have been the equals of men, even when it came to fighting, and in death they lie with their weapons. Perhaps as many as 37 percent of Scythian burials are of women warriors. Tombs of Viking women warriors from a later period have been found as well.

The west coast of Africa produced a modern-day equivalent to the Amazons in Dahomey, a state whose wealth and power came from slave trading and its highly militarized society. The Victorian traveler Richard Burton, who visited in 1863, described it as "this small black Sparta" and was struck by its elite corps of women warriors. In the early 1700s, so it is said, a ruler was short of men for his army, so he dressed a company of women in uniform to deceive his enemies. His pretense became actual as the women turned out to be a highly effective palace guard and combat troops. They may have made up as much as a third of the king's forces. The women were physically tough, well disciplined and armed with muskets and, later, rifles. They were reputed to be ferocious and implacable and much better fighters than the men. In Dahomey's last battles, in the second half of the nineteenth century, the women warriors fought to the bitter end. They were "remarkable for their courage and their ferocity," said a French marine, and threw themselves against the French bayonets "with prodigious bravery."

We remember such women warriors because they have been so rare in history. When women have been active participants in war, it has more often been as mistresses or wives accompanying their men, as nurses, cooks or purveyors of food or sex. The Spanish army in the Netherlands in the sixteenth century had 400 mounted prostitutes and another 400 on foot. In the American Civil War, the women who accompanied the Union general Joseph Hooker's Army of the Potomac generated a new word for prostitutes. Anglo-Saxon armies have been squeamish about official brothels, partly because of pressure from society, although the Indian Army ran them quietly on the side. The French army long had them as a matter of course. At the siege of Dien Bien Phu in Indochina in 1953, when a French force was surrounded by the Vietnamese nationalists—the Viet Minh—two mobile field brothels made up of women from Algeria and Morocco were trapped along with the defenders, and ended by sharing in the nursing of the soldiers. Often, as with the euphemistically named "comfort women" under the Japanese occupations of Korea and China, the women were forced into prostitution.

In Europe's early modern wars, the camp followers, and they could include men as well, often formed a long tail for relatively small forces. A Spanish force besieging the Dutch town of Bergen-op-Zoon in 1622 was, said a local, "such a small army with so many carts, baggage horse, nags, sutlers, lackeys, women, children, and a rabble which numbered far more than the army itself." The authorities often tried to limit the numbers, but until armies could provide their own supplies they were forced to allow the private suppliers. Moreover, it was almost impossible to prevent desperate women from following the armies; if their men abandoned them they and their children would probably die. If the men themselves died in battle or of disease the women would have to find other husbands or protectors as quickly as possible.

Although she came from a different social class to many of the camp followers, the Spaniard Juana Smith was equally vulnerable when she met her husband, Harry, during Wellington's campaigns in Spain. She was fourteen, penniless—her family was Spanish aristocracy but had been ruined by the French invasion and subsequent war—and alone in the world except for an older sister.

He was a British officer who, impetuous in this as well as in battle, fell madly in love with her. By marrying Harry, she gained a protector, at least while he lived, which, for a young officer at the time, was not likely to be long, but she cut herself off from her compatriots by marrying a Protestant. The marriage, most improbably, turned out to be a long and exceedingly happy one. Juana followed her husband through Spain, sharing the hardships of the campaign, as Wellington drove Napoleon's armies northward and she scoured the battlefields at Vitoria and then Waterloo to find him once the guns had fallen silent. She was with him when he fought in India and then in South Africa, where the city of Ladysmith is named after her.

While women have moved into other formerly male spheres in the twentieth century, armed forces have been slow to accept them as equals and use them in combat. The reluctance, or perhaps it is more accurate to call it resistance, has drawn on various arguments: that women are by nature nurturers, not warriors; that their presence on the battlefield might be bad for discipline as the men in their unit try to protect them; or that they are physically and temperamentally unfitted for the rigors of war. Or perhaps what really matters is that men fear that admitting women will destroy a cozy club. American male marines, said a woman officer, felt that the presence of women would make it impossible for them any longer to "fart, burp, tell raunchy jokes, walk around naked, swap sex stories, wrestle and simply be young men together." Why are you women, a teammate from a US special operations unit asked a female colleague, "trying to destroy the last good thing we [men] have left?" In recent decades most Western armies have gradually incorporated women as regular troops, but old attitudes die hard. In the 1990s an officer in the Russian navy greeted the first woman cadet to be admitted to its Naval Academy with "One girl alone cannot ruin the navy." American women going into the Marines, perhaps the toughest of all the services, have encountered hostility and misogyny, even sexual abuse. And often hostility has come from society at large. Women in uniform have been seen, contradictorily, as either sexless or oversexed. The British in the First World War eliminated the breast pocket on women's uniforms for fear it would call attention to the real thing underneath. In the Second World War a whispering campaign accused members of the American Women's Army Corps (the WACs) of being little better than prostitutes. Many of the women warriors Alexievich spoke to found that when they came home women who had not fought accused them of going off to the front to chase men. "We know what you did there!"

Women warriors have also struggled against the perception that they are softer than men. One of the comments that stood out for me during my Reith Lectures on war came from a young woman officer at York. She was the mother of two small children but, she said, when she was deployed to Afghanistan she forced herself not to think about them. While she was there her unit had an anthrax scare and they were all given injections, along with a warning that this might make women infertile. Again, she said, she simply could not think about it. The auditorium was completely silent.

The demands of mass war in the twentieth century meant that women had to be allowed into the armed forces, but typically they were assigned to noncombat roles, as nurses or clerks, driving vehicles or ferrying planes. The British discovered that women recruits were good at the painstaking work of reading aerial photography, perhaps, as one officer suggested, because they had experience in fine needlework. Even the Nazis, who had made such play of *Kinder, Küche, Kirche* (children, kitchen, church) as women's proper sphere, found they had to call them into service in the Second World War. By 1945 there were 500,000 women in the German armed forces in support roles. There were probably double that number in the Soviet forces. The Soviet authorities had always talked in peacetime about the equality of men and women (although the reality was rather different), but it was the devastating losses of men suffered during the German invasion that brought women into the armed forces, many of them as volunteers. Soviet women were at the front as medical staff but also as combatants, anti-aircraft gunners, partisans behind the German lines, infantry, tank crew and pilots. The Soviet air force had three all-women units of which the most famous was a bomber regiment nicknamed by the Germans the "night witches." Soviet men found their presence unsettling at first, partly because so many of the women were so young and partly because their presence reminded them of home. Olga, a medical assistant interviewed by Alexievich, remembered, "Once during the night I sat by a dugout and began to sing softly. I thought everyone was asleep and no one would hear me, but in the morning the commander said to me, 'We didn't sleep. Such longing for a woman's voice . . .'" The male commander of an anti-aircraft regiment initially said that women could not fit in: military affairs "from time immemorial had been considered men's work." What is more, the shells were too heavy for women to carry; their presence in the same dugout would be disturbing for the men; everyone knew that sitting on the metal control seats for hours on end was bad for women; and where, finally, "would they wash and dry their hair"? The needs of war forced both the women and the men in the unit to adapt. "We walked a hard path together," said one woman. The Germans were often particularly brutal to captured Soviet women soldiers, parading them to show how they were monsters or shooting them out of hand. The women warriors kept two bullets handy, one to kill themselves before the Germans could and the second in case the first misfired.

Some 27,000 Soviet women also fought as guerrillas against the Germans, and in Italy, it is said, 35,000 women were in the partisans during the Second World War and some were killed in fighting. Women fought and died in Yugoslavia, Greece, Poland and Denmark. The French Resistance tended to limit women to supporting roles, partly because the Gaullist Free French did not approve of giving guns to women. Or, as one male member of the Resistance told the British, "If women must be used, then it is preferable to use older women . . . less likely to be a source of temptation to colleagues . . ." From 1943, the formidable Maquis, which fought first in the mountains and hills of southeastern France, dispensed with women altogether. Since 1945 women have continued to fight in guerrilla wars against foreign occupiers or their own governments but when the fighting has stopped their contributions have often been downplayed or written out of the history. When the Sandinistas won in Nicaragua in 1979 most women were demobilized or moved to women-only units. After the Algerian War of Independence the women who fought were not given pensions.

Biology is clearly not a sufficient explanation for the long-standing gender differences which are only now, sporadically and fitfully, starting to change. Given the profound influences war and society have had on each other, we cannot ignore the ways in which war has shaped our understanding of what men and women should be. We know that culture, in its broadest sense of the values and beliefs a society holds dear and which help to keep it together, shapes humans as much as or more than biology. We hold such expectations before our young and we educate them in our ways.

War and masculinity have a long and intimate relationship in much of human history and we have tended to see woman's work as centered around the home and the family. In the *Iliad* Hector parts with his wife, Andromache, as he goes to fight the Greeks, saying:

> *So please go home and tend to your own tasks,*
> *The distaff and the loom, and keep the women*
> *working hard as well. As for the fighting,*
> *men will see to that, all who were born in Troy*
> *but I most of all.*

Mussolini declared, "War is to men what maternity is to women."
Fascists have been particularly enamored of traditional gender
roles. Vichy France made Mother's Day a major festival and
awarded medals to good mothers. Goebbels, the Nazi propaganda
chief, argued that "Man should be trained as a warrior and woman
as recreation for the warrior," a precept he put into practice in his
own life as far as the recreation was concerned. He also said sanc-
timoniously, "If we eliminate women from every realm of public
life, we do it not in order to dishonor her, but in order that her
honor may be restored to her." Such attitudes have not gone away
even in more liberal societies.

If men's views on women as warriors are ambivalent so too are
women's. Successive waves of feminists have been uncomfortable
with discussion of women fighting, preferring to see war as something men do. Jean Bethke Elshtain, a philosopher who, among
much else, explored gender roles and war, was struck by a special
issue of the *Women's Studies International Forum*, which, as its
name indicates, exists to encourage feminist research. The topic
announced, "Women and Men's Wars," she reflected, encourages
women to turn away. "War is men's: men are the historic authors
of organized violence. Yes, women have been drawn in—and they
have been required to observe, suffer, cope, mourn, honor, adore,
witness, work. But men have done the *describing* and *defining* of
war, and the women are 'affected' by it; they 'mostly react.'" While
there has been considerable research into the impact of war on
women, there is comparatively little on women as warriors or on
the broader topic of gender and war.

Yet in so many societies, in the past and now, boys are told to
be men and part of that is showing the sorts of qualities we associate with warriors. As they grow up they endure rituals, often
painful ones, to initiate them into manhood. As children boys are
given toy weapons, little uniforms or war games. In nineteenth-
century Europe conscription was often called "the school of man-
liness." Far more than women, men learn to fear being cowards.
Being accused of behaving like a woman carries connotations of

1. Vladimir Ilyich Lenin arrives at the Helsinki Station in St. Petersburg in April 1917. Without the First World War he and his tiny radical faction, the Bolsheviks, would never have had the opportunity to seize power in Russia. Among the many unintended consequences of war are great political changes as regimes falter and their publics lose patience.

2. Winter supply lines across Lake Ladoga during the siege of Leningrad, as St. Petersburg was then known. Sieges have long been part of warfare as a way of breaking the will of the enemy to fight on. In the Second World War, German forces besieged Leningrad for nearly 900 days. The city was able to endure but an unknown number of civilians, perhaps over a million, died.

3. The Confederate dead at the bloody battle of Antietam in 1862 during the American Civil War, by the famous photographer Alexander Gardner. He was known to have rearranged corpses for his shots and perhaps did here. Civil wars are often long and costly because of the passions they arouse. More Americans died in that war than in all other US conflicts put together.

4. The first great Republican offensive during the Spanish Civil War. Here the pioneering photographer Gerda Taro captures the house-to-house fighting near Madrid in 1936 as the Republicans who were defending the legitimate government tried to push back the right-wing insurgents led by General Francisco Franco.

5. A woman worker in Britain filling a shell during the First World War. Women took on what had been seen as "men's work" as the men went off to the battlefields. The chemicals used in munitions factories turned many of the women yellow and the "Canary Girls" often gave birth to babies of the same color. Women's contribution to the war effort helped to weaken social and legal obstacles to women working outside the home.

6. Soviet women pilots of the 588th Night Bomber Regiment, nicknamed by the Germans the "night witches." While the great majority of combatants in war throughout history have been men, there are many examples of women warriors from the Amazons to the present day. In the Second World War, Soviet women were also snipers, gunners, and partisan fighters.

7. A British Royal Air Force Vickers Vernon, which could carry troops and bombs, flying over Baghdad and the River Tigris in the 1920s. In an early example of the use of the new technology of air power in war, the British used planes like this to cow the rebellious Iraqis who found themselves under British rule after the First World War.

8. Women walk in a neighborhood damaged by air strikes in Idlib, Syria. Taken in March 2020, in the tenth year of the Syrian civil war, this photograph is testament to the costs that war exacts on civilians. While there has been no major war between nations since the Iran–Iraq conflict of the 1980s, long-running civil wars around the world continue to kill hundreds of thousands of civilians and make many more into refugees.

9. The first successful explosion of an atomic bomb at Alamogordo, New Mexico, in July 1945. The Manhattan Project, which made the calculations of physicists such as Albert Einstein into reality, gave the United States a new and immensely destructive weapon. Its use on the Japanese cities of Hiroshima and Nagasaki hastened the end of the Second World War in the Pacific but has remained controversial ever since. By 2020 nine powers possessed nuclear weapons, so far only as deterrents.

10. Greenham Common, United Kingdom, 1982: the Women's Protest against the deployment of American cruise missiles. Starting in 1981, groups of women, using nonviolent means, attempted to prevent the delivery of the missiles. Here some of the 30,000 protestors have formed a human blockade around the base. Attempts to limit or ban war totally have a history as long as war itself.

11. North Vietnamese soldiers walking past abandoned American military equipment. The Vietnam War of the 1960s, fought primarily between the United States and the North Vietnamese and their supporters in South Vietnam, ended in a truce in 1973. While the Americans were never defeated militarily, they lost the political battle at home and abroad. In 1975 North Vietnam took over the South.

12. An Austrian soldier on the Italian Front in the First World War. While we tend to think of battlefields as open spaces, war takes place on many terrains, from jungles to icy mountains. The fighting between Italy and Austria between 1915 and 1918 was often at high altitudes, which made moving men and equipment a particular challenge.

13. A scene from *Apocalypse Now* showing armored "Huey" helicopters attacking ground targets. In the Vietnam War, the United States had the technological edge, and "Hueys" were key to its command of the air. The Francis Ford Coppola movie, which was made in the Philippines, is an indictment of the madness and cruelty of war but also captures its excitement.

14. American marines fighting in 1950 in the early stages of the Korean War. While modern militaries have come to rely increasingly on technology, wars often still involve "boots on the ground." When North Korea invaded the South in 1950, the United States, acting under United Nations auspices, rushed ground troops there who managed to halt the invasion. This image was taken by the famous American photographer David Douglas Duncan.

15. American Army military police escorting a Taliban prisoner, Camp X-Ray Naval Base, Guantánamo Bay, Cuba, 2002. Rules governing the treatment of prisoners of war have existed in many cultures and were given greater shape in successive Geneva Conventions from the nineteenth century onward. The US has been much criticized for holding prisoners captured during its War on Terror, and not allowing them the protection of the Geneva Conventions.

16. China's National Day military parade. Here surface-to-surface guided missiles pass massed crowds and the Chinese communist leadership at the Tiananmen (Heavenly Peace) Gate in the center of Beijing in 2001. Despite civilian participation, the parade has become a showcase of China's military.

emotionalism and weakness. In military training, even today in modern societies, sergeants and officers shame new recruits by calling them "pussy" or "girl." So for women to fight alongside men threatens to undermine notions of what it is to be a man. As a noncommissioned officer from the elite US Navy SEALs (motto: "The Only Easy Day Was Yesterday") put it, "These guys were raised to think that girls were weaker and inferior, and put all their identity and manhood in what they do. So when these guys see women in the field, they panic, thinking, 'Oh my God, what does that make me?'"

Women have played a part in the making of the male warrior. She was convinced she had loved a coward, said an American woman during the Second World War, when she received a letter from her boyfriend in which he admitted that he wept during heavy fighting: "I never wrote to him again." Like the Spartan mothers in classical Greece or the women in the First World War who handed out white feathers to men of military age who were not in uniform, women have urged men to fight and shamed them for refusing. In different cultures women have taunted men by stripping naked or exposing their genitals to mock what they perceive as male cowardice. During the left-wing government of Salvador Allende in Chile, some of his conservative women opponents threw corn at the military because they were "chickens" afraid to remove him from office.

Women have opposed war, sometimes on the grounds that they create life and do not take it away, but they have also been its cheerleaders. "Do not think I am crying because my two older sons are dead," said a Bulgarian mother in the early twentieth century. "I'm crying because the two younger boys are not old enough to go and help drive out the Turks." In nineteenth-century Prussia patriotic women raised funds to build battleships. Those militant suffragists Emmeline and Christabel Pankhurst swung around after 1914 from demanding votes for women to supporting the war effort wholeheartedly, including the conscription of men. In the First World War a letter by a woman who described herself

as "A Little Mother" with a "Message to Pacifists" appeared in
1916 in the mass-circulation British paper the *Morning Post* and
sold 70,000 copies in under a week when it was reprinted as a
pamphlet. British women, she said, as mothers of the men who
were fighting to uphold the honor and traditions of the empire,
would not tolerate calls for peace. "There is only one temperature
for women of the British race, and that is white heat." We women,
she went on, "pass on the ammunition of 'the only sons'" to fill up
the gaps. Women, "gentle-nurtured" and "timid," had not wanted
the war but they had risen to their responsibility. "We've fetched
our laddie from school, we've put his cap away . . ." If, she concluded proudly, their sons did not come back, British women
would have the glorious memories of their men.

As Virginia Woolf wrote in *A Room of One's Own*:

> Women have served all these centuries as looking-
> glasses, possessing the magic and delicious power of reflect-
> ing the figure of man at twice its natural size. Without that
> power probably the earth would still be swamp and jungle.
> The glories of all our wars would be unknown. We should
> still be scratching the outlines of deer on the remains of
> mutton bones and bartering flints for sheep skins or what-
> ever simple ornament took our unsophisticated taste. Su-
> permen and Fingers of Destiny would never have existed.
> The Czar and the Kaiser would never have worn crowns or
> lost them. Whatever may be their use in civilized societies,
> mirrors are essential to all violent and heroic action. That is
> why Napoleon and Mussolini both insist so emphatically
> upon the inferiority of women, for if they were not inferior,
> they would cease to enlarge. That serves to explain in part
> the necessity that women so often are to men.

That Western exemplar of the great warrior, Achilles, who was
trained from childhood to become above all a superb killing ma-

chine, turned to his mother, the sea nymph Thetis, to help in his pain and anger when Agamemnon, commander of the Greek invaders of Troy, humiliated him. She promised him revenge and provided him with a special suit of armor. And there have been many parallels to Achilles in real life. Julian Grenfell came from an old aristocratic English family. He, his brother Billy and his two Grenfell cousins grew up before the First World War in great houses where visitors included prime ministers, leading writers, royalty—and distinguished officers. Grenfells were good at fighting and hunting, itself a preparation for war, at least of the old style. The family tree included admirals and generals and one field marshal. Grenfells won medals for bravery and Grenfells died bravely in Britain's wars around the world. When the First World War started, Julian was in South Africa, desperate to get back to Europe to join in the fighting. "It is horrible being tucked away here at a time like this," he wrote to his mother, Lady Desborough. "It must be wonderful in England now!" When he reached the trenches on the Western Front he wrote extraordinarily open letters to her about the experience of soldiering, his fears of being a coward and the thrill of battle. She circulated them proudly to her friends and persuaded the editor of *The Times* to publish them anonymously.

The most important thing for the Duke of Wellington was not that his officers could read a map or understand how a gun worked; it was that they should be brave. Before 1914 English public schools, their families and their friends taught that lesson to middle- and upper-class boys like Grenfell and his cousins: they were to learn to keep their upper lips stiff and their emotions well under control. If death came for them they must face it bravely. In great struggles like the First and Second World Wars it was almost unthinkable not to go when everyone about was enlisting and when civilians looked askance at men of military age who were not in uniform. It was not courage or his own initiative, said one Englishman, that led him to the front in France in the First World War: "On the contrary, I have been carried along on the crest of the world's event, that is all. It is weakness, the inability to resist the tide of time. No, it is not weakness; it is youth."

Cultures need heroes and so often the most vivid in our imaginations are the warriors. Hector, Achilles, Genghis Khan, Launcelot, Robert the Bruce, Julius Caesar, Babur, Frederick the Great, Napoleon, Baron von Richthofen, Geronimo, Richard the Lionheart, Saladin. The Old Testament is filled with stories of great warriors—Joshua, Gideon, David. We all have our own lists, but heroes cross cultural boundaries. Alexander the Great started his invasion of Asia by laying wreaths on what he supposed was the tomb of Achilles. Napoleon dreamed of Alexander when he invaded Egypt, and the unfortunate Napoleon III, his nephew, tried to emulate his great uncle by commanding his own troops in the Franco-Prussian War and so led them to disaster at Sedan. Nineteenth-century Europe rediscovered the Middle Ages and part of what attracted it was the image of the noble knight in armor prepared to battle and die for his own honor and that of his lady. An Austrian army handbook of 1889 read: "The strict interpretation of military honor ennobles the officer corps in its entirety and endows it with the character of knighthood." As a young soldier called Huntly Gordon leaned on the rail of the ship carrying him to France in 1914, his companion quoted lines from Shakespeare's *Henry V:* "Now, lords, for France; the enterprise whereof / Shall be to you, as us, like glorious." The young men who went off to war in 1914, whether they came from the great cities of Europe or the remoter parts of Canada or Australia, had been brought up on the classic myths and epics, on great literature, popular novels such as *The Three Musketeers* or the seemingly endless succession of boys' adventure stories.

War can offer adventure; it has also been a business, often a very profitable one. Mercenaries, free lancers as they were once known after their weapons, or guns for hire, have an ancient and frequently dishonorable history. In the thirteenth and fourteenth

centuries bands of armed men roamed Italy, hiring themselves
out to prosperous city-states for their struggles with their neighbors. Some were local men while others had drifted down over
the Alps, veterans perhaps from the Crusades or dynastic wars
with few skills beyond fighting. Their leaders signed a contract, a
condotta, to provide a certain number of soldiers. The men, the
condottieri, came with their own weapons and armor and usually
fought for as long as they were paid. If the funds did not come for
some reason they were quite capable of stopping in the middle of
a campaign, even during a battle, and holding their employer to
ransom. When campaigning, which usually took place in the dry
summer months, finished, the *condottieri* often roamed around
the countryside helping themselves to whatever they could lay
their hands on. Like a gang leader today with his boastful tattoos,
one *condottieri* captain proudly bore the motto on his breastplate
"Enemy of God, Enemy of Piety, Enemy of Peace." Machiavelli
loathed the mercenaries as dangerous parasites on the body poli-
tic and urged Italian rulers to institute militia made up of civilians
who would be imbued with the right sorts of virtues and have
true loyalty to their city and, equally important, be well disciplined and well trained. The challenge, he discovered, and it is a
perennial one, is how to take civilians—farmers, shoemakers, office clerks or schoolteachers—and make them into a cohesive
body of troops, prepared to obey orders and endure hardship, and
be ready to kill and be killed.

Like many of his contemporaries, Machiavelli consulted the
classical writers. "Victory in war," said the much-admired Vegetius, "does not depend entirely upon numbers or mere courage;
only skill and discipline will ensure it." The Romans, he went on,
conquered the world because they were continually training their
troops, they maintained strong discipline and they took the arts
of war seriously:

> Without these, what chance would the inconsiderable
> numbers of the Roman armies have had against the multi-

tudes of the Gauls? Or with what success would their small size have been opposed to the prodigious stature of the Germans? The Spaniards surpassed us not only in numbers, but in physical strength. We were always inferior to the Africans in wealth and unequal to them in deception and stratagem. And the Greeks, indisputably, were far superior to us in skill in arts and all kinds of knowledge.

In societies such as the Roman, the prevailing culture had already partly prepared young men to become soldiers. In other times and places, however, the hold of civilian society over recruits has had to be firmly severed, symbolically and literally, before they can be molded into good soldiers. Taking off civilian clothes and putting on uniforms, standardized haircuts and living in barracks all mark the passage from one world to another. Old loyalties, to family, friends or communities, must be superseded by newer ones to the regiment, the ship or the squadron. Standards, the bronze or silver eagles the Roman legions carried, for example, flags, stories of past triumphs or defeats are part of a new shared identity. When the Emperor Augustus recovered two Roman eagles which had been lost to the Parthians, he built a temple to house them and struck a coin in their honor. In the sixteenth century the fearsome German mercenary companies, the *Landsknechte*, greeted new members with an elaborate, quasi-religious ceremony. The recruits passed under an arch made from halberds and pikes for their enrollment, which included the inscribing of their names on a register and their acceptance of their first pay. They then listened to a reading of the fierce discipline code and took an oath to accept it. To keep their memories fresh, gallows, drawn or actual, marked off their territory. And the gallows would be used.

Military discipline has always depended in large part upon fear of punishment, from being confined to barracks to execution. From the ancient Greeks to the Iroquois, the military have used the gauntlet, with the victim running between his fellows as they strike at him. Prussian officers beat their men with the flats of their swords, while the Spanish used the ramrods from their muskets. For centuries the British army and navy used the cat-o'-nine-tails, which could lay a man's back open. The future admiral Jacky Fisher fainted as a thirteen-year-old cadet when he saw his first flogging. While the sorts of crimes soldiers can be accused of have changed—if blasphemy were still one most Western barracks would be largely silent—some remain remarkably consistent across time and space. Failure to obey orders, losing one's weapon and desertion are all a threat to order and unity and that is particularly dangerous in battle. "A soldier," said Frederick the Great, "must fear his officer more than the enemy." In a very different time, a very different man, the Russian revolutionary Leon Trotsky, said much the same thing: "A soldier must be faced with the choice between a probable death if he advances and certain death if he retreats." Like many others before and since, Trotsky's Red Army used summary executions on the battlefield, as did the Soviet armies in the Second World War.

In 1941 William McNeill, a young American who had been drafted, along with millions of others, encountered another, equally ancient way that the military make individuals into soldiers. On a dry and dusty Texas plain he had to submit to endless drilling as an "illiterate non-com" shouted orders. "A more useless exercise would be hard to imagine." Years later McNeill, by now a distinguished historian, realized that he remembered the drill with something like affection: "Words are inadequate to describe the emotion aroused by the prolonged movement in unison that drilling involved." He felt, he recalled, a sense of well-being and pleasure at being part of a collective ritual with his fellow soldiers. Marching became an end in itself: "Moving briskly and keeping in time was enough to make us feel good about ourselves, satisfied to be moving together, and vaguely pleased with the world at large." In our individualistic contemporary societies we laugh at and deplore the turning of humans into automatons, as in the mass gymnastics in Pyongyang or soldiers goose-stepping at military parades, but we also admire the teamwork that sends a rowing eight gliding across the water or a corps de ballet across the stage. McNeill eventually wrote a book about the importance of what he named "muscular bonding." Drill and discipline together create the warriors who will obey orders and perform tasks together like trained athletes and dancers even in the most difficult of circumstances. "It is only wonderful," said Wellington of his "scum of the earth," "that we should be able to make so much out of them."

We may deplore the very notion of training that turns men into parts of a greater machine, with their muscles automatically carrying on, but it is necessary if they are to function in battle. Having a clear task, as sailors do on their ships, for example, can keep panic at bay. Training and discipline also make the military do what is unnatural in risking their own lives and taking those of others. When discipline and training fail and units lose cohesion not only are they less of a threat to the enemy but they become vulnerable. At the Battle of Antietam the 16th Connecticut Infantry Regiment, which had only been organized a month before, was sent into combat with virtually no training. Its men barely knew how to fire their weapons and indeed they had only learned how to load them the previous day. The 16th's men did not know how to march or to wheel about as a body, something which is difficult in the best of times but especially on the battlefield, and their officers did not yet have either the authority or the knowledge to command them. When they were attacked on their flank through the tall stalks of corn by the toughened and experienced Confederate soldiers, there was chaos. The 16th's officers, as inexperienced as the men, had no idea what to do. One said desperately to his colonel, "Tell us what you want us to do and we'll try to obey you." The men simply panicked and fled. A Confederate soldier described a crowd of terrified Union soldiers, at the bottom of a hill "in a crouching disorderly line," unable to move. "We poured into them," he said, "volley after volley, doubtless with terrible execution." The 16th lost 25 percent of its strength that day.

Military hierarchy, cohesion and strong morale can bring their own dangers. In October 1943 an officer spoke to a group of his men: "Most of you will know what it is like when a hundred corpses lie together, when there are five hundred, or when there are a thousand. And to have seen this through, and—apart from exceptional cases of human weakness—to have remained decent, has made us hard and is a page of glory never mentioned and never to be mentioned." The speaker was Heinrich Himmler, Hitler's devoted lieutenant and head of the Nazis' own military, the Schutzstaffel or SS, which was responsible for their worst atrocities. His audience were SS officers in German-occupied Poland and the page of glory he was talking about was the extermination of Europe's Jews. While some soldiers come to enjoy the sadistic pleasure of torturing and killing the helpless, others simply treat it as a job to be done.

A strong sense of comradeship and a willingness to follow orders, which make men fight and endure together, can lead to systematic organized cruelty and evil. *Ordinary Men* is what the historian Christopher Browning entitled his study of a German police battalion that massacred Jews in Poland. Some were anti-Semites but most seem simply to have been obeying orders. The men were given the option to transfer out of the battalion if they found the task too hard; of 500, fewer than a dozen left. In 1944 an SS company went to the small French town of Oradour-sur-Glane and killed everyone, men, women and children, they could find, later giving as an excuse the fact that the town was heavily involved in the Resistance. Some 642 died, even though the SS had not found any evidence of Resistance activity. One of the SS killers later said to another German veteran, "Speaking as one old SS man to another, Herr Müller, it was nothing. In Russia, we did such things every day." The ruined village has remained empty ever since, as a memorial to that dark time. We cannot take comfort, however, in the fact that the "ordinary" men of the police battalion or those in the SS were Nazis. Even the military from good democratic regimes with strong liberal values are capable of committing atrocities. One of the perennial challenges facing even those societies that deplore such wanton violence is to make their military into killers but controlled ones. The delicate balance is between training recruits to overcome the normal human inhibitions against killing—otherwise they will not be useful in combat—and reining them in from going too far.

War has its own laws and one of the oldest and most persistent is that those who have surrendered and civilians, where possible, should be spared. Yet we all know the stories or have seen pictures of the sacking of cities, the execution of prisoners of war, the shelling of churches filled with refugees, or the farm buildings deliberately set on fire, and we remember names such as Oradour or Wounded Knee or Nanjing. For any American who lived through the Vietnam War the incident at My Lai, when a representative group of ordinary American soldiers rampaged through a village, has come to represent the barbarism of much of that war. (The Vietnamese forces committed their own atrocities, but Vietnam has been slow to come to terms with them.) In 1968 American reporters in the country started to hear stories about the murder in cold blood of some 500 villagers, of all ages, by an American patrol. One courageous helicopter pilot who was there did his best to save the Vietnamese and later filed a report with his superiors, who did nothing. Senior officers in Vietnam and later in Washington did their best to cover the incident up. In 1969 one of America's most respected journalists, Mike Wallace, interviewed Paul Meadlo, one of the soldiers responsible, who admitted freely that he had fired at point-blank range into helpless civilians. "And you killed how many?" asked Wallace. It was hard to tell, replied Meadlo, because with an automatic rifle you just spray the bullets about. Possibly, he added, ten or fifteen. "Men, women, and children?" Yes, said Meadlo. "And babies?" said Wallace. "And babies." Meadlo's mother, who was interviewed by Seymour Hersh, who had first broken the story, said of her son, "I gave them a good boy and they sent me back a murderer."

CHAPTER 6

FIGHTING

———

"No one has been able to capture the real feeling of
what combat is like. Many books have been written,
hundreds of feet of film have been made, thousands of
words have been spoken, all of these means have failed
to give the true horrible picture, the awful noise, the
smell, and the fear that makes one stand up and
scream out the horror that is pent up inside of you.
And yet, under all this there is really something
beautiful about combat."

—FROM THE DIARY OF AN AMERICAN SOLDIER
IN THE PACIFIC DURING THE SECOND WORLD WAR

WAR IS A MYSTERY BOTH TO THOSE WHO FIGHT AND THOSE
of us who are on the sidelines. And it is a troubling and unsettling
mystery. It should be abhorrent, but it is so often alluring and its
values seductive. It promises glory and offers suffering and death.
We who are noncombatants may fear the warriors, but we also
admire, even love, them. And we cannot pretend that we are not
part of the same family, with the same potential for fighting. Perhaps the Australian writer Frederic Manning, who wrote one of
the greatest novels about the First World War, *The Middle Parts of
Fortune,* was right when he said, "War is waged by men; not by
beasts, or by gods. It is a peculiarly human activity. To call it a
crime against mankind is to miss at least half its significance; it is
also the punishment of a crime."

From the time of the earliest cave paintings we have been trying to portray war and to grasp its complex essence in the arts, in
diaries, letters, memoirs, poems, histories, novels and movies. Yet
how much can we rely on these? Memories are fallible and the
more complex and intense the events, the more difficult it is to
recollect what actually happened. Moreover, each generation has
its own strong conventions about how war should be portrayed
and each fixes on some things more than others. It depends too
on who is doing the telling: a general or an admiral may see the
battle as a whole, the ordinary soldier or seaman only his part.
And being in the air or on or under the sea is very different from
being on the ground. Also, for much of history the records were
made and kept by that minority who could read and write. We
know what the knight on horseback or the captain on his poop
deck thought or felt but not the humble foot soldier or seaman.
The First World War was groundbreaking, as in much else, in
having a majority of combatants who could read and write. As a
result much of what we know about the experience of fighting
comes from those four years of conflict. Even so, most of the published writers in that war came from the educated middle and
upper classes; recovering the voices of the lower classes has been
difficult, although it can and has been done indirectly by, for example, looking at what officers reported from the letters of their
men that they were censoring.

We have to be careful too not to let a few accounts stand in for
all the great variety of experiences in war. After the First World
War, the Western Front—with its images of mud, lice, rats, death,
futile attacks, callous and incompetent generals—came to dominate memories especially in Western Europe. Of all the hundreds
of novels, memoirs and poems published by those who fought,
only a handful, such as the memoirs of Robert Graves and Siegfried Sassoon or Wilfred Owen's and Sassoon's poetry in Britain,
Henri Barbusse in France or Erich Maria Remarque in Germany,
whose *All Quiet on the Western Front* became an international
bestseller, have come to shape a particular and powerful view of

the war. Many soldiers in the First World War, however, and this is true of many other wars as well, did not see combat at all or were on quiet fronts where there was little action. There were many different types of battlefields during the war, on the long Eastern Front, in the Balkans, the Middle East, Africa or Asia, or on the seas, and many different experiences of the war, and many styles for describing them. So whatever I say here is only a sampling of what exists and what can be said about the experience of war.

My examples come mainly from land fighting. Naval and aerial war are as intense for those involved, but we the bystanders find it harder to put ourselves in the shoes of aviators and sailors. We cannot tour the battlefields of the skies and, unless we are divers, we cannot visit the sites of great naval battles or the graves of those who died at sea. It is true that the crews of galleys and even early sailing ships once grappled with each other, but with the advent of better steering and then steam, naval war came to be about vessels trying to sink each other. By the twentieth century the seamen often never saw the enemy ships because they were over the horizon. The flying aces in the First World War often saw each other's faces as they fought and even knew each other by name. They were seen by the troops struggling in the mass war below, and often saw themselves, as modern equivalents of knights in armor, giving war a human dimension. Air war has moved on so rapidly, however, that pilots are becoming obsolete and future aerial combat will be between machines. For the most part the heroes we have and the stories we know are largely from land war. The Smithsonian's 2018 bestseller *Battles That Changed History* lists forty-two battles between the start of the seventeenth century and Pearl Harbor in 1941 and only five of them are naval.

Do we have any hope of understanding or feeling what it is to be in combat with and against other human beings? The smells, sounds and sensations of the fighting, the presence of fear and of death, the madness that can grip the soldiers in attack, the panic of the defeated? Even while the goal is elusive we keep trying, because war is so much part of being human and of our history and development. And perhaps, in the cacophony of voices from so many times and so many places, we can pick out certain things that characterize fighting. The ever-present possibility of death to start with, although warriors from different cultures face it in different ways. The ancient Greeks knew the horrors of battle but their writers described them dispassionately, with a cool appraisal of the wounds given and received and with scant grieving over the waste of lives. Death was something that happened to warriors. In the *Iliad* spears and arrows go into guts or eyes or chests or groins and the men die in agony. As Homer says of one, "gasping out his life as he writhed along the ground / like an earthworm stretched out in death, blood pooling, / soaking the earth dark red . . ." And no heaven waits for them as a consolation; they are borne away into the dark. By contrast, in Christianity and Islam there is the promise of eternal life as a recompense for suffering and sacrifice on earth.

Muddle and confusion have also been part of war as long as it has existed. Battle is at once one of the most organized of human activities and one with the greatest likelihood of things going wrong. "No plan," said von Moltke the Elder, the father of Prussia's victories in the nineteenth century, "survives first contact with the enemy." In *War and Peace* Pierre Bezukhov wanders, bewildered, about the battlefield at Borodino. He has little idea of what is happening, whether the Russians or the French are winning or losing, and nor do the officers and men he encounters, and, as Tolstoy points out, or the generals on either side. Generals' memoirs written after the event may tell the story of a grand strategic plan duly unfolding but the reality is much messier. Even the great commanders, whether it was Napoleon trying to find a hill or a tower which would let him see the battlefield, or General Norman Schwarzkopf in the First Gulf War with electronic eyes on the ground, can only peer into the confusion and try to gauge where the battle is going. In the midst of battle, orders can come too late, are impossible to carry out or never get there, and the recipients misunderstand or disobey. The catastrophe of the Charge of the Light Brigade, when the British Light Cavalry charged into the mouths of the Russian guns, was the result of an unclear order and the rash command of the Earl of Cardigan, who wanted glory for himself. At the Battle of Crécy in 1346, when the English were badly outnumbered, the French king could not hold back his knights, who charged over France's bow-men and each other. As a chronicler reported, "Those behind would not stop until they had caught up with the front ranks. And when the leaders saw the other coming they went on also. So pride and vanity took charge of events. Each wanted to outshine his companions."

For soldiers from the early modern age until the second half of the nineteenth century, war was literally in a fog and was also and remains so in a figurative sense. Julian Grenfell wrote to his mother when he first arrived in France in 1914, before the war had settled down into trenches, that his force was doing marches and countermarches while the guns boomed in the distance and no one seemed to know what was happening. As the American Tim O'Brien wrote about Vietnam in his great novel *The Things They Carried*, "For the common soldier, at least, war has the feel—the spiritual texture—of a great ghostly fog, thick and permanent."

Michael Howard, who later became a great historian of war, landed as a young officer at Salerno, partway up the Italian boot, south of Naples, in the autumn of 1943. In his first encounter with the German enemy, he was sent out at night to take a hill. He and his small force got lost in the dark and arrived later than planned and in some disorder at their starting point after the barrage which was meant to give them support was already under way. As he and his men sheltered behind a stone wall, German bullets whizzed overhead. He felt, he recalled, as though he was in a B movie playing the gallant platoon commander: "All right, I thought, if I was cast as David Niven I had better behave like David Niven; so I hissed, 'Right—over with me!'" The British stumbled down a slope in the dark through trees and across terrace walls. "Everything thereafter became so confused that it is hard to make any coherent narrative out of it," he wrote, but he remembered shouting like a madman and the flashes and bangs from German grenades and guns. The action was successful and the Germans retreated. The next morning the British buried the German dead, "shrunken pathetic dolls."

Many combatants have also tried to describe the pressures they feel and the intensity of the experience, with the mingled fear of death, the need to keep following orders and the strange elation that can come in battle. David Thompson, a private from New York, tried to sketch out his reactions at Antietam. "The truth is," he wrote, "when bullets are whacking against tree-trunks and solid shot are cracking skulls like egg-shells, the consuming passion in the breast of the average man is to get out of the way." Yet he got up and went forward when the order came. "In a second the air was full of the hiss of bullets and the hurtle of grape-shot. The mental strain was so great that I saw at that moment the singular effect mentioned, I think, in the life of Goethe on a similar occasion—the whole landscape for an instant turned slightly red." Manning, whose novel is based on his own experiences at the Somme, talked about "one bright hard point of action." "The most terrible thing, of course," said one of the Soviet women fighters Svetlana Alexievich interviewed, "is the first battle. It's because you don't know anything yet ... The sky throbs, the ground throbs, your heart seems about to burst, your skin feels ready to split. I never thought the ground could crackle. Everything crackled, everything rumbled."

Sometimes, in the midst of battle, a strange calmness can come over the participants. In his great First World War memoir *A Soldier on the Southern Front*, the Italian Emilio Lussu remembered taking part in one of the many futile attacks against the

Austrian lines. The Italians were walked down an open hill that was raked by Austrian machine guns. He wrote:

> For a minute or so, I was overcome by a sort of mental torpor, and my whole body felt heavy and slow. Maybe I'm wounded, I thought. Yet I could feel I wasn't wounded. The machine gun bullets whizzing by and the constant rush of the units on our heels woke me up. Instantly I regained consciousness of my situation. Not anger, not hate, as in a brawl, but utter calm, absolute, a sort of infinite weariness wrapped around my now lucid mind. Then even that weariness subsided and I was running again fast.

One thing that comes out from many of the accounts by those who fought was their fear—of being wounded or killed of course, but also of not meeting the test of war, of giving way to panic and behaving badly. Tim O'Brien, who fought in Vietnam himself, wrote, "Men killed, and died, because they were embarrassed not to. It was what had brought them to war in the first place, nothing positive, no dreams of glory or honor, just to avoid the blush of dishonor." Even Julian Grenfell felt fear, as he admitted to his mother after his first action in France. He wanted to claim that he had enjoyed it, "But it's bloody. I pretended to myself for a bit that I liked it; but it was no good; it only made one careless and unwatchful and self-absorbed. But when one acknowledged to oneself that it was bloody, one became all right again and cool." While it is difficult to predict in peaceful conditions who will be brave and who won't, training and discipline and sometimes leadership can help to carry the warriors through the most perilous of combats. At the Battle of Gettysburg, a crucial hill, Little Round Top, nearly fell to the Confederates. The day was saved for the Union by a small, outnumbered force under the command of a college professor. Against what seemed like impossible odds, the Union forces charged with bayonets and the Confederates broke.

Sometimes, as Howard recalled, playing the part of a soldier took over as much to impress others as the fighter himself. In another attack, this time in the day, he found himself sheltering in a trench with a fellow young officer. "This is like a bad American film," said Howard. "Yes," his companion replied, "but not such fun." In Vietnam O'Brien's soldiers talked tough: "They used a hard vocabulary to contain the terrible softness. *Greased* they'd say. *Offed, lit up, zapped while zipping.* It wasn't cruelty, just stage presence." And to cope with death soldiers have often made a joke of it, propping up enemy corpses with cigarettes in hand, for example, in the two world wars. During the Falklands War between Britain and Argentina, the British destroyer *Antrim* was hit by Argentinian aircraft and, with leaking fuel, was in danger of fire. At the tensest moment, as warning buzzers and bells were sounding and the crew were scurrying about, a stoker suddenly appeared. "STOP!" he shouted. Everyone, from officers to ordinary seamen, froze. He pointed down a passageway. "Zulus! Thousands of them!" and disappeared. (The movie of the nineteenth-century Zulu Wars in southern Africa is apparently the favorite of the British military even though the Zulus do rather well.) A young Chris Parry, a future admiral, remembered the moment for its relieving of tension.

Religion or ritual has long been a part of battle in many different cultures. Over the centuries warriors have used dances, rituals and prayers to prepare for battle and have worn amulets or observed superstitions to keep them safe. The Boxers who rebelled against the Manchu dynasty and attacked foreigners at the end of the nineteenth century believed that their martial exercises made them invulnerable to bullets. Ritual can also bring catharsis at the end of battle. When Aeneas persuades his father to flee from Troy he asks the old man to carry their most sacred things: "Father, take in your arms the sacred emblems of our country's household gods; for me, fresh from fierce battle and recent slaughter, it would be sinful to handle them until I have washed myself clean in running water . . ."

Drink and drugs can have similar effects in helping warriors prepare for battle and deal with it afterward. The British army, like many Continental ones, used to give their troops strong drafts of brandy or rum; in Vietnam the American soldiers took drugs to dull their fears. In his recollections of the First World War, Lussu describes how the Italians were once nearly overwhelmed by the waves of brandy fumes coming from the Austrians as they attacked. His fellow officers drank deliberately as well, as much to endure the madness of war as anything else. He saw an Italian officer trying to put his pistol on his head and shoot with his helmet. "I defend myself by drinking," said one to him. "Otherwise, I'd already be in the nuthouse." Neither side could see each other yet they kept trying to kill. "It's horrible! That's why we're drunk all the time, on one side and the other." Today, modern armies have developed a better understanding of treating stress but it is inescapable in battle.

While some soldiers seek death, like the last Byzantine emperor, who wandered in vain about his breached city walls in 1453 in the hopes that the Ottoman conquerors would kill him, most actively try to avoid it or at least hope that it will come for others but not for them. Death in battle so often comes suddenly and randomly. Lussu was on the high plateau between Italy and today's Slovenia, then part of Austria-Hungary. Badly equipped and led, the Italians were forced into repeated costly attacks on Austrian lines. He remembered sitting with a friend from university waiting for orders for a fresh attack. They shared cigarettes and a flask of brandy and chatted about Homer, wondering whether, if the great Trojan warrior Hector had had brandy, he might have been able to deal with his Greek nemesis, Achilles. "I've forgotten a lot of things about the war," wrote Lussu, "but I'll never forget that moment. I was watching my friend smile between one mouthful of smoke and another. A single gunshot rang out from the enemy trench. He bowed his head, the cigarette still between his lips, and from a newly formed red spot on his forehead, a thin line of blood came streaming out. Slowly he folded in on himself and fell on my feet. I lifted him up, dead."

While combatants mourn the dead, they cannot afford to linger on their loss. "One suffers vicariously," wrote Frederic Manning, ". . . with the inalienable sympathy of man for man." One forgets quickly, he went on, and there is relief too in still being alive. "The mind is averted as well as the eyes. It reassures itself after that first despairing cry: 'It is I!' . . . No, it is not I. I shall not be like that."

The knowledge of death makes life even more precious. After coming out of a battle on the Western Front in 1917, in which his unit took losses, Ernst Jünger, author of *Storm of Steel*, one of the classic war memoirs, said the village where the survivors were billeted resounded with the sounds of cheerful reunions. "Such libations after a successfully endured engagement are among the fondest memories an old warrior may have. Even if ten out of twelve men had fallen, the two survivors would surely meet over a glass on their first evening off, and drink a silent toast to their comrades, and jestingly talk over their shared experiences." In Burma in the Second World War George MacDonald Fraser was surprised and perhaps a bit shocked when, after a battle in which one of their number had died, none of the other soldiers in the section said much about it or the dead man. "They expressed no grief, or anger, or obvious relief, or indeed any emotion at all; they betrayed no symptoms of shock or disturbance, nor were they nervous or short-tempered. If they were quieter than usual that evening, well, they were dog-tired." Yet, and again he was shocked, before they turned in they spread out a groundsheet and placed on it all the dead man's possessions and each took one. It was, Fraser came to understand, a way of remembering and honoring him.

Of course, being in a war is not only about fear, death or action; it is also about waiting around, boredom and grumbling about food, lice, the rats, weather or the senior officers. Roman soldiers wrote letters home from the frontiers full of complaints and, if they were unfortunate enough to be on Hadrian's Wall in the north of England, asking to be sent warm clothing. Two millennia later, Japanese soldiers in China begged their families to send them socks and underpants. A fragment of papyrus found in Egypt has a Roman soldier with another perennial complaint: "But you never wrote to me concerning your health, how you are doing. I am worried about you because although you received letters from me often, you never wrote back to me so that I may know how you ..." In the trenches in the First World War soldiers could find an escape, or at least a way of dealing with reality, in writing down what was happening to them. (And in this war, the majority, certainly on the Western Front, were literate.) In the French army Robert Dorgelès, who had been a tinsmith in civilian life, said he was stupefied and overwhelmed at leaving civilian life for the military. "I believed I was taking the unknown track of a world turned upside down, and on the very day of my departure, I had already turned into a war writer." Manufacturers advertised special pens and small notebooks for recording life at the front, and newspapers by and for soldiers provided outlets for their work. The American *Stars and Stripes* published 100,000 lines of poetry by American soldiers in the short period the United States was in the war.

Home is distant to those who are fighting, and not just in terms of geography. War, even more than military life in peacetime, can upend normal expectations of life and concepts of time and space. Winter is a foe if you are Napoleon in 1812 or the German army in the Second World War but a friend if you are the Russians defending your homeland. Time can drag out unbearably before a battle but in combat each second seems to matter. Fraser's first face-to-face fighting with the Japanese, around a small temple, lasted, he thinks, for about a minute but he remembered the scenes vividly for the rest of his life and his feelings: "A continuous nervous excitement was shot through with occasional flashes of rage, terror, elation, relief and amazement." A British soldier who fought at Mons in the First World War said, "A battle was a wonderfully exciting thing when it was in progress ..."

A German soldier who was on the other side experienced, as he advanced, "a shout of triumph, a wild, unearthly singing surged within me, uplifting and inspiring me, filling all my senses. I had overcome fear; I had conquered my mortal bodily self."

War inverts what we think of as the natural order and morality in society. It is right and indeed necessary in wartime to blow up buildings, bridges or railways, the infrastructure that allows societies to survive, and to murder and hurt others. What is grotesque or appalling in peacetime—the smell of death or unburied corpses, dirt, rats, lice, foul water or rotten food—is simply part of the fabric of war. The possessions—fashionable clothes perhaps or sporting equipment—we surround ourselves with in peacetime lose their value, while objects we never much thought about, such as wire cutters or foot powder, become enormously important. In his *The Things They Carried*, O'Brien provides those lists which vary from soldier to soldier but always include the steel helmet, the compress bandage in case they were hit, mosquito repellent, rations and water. In the summer of 1919 the Canadian artist David Milne was sent to record the now quiet battlefields of the Western Front where Canadians had fought. In a letter to a friend he listed the contents of a single shell hole: tinned food, shells, hand grenades, water bottles, bandoliers, gas masks, helmets, clothing. Just a year before, what Milne called "the great mass of junk" had been essential equipment of soldiers.

War changes and disrupts the patterns of daily life. On the Western Front in the First World War, night was safe and day was dangerous. Soldiers were exposed by the sun to the watching eyes on the other side. Day was for resting, night for work, whether bringing up supplies, repairing or building new trenches, tunneling or making raids into no-man's-land. The full moon was not something to admire; it was an enemy. Fireworks in the skies were not festive but guides for death and destruction. The meanings of landscapes changed too: rivers and canals were no longer for transportation or for watering crops but defenses or obstacles to attack. Mountains, forests, hills and valleys were parts of battle plans, tactical goals to be captured or held. Vimy Ridge in northern France is only some 200 feet above the plain below but it cost the Canadians 10,000 casualties to take it from the Germans in 1917. Open fields and farms did not produce new life but death and harvests of ordnance, and still do as the winter frosts continue to heave up unexploded shells along the Western Front which can still claim lives.

Behavior that may be unacceptable in peacetime—swearing or blaspheming, for example—becomes normal in war. So does scrounging, or what in peacetime might be called stealing. When Fraser's section was once assigned to help unload air-dropped supplies, he was offended on the men's behalf that the commanding officer greeted them with deep suspicion and warned them not to take anything. The men, to his surprise, accepted it all in good part and worked energetically and uncomplainingly throughout the long hot day. At its end they were congratulated for their diligence and honesty by the commanding officer and given a few packages of cigarettes as a reward. When they were back in camp the men spread out a groundsheet and Fraser watched with astonishment and admiration as they emptied their water bottles of mounds of sugar and from their clothes and under their hats took loose tea, cigarettes, tobacco and tins of food. "By the time they had finished that groundsheet looked like Harrods food hall."

Sexual norms alter in wartime too. We think at once of rape, an act of dominance and destruction, but in war sex can also be a reaffirmation of life. The knowledge that death may be near makes peacetime prohibitions and restrictions pointless. "By most people's standards we were immoral," said an American soldier of the Second World War, "but we were young and could die tomorrow." Emotional contact with another human being mattered, even if it came through paid sex. "I've noticed it before," said the owner of a brothel in New Orleans during the First World War, when the city filled with American servicemen, "the way the idea of war

and dying makes a man raunchy." It was not so much for the pleasure, she noted, "but a kind of nervous breakdown that could only
be treated with a girl and a set to." Manning's main character,
Bourne, is strangely moved and touched by a young French farm
girl who serves him supper, partly because she makes him aware
of his own mortality and loneliness: "In the shuddering revulsion
from death one turns instinctively to love as an act which seems
to reaffirm the completeness of being." He does not think about
women when he is at the front, he notes. As a number of experts
have suggested, the closer men and women are to the battlefield,
the less important sex becomes, perhaps because they are focused
on survival and too busy, frightened or simply tired.

There can be a curious exhilaration in breaking taboos of all
sorts and in the sheer destruction that war brings. In July 1917
Huntly Gordon, a young Scottish artillery officer on the Western
Front, wrote to his mother about a visit at night to the ruined city
of Ypres, which had just received yet another heavy bombard-
ment by the Germans. He found, he said, "a strange beauty" in the
deserted streets where a few houses still stood. One, like a giant
doll's house, had its front ripped off to expose the rooms, some
still with their furniture and a picture or two hanging aslant. As
he headed toward the Menin Gate, he crossed the great square
with the remnants of the great Gothic masterpiece, the Cloth
Hall. "I've heard of the Taj Mahal by moonlight—but for me it
could never be so impressive as this ruin. The stones and masonry
gleamed snowy white and the massive tower stood there, raising
its jagged turrets against the dark sky like some huge iceberg." As
he hurried across he just had time to notice the crumpled body of
a soldier by a lamp post.

By the time of the Second World War the long-range bomber
meant that civilians increasingly found themselves part of the
battlefronts and they too experienced that thrill of destruction. A
young Canadian diplomat, Charles Ritchie, came out of a cinema
in the center of London after a severe bombing in October 1940.

"It seemed," he wrote in his diary, "as though the whole of Piccadilly were on fire. Tongues of flames were licking the colonnade at the top of the London Pavilion. We drove to the Dorchester through bombs and shrapnel—there seemed to be fire everywhere." He and his companion were "childishly excited" and elated. "There is an exhilaration in this orgy of destruction and in the danger, but the next day was the morning after the debauch. I was awakened by the sound of shovelling glass." On August 6, 1945, a Japanese lecturer, Ogura Toyofumi, was heading into Hiroshima. Suddenly there was a massive flash. He stood transfixed by the giant swirling cloud that grew and spread. He had, he recalled, no adequate ways to describe it: "The unsophisticated concepts and fantasies dreamed up by the ancients were useless to describe this horrible pageant of clouds and lights staged in the firmament." He kept walking toward the city, drawn by an impulse to experience the destruction, which he later described as "the greatest of its kind man had ever experienced."

Explaining what being in war is like is never easy. It is hard to find the words and images; hard too when those who are at home do not want to hear about the realities of life in combat. Gordon, the young Scottish officer, complains in his memoirs of being home on leave in Edinburgh and the endless stream of visitors with their "inane" questions about what it is really like at the front. "Fine, thanks, just fine," is all he replies. "What else could one say? How could they begin to understand? We were now simply in different worlds." Modern war makes the contrast between those different worlds particularly sharp. Today combatants can be plucked from the battlefield and whisked around the world, but even in the First World War it was possible for soldiers on the front to be in the trenches one day and home in their own countries the next.

What can also upset those who are fighting is the impression that many at home are profiting from the war. The ordinary soldiers in Manning's novel or in Fraser's memoir complain repeatedly about the high wages workers in mining, for example, or war industries are getting; about the profits manufacturers are making; or simply about how civilians might be enjoying themselves. Another young Scottish officer, John Reith (later to be Lord Reith and the long-serving head of the BBC), spent part of his first leave during the First World War in London. He had dinner with his brother but could not enjoy the rich food and the sumptuous surroundings. He noticed how many men were not in uniform. "Anyhow, it all jarred; I was out of touch with this sort of life and felt resentful of it."

During the Japanese invasion of China in the late 1930s a Japanese soldier wrote, "I wonder if the people at home, overjoyed with the thought of ever-victorious Japanese soldiers, understand the unending pain that comes with this victory." Erich Maria Remarque's *All Quiet on the Western Front* is a novel but it draws on Remarque's own experience as a German soldier, and the scenes when his protagonist Paul Bäumer tries to describe what the war is really like are echoed in countless memoirs and letters from the First World War. When Bäumer goes home on leave he finds himself unable to communicate anything about the reality of the war to his acquaintances or his family. He does not want to upset his dying mother or his father, and the others want the sorts of stories, about glorious deeds or the coming victory, that he cannot tell. He reflects sadly that he never should have come home.

Another gap that opens up between the war and home fronts is that civilians often hate the enemy more than those doing the fighting. In the Second World War a British study showed that people who lived in rural areas not affected by the Blitz were more likely to want German cities bombed in reprisal than those who actually lived in cities that had been badly hit. A survey done of US servicemen in the same war showed that those who had not yet left the United States were much more likely to agree that the Japanese should be wiped out "altogether" than those already in the Pacific. The combatant who admits, like Ernst Jünger does,

that he went into battle "in the grip of a berserk rage" and longing
to kill is rarer than the British officer in the Second World War
who said of the enemy, "In fact we respected them as brave soldiers, but our job was to defeat them and win the war." In the
Iliad, when Achilles calls one of the Trojans he is about to kill
"friend," he is recognizing that they are both warriors who are
doing what they must. "One cannot blame them," writes Gordon
of the Germans in the First World War, "for defending themselves and shelling us." He cannot hate them, he finds; indeed he
feels a sort of pity for them since they may be having an even
worse time than the British. The Christmas truces on the Western
Front, which broke out spontaneously along the lines until the
military authorities put a stop to them, and the informal live-
and-let-live arrangements—to let each side collect its corpses undisturbed, for example—reflect a sense that shared hardships and
humanity cross lines. Frank Richards, whose *Old Soldiers Never
Die* is one of the rare First World War accounts by an ordinary
soldier, took part in such a truce in 1914. The men came out first
and the officers followed. "We mucked in all day with one another," he said. The Germans sent a barrel of beer over to the British trenches and the British sent back plum pudding in return.
"One of their men, speaking in English," Richards recalled, "mentioned that he had worked in Brighton for some years and that he
was fed up to the neck with this damned war and would be glad
when it was all over. We told him that he wasn't the only one that
was fed up with it."

That fellow feeling holds true for other wars in other times and
places. A Japanese soldier in China in the late 1930s is saddened
when his commander orders wounded Chinese soldiers to be in-
terrogated and then killed: "Even though they're our enemies,
they're human beings with a soul like all other living things in
this world. To use them as helpless tests for one's sword is truly
cruel." A Soviet woman who was a medical assistant in a cavalry
regiment during the Second World War recalled the remorse she

felt when she shot two German soldiers: "One was such a handsome young German. It was a pity, even though he was a fascist,
all the same . . . That feeling didn't leave me for a long time. You
see I didn't want to kill. There was such hatred in my soul: why
had they come to our land? But when you yourself kill, it's frightening . . . " A much-cited study of American soldiers in the Second World War concluded that only 15 to 25 percent were prepared
to aim and fire at the enemy; the rest either did not shoot at all or
aimed wide. Similar studies of Germans and Japanese in the war
showed much the same results. Not surprisingly, such findings—
and they have been challenged since—spurred an increased interest into how the insights and tools of psychology could be
incorporated into military training to turn recruits into efficient
killers who would not flinch on the battlefield.

Leaders sometimes but not always can make a difference to
how men and women behave in battle. Alexander, Julius Caesar,
Admiral Horatio Nelson, General George Patton and Napoleon
all seem to have had an uncanny ability to motivate their men to
kill and to face death boldly. Each consciously played the part of
leader, encouraging the legends that surrounded them and manipulating symbols and portents. Alexander would use artifice to
add signs for "victory" when the livers of animals were inspected
for omens by his priests. When someone offered him a helmet
full of water in a dry desert, he dramatically poured it out to show
that he would rather suffer with his men. A legendary Chinese
general, when given a keg of sweet wine, ordered it to be poured
into a river so that he and his soldiers could all drink the mingled
water and wine. Napoleon's propaganda made much of his dramatic gallop over the Alps, when in reality he sat on a slow-
moving mule, and of his claim that, when he rested in the
monastery at the St. Bernard Pass, he found a copy of Livy and
read the passage on Hannibal, who had made the journey before
him.

Great commanders also have that indefinable quality of charisma, with a presence that seems more than human and an ability to see into the human soul. The battle-hardened General Dominique-René Vandamme said of Napoleon, "So it is that I, who fear neither God nor the Devil, am ready to tremble like a child when I approach him." Napoleon's great adversary the Duke of Wellington once said that the emperor's presence on the battlefield was worth 40,000 men. After his final defeat, when Napoleon went on board the ship carrying him to his lonely exile on St. Helena, he immediately charmed the entire crew and officers. And lesser officers have had a similar impact on the battlefield. Physical courage matters but there is more to it than that. Captain Malet, in Manning's novel, had a huge presence: "The impression he left on the mind was not one of mass, but of force and speed. It was his expression, his manner, something in the way he moved and spoke, which made one feel that only an enormous energy enabled him to bridle the insubordinate and destructive energy within him. Perhaps in battle it broke loose and gratified its indomitable appetites." His men admired his nonchalance and daring, as when he walked along the top of the trenches or went back into no-man's-land to get the ash stick which he had left behind. Some leaders, like General Patton or Field Marshal Montgomery, were flamboyant, playing to the audience. Others, like General Slim, whom George MacDonald Fraser encountered in Burma, impressed in a different sort of way. He was the only man he had ever seen, said Fraser, "who had a force that came out of him, a strength of personality that I have puzzled over since, for there was no apparent reason for it . . ." It was not his appearance—to Fraser, Slim looked more like a yard foreman who had been promoted to managing director, or a farmer—nor was it his way with words, for he sat with the men chatting simply and unpretentiously about the campaign against the Japanese. Yet Fraser came away with the feeling that Slim understood the ordinary soldier. "I think it was that sense of being close to us, as though he were chatting offhand to an understanding nephew (not for nothing was he 'Uncle Bill'), that was his great gift."

For the most part, however, ordinary soldiers and sailors seem to have tolerated their officers where they have not actively despised them for their impossible orders, their lack of understanding of conditions on the ground and, especially for the higher ranks, their remoteness from the realities of battle. Emilio Lussu has left a vivid account of one of his generals in the First World War who was bent on glory whatever it cost the troops. "Do you love war?" the general asks, his eyes spinning madly like the wheels of a racing car. When Lussu says that he does not particularly, the general explodes with contempt: "So you're for peace, are you? For peace! Just like some meek little housewife..." Although the Italians do not yet have any artillery, the general is determined to attack the Austrians, which he does with predictable results. When his mule dances close to the edge of a cliff and tries to shake him off one day, not one of the Italians moves. The soldier who eventually rushes forward to save him is later beaten by his fellows and denounced as a disgrace to his unit.

Abstract ideals, powerful though they might be, and even great leaders, are not and have never been the most important forces sustaining those in battle. The Greek hoplites in their lines, the Swiss in their squares, sailors whether on galleys or aircraft carriers, pilots in squadrons, all rely on and fight for each other. As Plutarch said, "Men wear their helmets and breastplates for their own needs, but they carry their shields for the men of the entire line." You love your comrade so much, said a fourteenth-century knight, "you are prepared to go and die or live with him." Soldiers might be rough with each other but they could also be surprisingly gentle. "Friendship" seems too pallid a word and "love" too romantic, although there are elements of both in what combatants have tried to express down through the centuries. The best that English can do is "comradeship." Manning called it "an intensity of feeling which friendship never touches." People are thrown together often haphazardly in war and yet they can develop such strong attachments that they will give up their lives for each other. Siegfried Sassoon came to hate the war as a "dirty trick" played on his generation, but he still went back to his unit for the sake of his comrades. When Bäumer from *All Quiet on the Western Front* rejoins his friends after his leave, he says simply, "This is where I belong." Jünger remembered coming back to the front after being wounded: "It was like returning to the bosom of a family."

When the French were besieged at Dien Bien Phu, in their ill-fated attempt to bring victory against the Vietnamese in Indochina, the fort's outposts fell one by one and their garrisons were taken off to prison camps. Among the prisoners were Germans from the Foreign Legion who decided to look out for themselves. They told the Viet Minh camp commander that they had seen the light and no longer supported the French. As a result, their treatment and rations dramatically improved. Every morning they would stand to for a lecture from the commander, who would talk about the Viet Minh victories the day before. The German legionnaires would cheer and sing "The Internationale," the anthem of the international communist movement. Then one day the commander announced that hills held by legionnaires had been taken after hard fighting. The German prisoners remained silent. "Come on, sing!" said the camp commander. "What are you waiting for?" The Germans looked at each other and then broke into a song which dates back to the Napoleonic Wars: "*Ich hatt'einen Kameraden / Einen bessern findst du nicht . . .*" ("I once had a comrade / you couldn't find a better one . . ."). They were stripped of all privileges.

Those who have fought may want to forget the horrors of war—or try to—but many veterans also look back nostalgically to that comradeship and the ways in which life was simpler, with fewer alternatives or choices. And some miss the excitement. "Probably he would never look down on the lines again," wrote a British pilot after the First World War, ". . . never search the sky for Huns, never fire his guns at a living target, never hear the infernal staccato behind him, never see tracers come up from the ground; all that was over and past. Never more the dawn patrol and the hard-boiled egg; never more the terrific binges and the inimitable comradeship; never more the frantic excitement and the ghastly fear; all that was over, and life was empty." There is a memorable scene in Kathryn Bigelow's film *The Hurt Locker* where the hero, William James, a bomb disposal expert who risks his life repeatedly in Iraq, is home at the end of a tour of duty and his wife asks him to get some breakfast cereal in a supermarket. He stares in bewilderment at shelf after shelf of different brands. Shortly afterward he reenlists.

Frank Richards used to meet a friend in a pub for years after the First World War to swap stories. "We generally wound up our evenings with the old song, set to the tune of a well-known hymn, 'Old soldiers never die, they simply fade away.'" When the strongly antiwar musical *Oh, What a Lovely War!* opened in London in the early 1960s, many of those who had fought in the First World War were still alive. A friend of mine was there one night when several busloads of veterans were in the audience. They sang along with the old tunes and jammed the bar reminiscing happily—not, one assumes, a reaction the cast and its left-wing director Joan Littlewood were counting on.

This enjoyment of war is something that makes civilians in peaceful societies uncomfortable. A Canadian general I was once interviewing for an educational radio program spoke about the excitement of war but only after I had turned off my tape recorder. It was, he said, like riding a very fast motorcycle. The knowledge that you could crash and die at any moment added to the thrill. Even more disturbing is the realization that some combatants actually enjoy having the power of life and death over another and take pleasure in killing and destruction. The Australian Ion Llewellyn Idriess, who was a sniper in the First World War, said that he felt "only hot pride that in fair warfare I had taken the life of a strong man." In the Second World War a British pilot found that he could not sleep after downing two German aircraft: "There was nothing else I could talk about for days after; there was nothing else I could think about for weeks after ... it was sweet and very intoxicating." One of the shocking things about Jünger's memoir is the way he lays out his feelings without any apology or explanation. In an early edition, which he later revised to make it somewhat less brutal, he talks about shooting an Englishman: "He snapped shut like the blade of a knife and lay still." In another passage, which he did leave in, he talks about how he and his fellow soldiers poured fire into a British advance: "The enemy were bewildered, and started hopping about this way and that, like rabbits, while clouds of dust were whirled up between them."

Julian Grenfell's letters to his mother are equally open and are full of references to how lucky he is to be in the war and to what fun he is having: "I adore war. It is like a big picnic without the objectlessness of a picnic. I have never been so well or happy. Nobody grumbles at one for being dirty." The excitement of fighting "vitalizes everything, every sight and word and action." He had an odd feeling, he admits, the first time he shot a man, "but very soon it gets like shooting a crocodile, only more amusing, because he shoots back at you." Like Jünger, he watches death as he metes it out with mild curiosity. "He just gave a grunt and crumpled up," he says of one German. He hopes, he tells his mother, that the war will go on for a long time, "but pigsticking will be the only tolerable pursuit after this, or one will die of sheer ennui." He was shot in the head and died in May 1915. His brother and two cousins also died in those first months of the war.

When the BBC's Lord Reith wrote a memoir in the 1960s about his time as a young British transport officer in the First World War, he had trouble finding a publisher because his memories did not fit well with the prevailing view that the war was loathed by everyone who was unfortunate enough to be in it. He was happy and thrilled to be in France. When he rode at night through Armentières, his reaction was: "How queer it all was.

How vastly exciting. Exciting to be on a horse at all; on a horse in the dark streets of this deserted foreign town instead of, just at this time, setting out with one's mother to go to evening service in Glasgow." Although being a transport officer meant that he was billeted behind the lines in relative comfort, he faced the possibility of death every time he and his men crossed open ground with their horses and wagons. He was pleased to discover that he was not afraid but put it down to chance more than any virtue he might possess. It was interesting, he noted, "to walk across a turnip field knowing that at any moment one will stop walking for the most conclusive of all reasons." He wondered perhaps if his Christian faith was a help: "I felt there were special transport facilities from the racked battle-field on which we stood to the green pastures and still waters beyond." When he was invalided out after being badly wounded in the face, he wrote to his parents, "I am more disgusted than I can say. I was getting on so well and enjoying the work and everything."

He also noted in his memoir the beauties that war can produce; the daylight in the summer, the wild flowers in no-man's-land, the blue sky flecked with the white of anti-aircraft shells bursting. Night fighting could be even more spectacular. Lussu described an Austrian artillery attack: "It looked as though all those fireworks, exploding over that forest of fir trees, were lighting up the columns and the naves of an immense basilica." The nearness of death can make the world lovelier and more precious. You sit in a filthy paddy being shot at, wrote O'Brien, "but for a few seconds everything goes quiet and you look up and see the sun and a few puffy white clouds, and the immense serenity flashes against your eyeballs—the whole world gets rearranged—and even though you're pinned down by a war you never felt more at peace." Books and movies cannot get it, said a Russian woman veteran of the Second World War. "No, not it. It doesn't come off. I start talking, myself—that's also not it. Not as frightening and not as beautiful. Do you know how beautiful a morning at war can be? Before combat . . . You look and you know: this may be your last. The earth is so beautiful . . . And the air . . . And the dear sun . . ."

Like war itself, the peace afterward affects those who fight in many different ways: nostalgia, pride, hatred of war, post-traumatic stress, anger, sorrow. An American veteran of Vietnam said of that war—and it is impossible to tell if he was glad or not—"It had burned away the boy in him and left a man of tempered steel." Zinaida Vasilyevna, who had been a medical assistant in a Soviet infantry company in the Second World War, told Alexievich, "In war your soul ages." Some veterans cannot bear to talk about their war experiences at all. A woman who had been a sergeant in the anti-aircraft artillery told Alexievich, "There was no one I could tell that I had been wounded, that I had a concussion. Try telling it, and who will give you a job then, who will marry you? We were silent as fish." Sometimes veterans can talk to their grandchildren, perhaps because war is so far away for these young people and perhaps because the children will not really grasp the meaning of what they are hearing.

As Alexievich says, "War remains, as it always has been, one of the chief human mysteries." Perhaps the final word should go to the great Confederate general Robert E. Lee, who, as he watched the Union troops make one futile and costly charge after another at Fredericksburg in 1862, said, "It is well that war is so terrible, or we should grow too fond of it."

CHAPTER 7

CIVILIANS

═

"The people must be left with nothing but their eyes
to weep with over the war."

—GENERAL PHILIP SHERIDAN

APRIL IN BERLIN IS USUALLY A BEAUTIFUL MONTH: THE winter cold and snow have vanished and in their place are soft green leaves and spring blossoms. Berliners go out to the city's many parks and lakes to celebrate the new season. In 1945 they were not celebrating. Soviet armies were rolling westward, the Nazi regime was collapsing and many of its leading members were scurrying west and south to try and save themselves. By the twentieth of the month, the anonymous author of the harrowing *A Woman in Berlin* records in her diary, the distant sound of Soviet guns has turned into a constant roar: "We are ringed in by barrels and the circle is growing smaller by the hour." People gossip uneasily on street corners; no one really knows what is happening but everyone fears the worst. Rumors run through the city, some false—that, for example, the Americans and the British have fallen out with the Russians and will do a deal with Germany—and some true—that the authorities have released the food stocks they have been hoarding. Those who are able rush to the shops to seize what they can carry away even as the artillery shells send them diving for shelter. "Then all of a sudden," writes the author, "you remember that it's spring. Clouds of lilac perfume drift over from untended gardens and go wafting through the charred ruins of apartment houses." That night, as the Soviet shells continue to fall, she and her neighbors huddle in their basement shelter wondering when the Soviet troops will arrive and what they will do to the women.

Too often we concentrate on the warriors, their battles, their victories and their losses, and do not pay enough attention to civilians who are caught up, willingly or not, in war. Civilians, as we know, can be its cheerleaders, urging their governments or communities to war, as French revolutionaries did in the 1790s, as many did in the First World War and also many of those waiting in Berlin that spring for the Soviets to arrive. Civilians, as combatants often note in their writings, often hate the enemy more than those at the front. And war is not invariably bad for civilians; they can benefit, whether through sharing in the spoils of victory or finding better opportunities to make money, get ahead or break taboos. Yet civilians are also war's innocent victims, paying the heavy penalties of defeat in the coin of starvation, murder, rape, slavery, forced labor or mass deportations.

As that conversation in the cellar in Berlin in April 1945 about what the Soviet troops might do shows, women civilians fear a particular fate in war. Throughout history, in different times and different places, they have been warriors' prizes, to be carried off and made part of their households or raped on the spot. "You are allowed to rape," said the French commando leader to his men in Algeria during its war of independence, "but do it discreetly." Stalin managed to shock the battle-hardened young Yugoslav communist Milovan Djilas when he defended the rapes by Soviet troops in the territories they were liberating from the Nazis. "Imagine a man," said the Soviet dictator, "who has fought from Stalingrad to Belgrade—over a thousand kilometers of his own devastated land, across the dead bodies of his comrades and dearest ones. How can such a man react normally? And what is so awful in his having fun with a woman, after such horrors?"

In Germany alone in 1945 it is estimated that as many as 2 million women were raped by Soviet forces, some of them by multiple men, over a short period of time. The diary of the anonymous woman in Berlin records the apprehension as she and her neighbors wait for the first arrival of Soviet soldiers. The Berliners' relief that the men they at first encounter seem to be friendly with good-natured faces—"only men" after all—turns to dismay and terror as the drinking starts. The Soviet authorities made little effort initially to keep their men under control and allowed the widespread looting of alcohol stocks, which helped to release any inhibitions the soldiers might have felt. The author of the diary manages to persuade the soldiers to leave a young girl who has been wounded alone but is herself raped repeatedly that night and for several days thereafter until she finds a protector. She even sees there is a sort of gallows humor in her situation. She notices that the Soviet soldiers go first for the fatter women, like the local distiller's wife, who had managed to eat well during the war.

It was only when complaints started coming in from German communists that their wives and daughters were being raped that the Soviet leaders realized that brutalizing the German population was not an effective way of winning it over to the cause of socialism and was damaging the reputation of the Soviet Union among well-wishers in other countries. "Such deeds and unsanctioned behavior," said an order issued in August 1945 by Marshal Georgy Zhukov, the commander of the Soviet occupation zone, "are compromising us very badly in the eyes of German antifascists, particularly now that the war is over, and greatly assist fascist campaigns against the Red Army and the Soviet government."

As the anonymous woman in Berlin makes clear, the Soviet soldiers who raped had several motives: sexual release, the companionship of a woman and, symbolically, to demonstrate their power over her and her society. Rape was a violent act by the Soviets to humiliate and disgrace German women and the German nation. Victory and defeat in war are often expressed in gendered terms—a test of virility or a corresponding loss of virginity or emasculation. In the ancient world, and it still happens sometimes today, defeated men could be castrated and raped. In Bosnia in the 1990s, where between 20,000 and 50,000 women (and some men too) were raped, all sides committed the crime although the majority of victims were Bosnian Muslims. The rape of women, as the bearers of children, carries the added meaning of destroying a particular ethnic group. Serb rapists took pleasure in telling Muslim women that they would give birth to future Serb warriors. Serb nationalist forces set aside women in "rape camps" or brothels and Serbian fighters carried out public rape to intimidate and gain information as well as to encourage non-Serbs to flee.

Women who have been raped in war not only have to live with their injuries, both physical and psychological, but often also bear the additional burden of being shunned by their own communities. German women who had been raped in 1945 found comfort in talking about their shared experience but they were often given a hard time by the men in their lives. The fiancé of the anonymous woman in Berlin thought her shameless for mentioning rape at all and walked out on her. The women dealt as best they could with both the cruelty and the reality of what had happened to them. One said she simply repressed a lot "in order, to some extent, to be able to live."

Because women are often seen as the progenitors of the nation, societies can react savagely to any hint that they might willingly consort with the enemy. In France, after the liberation, women who had entered into relationships with Germans were publicly shamed by having their heads shaved. During the war in Germany, where the Nazis made much of women's role as wives and mothers, there was particular panic at the prospect of Polish slave laborers, who had been brought in their thousands to work mainly on German farms, having sexual relations with local women. "We can and may not stand idly by," said the head of the Office of Racial Purity, "while they invade the vital essence of our people, impregnate women of German blood and corrupt our youth." The Gestapo did not stand idly by; it carried out public hangings across Germany of Poles for "forbidden contact." German women sometimes shared in the punishment. In the pretty town of Eisenach, birthplace of Johann Sebastian Bach, one was made to stand, head shaved and tied back-to-back with her Polish lover, in the main square with a sign reading: "I let myself go with a Pole." After 1945 women who had affairs with Allied soldiers, often simply out of the need to survive, became the subject of a bitter joke: "It took six years to beat the German soldier, but it only took five minutes to win over a German woman."

There have been many attempts over the centuries to come up with ways of protecting the innocent from the ravages of war. In many times and places, civilians have been regarded as a separate category from warriors and there have been rules about how each should be treated: that civilians, for example, should not be regarded as combatants and their lives, persons and often their property should be spared. Rules are easily broken or ignored, however, in the passions raised by war and civilians suffer horribly if they are close to the battlefields or in sieges. When the German siege of Leningrad started in September 1941, the city had a population of around 7 million; by the time it ended in January 1944, 1.75 million had managed to escape and 1 million had died. It is usually the weak who die first—the children, the elderly, the poor. Sometimes civilians are, in that chilling phrase of military strategists, "collateral damage," but often they are deliberately targeted to weaken the enemy. The total wars of the twentieth century presented humanity with enormous bills. In the Second World War between 50 and 80 million civilians—we will never know with any certainty—may have died. The range is so broad partly because, as has happened so often before, records were often not kept or were destroyed and because of differences over what to count: deaths from weapons or from starvation and disease as well.

Thucydides notes without comment that when the people of the island of Melos surrendered unconditionally to Athens in the sixteenth year of the Peloponnesian War the Athenians "put to death all the men of military age they took, and sold the women and children as slaves." In their sack of Nanjing in 1937, the Japanese may have killed up to 300,000, raped 20,000 and as well burned a third of the city's buildings. In the Second World War in Europe, Germany not only used prisoners of war as slave labor—against conventions which it had itself signed up to—but it forced some 4 to 5 million civilians mainly from the occupied Soviet Union but also from Poland, France and eventually Italy and elsewhere in Europe to labor for its war effort. The slave laborers were kept on starvation rations and abused. Those unable to work—"useless mouths"—were deliberately killed. Women were sterilized or forced to have abortions. Stalin deported various non-Russian minorities, from some 1.2 million Volga Germans, whose ancestors had come to Russia generations before, to 180,000 Crimean Tartars, on the grounds that they were collaborating with the enemy. And war or the threat of war has also been used to get civilians to flee, as Zionist militias did in Palestine in 1948 or Serb ones in Bosnia in the 1990s.

Beirut, where I gave one of the Reith Lectures, made me reflect again on what war means for civilians. The city has recovered, apparently, from the civil war which ravaged Lebanon between 1975 and 1990, but if you look closely the reminders are there, in the bullet pockmarks on the buildings or in the ruins of the Holiday Inn in the city's center. In the National Museum you can see the hole smashed through a Roman mosaic so that a sniper could sight his gun on the Green Line dividing the different factions which ran just outside. I met people who had lived through the war; they learned, they told me, to distinguish the sounds of the different guns and artillery, to snatch sleep in shelters and to carry on with their daily lives as best they could amid the ruins of their beloved city. "*Sihtak bil dinya* [Your health is worth everything in the world]," they would say to each other when someone's home or shop had been blown up.

As a major seaport at the eastern end of the Mediterranean, Beirut has known war many times during its 5,000-year history. Its inhabitants believe that it has been destroyed and rebuilt at least seven times. Hittites, Phoenicians, ancient Greeks and Romans, Byzantines, Mameluks, Ottomans and latterly the French and Syrians have all coveted it. In 1110, at the end of the First Crusade, the city and its inhabitants were attacked with wooden scaling towers and swords, not rockets and Kalashnikovs, but the sufferings of the civilians, as so often before and since, were great. The Crusaders, led by King Baldwin of Jerusalem, had surrounded the city on land and from the sea and no support from friendly fleets was able to reach the largely Muslim inhabitants. For two months, said a chronicler some years later, the besieging forces kept up their attack so continuously "that neither by night nor by day were the defenders granted respite even for an hour. Thus working by turns and succeeding each other in relays, the Christians exhausted the strength of their foes by unendurable labor." When the city finally fell, the desperate citizens fled toward the sea, only to face an onslaught from the Christian troops who leaped from their ships. "The unfortunate townspeople," said the chronicler, "unluckily caught between two hostile bands, beset now on one side and now on the other, perished by the sword between the two." Some thousands are said to have died until Baldwin himself grew tired of the slaughter and ordered an end to it.

The sacking of cities and the rape and slaughter of their inhabitants have a long and dishonorable history. Sometimes commanders try to control their soldiers; too often they order them to commit atrocities or simply encourage them to behave as they will to civilians. When the Japanese army took the Chinese city of Nanjing in 1937, its officers directed their men to torture, kill and rape Chinese civilians. The new recruits were shocked at first when they witnessed what was happening, said one officer, "but soon they will be doing the same things themselves." The longer or more costly a siege is, the more likely it is that the citizens in a town after its surrender will suffer a dreadful fate, because the attacking soldiers see resistance as having prolonged the hardships that they, the attackers, have endured. When Spanish soldiers seized Maastricht from Dutch rebels in 1579, a third of its inhabitants were slaughtered. The fate of Magdeburg in the Thirty Years War was remembered for centuries after as an example of the cruelty of war for civilians. The largely Protestant town had some 25,000 inhabitants when Habsburg imperial troops and the Catholic League started their siege in March 1631. When Magdeburg finally fell that May, imperial troops set it on fire; 1,700 out of 1,900 buildings were destroyed. Soldiers running amok raped women and young girls. Some 20,000 civilians died and a census the following year showed only 449 still living in the town.

In Shakespeare's *Henry V,* the British king urges his troops on to attack the French town of Harfleur in a speech which has become a treasured part of English literature: "Once more unto the breach, dear friends, once more; / Or close the wall up with our English dead." These heroic sentiments from a much-admired warrior king are equally popular with sports commentators, stock market analysts and politicians in the United Kingdom. They should read Henry's next speech, however, which comes two scenes later, after a comic interlude. He tells the governor and citizens of Harfleur that his soldiers will not be merciful if they have to fight to take the town. Surrender, he tells the men of Harfleur as they look down from their walls, while they still can.

> *If not, why, in a moment look to see*
> *The blind and bloody soldier with foul hand*
> *Defile the locks of your shrill-shrieking daughters;*
> *Your fathers taken by the silver beards,*

And their most reverend heads dash'd to the walls,
Your naked infants spitted upon pikes,
Whiles the mad mothers with their howls confused
Do break the clouds, as did the wives of Jewry
At Herod's bloody-hunting slaughtermen.
What say you? will you yield, and this avoid,
Or, guilty in defense, be thus destroy'd?

War does not come courteously and give civilians a choice about whether or not they want to be involved. Generals order a scorched-earth policy as they and their armies retreat. During the closing days of the Second World War in Europe, the German high command cared so little for its own civilians that it ordered the defense of "every block of flats, every house, every hedgerow, every crater to the last man and the last bullet." The order was issued in March 1945, when Germany's final collapse was clearly only a matter of weeks away. The author of *A Woman in Berlin* watches as German troops march past her neighborhood. "What's going on?" she asks. "Where are you headed?" One mumbles that they are following the Führer even to their deaths. "They're obviously not too concerned about us," she writes in her diary.

In war all armies, even friendly ones, march through peaceful countryside scooping up the available food as they go. Farm buildings go up in flames and cattle are driven off. Navies sink merchant shipping or blockade ports. Bombers drop their bombs on targets which might have some military use but often include housing, schools and hospitals. Civilians must survive as best they can, but disease and hunger will join their killers. In the first quarter of the sixteenth century children in the Italian city of Pavia cried from hunger in the streets lined with their magnificent Renaissance buildings. The town's population fell from 16,000 in 1500 to under 7,000 in 1529. A century later, in the Thirty Years War, the population of different German states went down by between 25 and 40 percent. Some of those deaths were deliberate, but many were the by-product of the movements of large numbers of troops carrying diseases which hit populations already weakened by shortage of food. The deadly influenza epidemic which struck the world just at the end of the First World War, killing up to 50 million people, was probably spread rapidly around the world by the massive movements of troops to the battlefronts.

The deliberate targeting of civilians has long been a tactic of war, whether to squeeze resources out of them, force the enemy to stand and fight or weaken his will to carry on. For centuries besieging armies in Europe demanded treasure to spare towns and monasteries from destruction and the murder of their inhabitants. The anarchy war so often brings opens the way for private entrepreneurs to prey on civilians as well. In the fourteenth century, during the Hundred Years War between the English and the French, private gangs calling themselves such names as Smashing Bars and Arm of Iron roamed across France extorting, brutalizing and murdering, much as armed gangs did in the Lebanese civil war and do today in Libya or parts of the Congo. Between 1356 and 1364 more than 450 places in France were obliged to pay ransom. Sometimes, like the Mafia or the Cosa Nostra, the armies and private gangs demanded regular protection money. In the sixteenth century in Germany and the Netherlands, householders could get a certificate (in German a *Brandschatzung* or fire tax) to show that they had paid up. The military authorities even had preprinted forms with blanks to be filled in for the amounts and dates. Failure to pay recurring taxes on time led to what was called "execution," often the burning down of villages or even execution of locals. Even when invading armies obey their own rules, civilians are still seen as there to be exploited, their supplies and savings to be used and their houses appropriated for billeting soldiers. Armies have sometimes tried to pay but the promissory notes and scrip they offer often turn out to be worthless.

In his *History of the Peloponnesian War* Thucydides describes how the devastation of Attica by the Spartans in the first year of the war was intended to entice the Athenians to come out from behind their walls and fight to defend their farms. A territorial dispute between the Kingdom of Poland and its ally the Grand Duchy of Lithuania and the Teutonic Knights led to the Hunger War in the summer of 1414, when both sides used scorched-earth tactics to starve the other into submission. In the Europe of the Middle Ages the knights, whose chivalric code has been so admired, used the *chevauchée,* an innocent word for a brutal tactic. True they rode, as the name suggests, but the *chevauchée's* purpose was to take, burn or level everything—animals, crops, buildings, people—in their path. That is why in parts of France you still see fortified farmhouses and churches where the poor took refuge. Not that it always saved them, because buildings could be stormed or set aflame. "War without fire," said the real Henry V, "is as worthless as a sausage without mustard." In 1360, during the Hundred Years War, 100 peasants were slaughtered when the English broke into the church at Orly. The noble warriors used the destruction, including that of peasants and serfs whom they saw as their inferiors, to force their opponents out of their fortified castles to defend their property. (And the looting and pillaging were ways of keeping the ordinary soldiers happy.) Near the start of the Hundred Years War the British conducted a famous *chevauchée* twenty-seven miles wide which left a ruined countryside in its wake. An Italian poet who came back twenty-five years after the war began said he "had to force myself to believe it was the same country I had seen before."

The speech by the Duke of Burgundy, the Marshal of France, in *Henry V,* is a telling counterpoint to the glories of war Shakespeare's characters talk about elsewhere in the play. Burgundy urges the French and English kings to end the fighting:

> *If I demand, before this royal view,*
> *What rub or what impediment there is,*
> *Why that the naked, poor and mangled Peace,*

Dear nurse of arts, plenties and joyful births,
Should not in this best garden of the world
Our fertile France, put up her lovely visage?

And he tries to tell them of the human costs:

And as our vineyards, fallows, meads and hedges,
Defective in their natures, grow to wildness,
Even so our houses and ourselves and children
Have lost, or do not learn for want of time,
The sciences that should become our country;
But grow like savages,—as soldiers will
That nothing do but meditate on blood . . .

Brutality against civilians is also intended to keep them submissive and teach them that resistance does not pay. During Tyrone's Rebellion, which started in the 1590s when the Irish rose up against the English Tudor conquest, the English reacted with the utmost severity. Sir Arthur Chichester, the ruthless governor of Carrickfergus, boasted in a letter to his superior of a raid along Lough Neagh, just west of Belfast (today a peaceful lake known for its eels and its opportunities for birdwatching), "We have killed, burnt and spoiled all along the lough within four miles of Dungannon." He counted, he said, at least a hundred dead and he had burned out as many or more. "We spare none of what quality or sex soever, and it has bred much terror in the people . . ." Humanity has never abandoned such measures. In 1942 during their war against China, the Japanese adopted a similar policy in their Three Alls: Burn All, Kill All, Destroy All. Today Syrian government forces lay waste to rebel towns and villages.

In the American Civil War not only did General Sherman use mass reprisals against civilians to deter attacks, on Union ships on rivers, for example, but, like the Americans later in Vietnam, he became convinced that the key to victory lay in cutting off the support—from providing intelligence to food—that Southern civilians could give their forces in their home territory. As he said in a letter to the Secretary of the Treasury, "The Government of the United States may now safely proceed on the proper rule that all in the South are enemies of all in the North; and not only are they unfriendly, but all who can procure arms now bear them as organized regiments or as guerrillas." Sherman viewed every Southern civilian, young, old, men and women, as an enemy. In pursuit of victory he singled out civilians in key Confederate states such as Mississippi, Georgia, and South Carolina for special treatment, expelling the inhabitants of selected towns and cities and setting buildings on fire, appropriating horses and cattle and destroying crops. The March to the Sea, through Georgia in 1864, left a trail of ruin some sixty miles wide across the state and in the following year South Carolina suffered the same fate.

The Europeans regarded the American Civil War with a certain amount of pity, as evidence that the Americans had not yet advanced in civilization as far as they so evidently had. In the decades before the First World War, Europeans increasingly thought that war was something that only less advanced and less civilized parts of the world still engaged in. After the Franco-Prussian War of 1870–71 the only conflicts in Europe were in the Balkans, which could be explained away on the grounds that nations such as Serbia, Bulgaria, Romania and Greece had only just emerged from under the dead hand of the Ottoman Empire and therefore had some catching up to do. The new Carnegie Endowment for International Peace wrote a report on the First and Second Balkan Wars of 1912 and 1913 and commented on the atrocities committed by all sides against civilians. "In the older civilizations," it said comfortingly with a reference to the rest of Europe, "there is a synthesis of moral and social forces embodied in laws and institutions giving stability of character, forming public sentiment, and making for security." The report came out in the early summer of 1914, just as Europe was about to embark on a war which showed how capable it was of its own cruelties against civilians.

The move toward total war in the twentieth century blurred the line between the battlefront and the home front. After all, so it was reasoned, the woman who made the bullets in a factory was as much a part of the war effort as the soldier who fired them. The growth of nationalism and the mass participation of citizens in their own societies provided the fuel and justification for an all-encompassing hatred of the enemy, combatants and civilians alike, and the great advances in industry, science and technology gave greater means to act on that, although older tactics—the naval blockade, forcible billeting of soldiers, seizing of assets, scorched earth—were also used against civilians.

For a long time after the First World War it was assumed that the stories of German atrocities in Belgium were the creation of skillful Allied propaganda. In fact, as historians have shown recently, many of them were true. German troops did shoot innocent Belgian civilians out of hand or use them as human shields, and deliberately set buildings on fire. Germany did strip Belgium of much of its wealth, from gold to cattle. And Belgian civilians, some 120,000 of them, were forcibly taken to work, usually under appalling conditions and on short rations, in Germany and German-occupied northern France. The Germans were not the only ones guilty of maltreating civilians. The British blockade of Germany, which included foodstuffs, remains controversial to this day. Recent work by a young British historian, Mary Cox, shows that poor children in Germany, whose parents could not afford to buy increasingly expensive food for them, were undernourished and their growth affected during and just after the war, when the British continued the blockade to put pressure on the Germans to agree to their peace terms. When their armies withdrew in the face of German advances in 1915, the Russians not only used scorched-earth tactics but forced non-Russian minorities to leave. Some 300,000 Lithuanians, 350,000 Jews and

750,000 Poles were sent eastward into Russia. Jews were singled out for special attention and pogroms against them continued through the war in Russian-held territory. When Austria invaded Serbia in 1914 and again, with greater success, in 1915, its troops behaved brutally toward the local population. Over 1,000 civilians, including women and children, suspected of helping the Serbian army were killed, "under circumstances of the most revolting cruelty," said one foreign observer. In the Ottoman Empire the ruling Committee of Unity and Progress, nicknamed the Young Turks, used the war as an excuse to carry out a systematic genocide against its Armenian minority. Between 1 million and 1.5 million died, as a result of executions or the hardships they suffered on the forced march from their homes in the northeast across the desert to Syria.

Between the wars improvements in technology—better and more deadly bombs, longer-range and more powerful aircraft, submarines, poison gas and the atomic bomb—made it possible to kill on a greater scale and from a greater distance. For all the revulsion against the massive death tolls in the aftermath of the First World War, Western governments found bombing from the sky a cheap and easy way to bring recalcitrant civilians under control, especially if they were regarded, as was so often the case, as less-civilized peoples. The British used bombers against villages in Iraq and Afghanistan in the early 1920s, as did the Italians when they invaded Ethiopia in 1935. (Mussolini's son-in-law Count Galeazzo Ciano thought the exploding bombs looked like flowers from the air.) Aerial bombing of civilians finally came to Europe in 1937 during the Spanish Civil War when Nazi and fascist pilots acting for General Franco's forces destroyed the Basque town of Guernica, killing some several hundreds.

At the start of the Second World War, there were still some questions, at least on the Allied side, about what constituted a legitimate target (a British Cabinet minister is said to have protested in 1939, "But that's private property," when the possibility of bombing German industry in the Ruhr came up). The all-out nature of the war swept such issues aside, although, again on the Allied side, they never completely disappeared. All the belligerents used bombing of civilians to disrupt enemy war efforts and weaken the will to fight on. Ports, factories, railway marshaling yards, oil depots, dams and bridges were all targets, but so too were housing and city centers. Hermann Goering promised Hitler in the summer of 1940 that he could force Britain to sue for peace by bombing its airfields and key cities, especially London. Sir Arthur Harris, chief of Britain's Bomber Command, was convinced, and managed to persuade his superiors, including Winston Churchill, that the war against Germany could be won by the bomber and that the critical target was German morale. The aim was, said Harris in a top-secret memorandum in October 1943:

> The destruction of German cities, the killing of German workers, and the disruption of civilized community life throughout Germany . . . the destruction of houses, public utilities, transport and lives; the creation of a refugee problem on an unprecedented scale; and the breakdown of morale both at home and at the battle fronts by fear of extended and intensified bombing, are accepted and intended aims of our bombing policy. They are not by-products of attempts to hit factories.

In 1943, 40,000 died in the German city of Hamburg, many in the firestorm that swept the city as a result of Allied bombing, and in 1945 perhaps a further 35,000 in Dresden. (The figure for the latter, like the choice of the target itself, remains highly controversial.) The American bombing of Tokyo that same year with incendiary bombs (a weapon chosen deliberately because so many structures in the city were made of wood) destroyed sixteen square miles and left 80,000 to 100,000 dead and 1 million homeless.

Major General Curtis LeMay, whose responsibility the raid was, said the Japanese were "scorched and boiled and baked to death." It was no oversight that mass bombings were not included in the Allied indictment of Nazi leaders at the Nuremberg trials.

Total war also blurred the distinction which had been established in the preceding centuries between the proper roles of combatants and noncombatants. Uniforms, hierarchy, discipline and rules were meant to mark out the military from civilians. The former had the right to use force; the latter did not. But what happened when civilians took up arms or resisted armed invaders? Did the rules of war apply to them or not? Could and should such civilians be punished—as General Sherman did in the American South, for example? Questions like these were part of larger and continuing attempts to control and regulate war, but they also point to the increasing importance of civilians in war.

Before the modern age, civilian support for war was not something rulers cared much about, but with the appearance of nationalism and the growing complexity and demands of war, civilians—their approval and their labor—became increasingly important to the war effort. Civilian volunteers, such as the patriotic women's associations in Prussia during the Napoleonic Wars or the International Red Cross, founded in the mid-nineteenth century, could look after the military or victims of war, raise money for soldiers' families, provide and staff hospitals for the wounded, or buy bonds to finance the war effort. Women, the young and the old could take on jobs to free men for the front or help the authorities by volunteering to monitor blackouts or watch for fires. Conversely, when the public, or enough of them, withdraw their support for wars, as they did in Russia in 1917, in Germany in 1918 and in the 1960s and 1970s in the United States during the Vietnam War, it is difficult if not impossible for governments to fight on. Even while a war continues, civilians can sabotage and weaken their country's war effort in a variety of ways. One extreme is direct resistance, whether of pacifists who lie across railway tracks or block recruiting centers or of resisters who take up arms against either their own governments or occupying forces. At the other end of the scale is unwillingness to cooperate, refraining from buying war bonds, for example, or refusing to work extra hours. When the Soviet Union and Germany signed their Non-Aggression Pact (also known as the Molotov–Ribbentrop Pact after their two foreign ministers) just before the outbreak of the Second World War, Communist Parties around the world were ordered by Moscow to reverse their positions completely from hostility toward Nazi Germany to attacking the democracies. (It was this that helped to inspire George Orwell's *Nineteen Eighty-Four*.) In France the powerful Communist Party switched overnight from urging war on Germany to advocating peace. When the government decreed mobilization, communists shouted, "Don't go!" and "Peace! Peace!" at the railway stations and there were reports, difficult to substantiate, that communist workers sabotaged munitions' production.

The Second World War saw vast territories with millions of civilians under enemy occupation. In Europe 180 million came under the Axis powers of Italy and Germany and their smaller partners, while in Asia the Japanese ruled over 460 million. Some civilians collaborated, often enthusiastically, with the conquerors. In China the leading nationalist Wang Jingwei agreed to head a puppet regime for the Japanese, in part because he believed that his country and Japan in partnership could expel Western imperialism and build a new Asia. The Belgian intellectual Henri de Man thought Nazi rule "a deliverance" from liberal democracy. The ruling elites and their supporters in the puppet state of Vichy France saw an opportunity to turn back the clock to what they believed were France's eternal Catholic and conservative values. When the Germans demanded that French Jews be handed over for shipment to the extermination camps, Vichy cooperated willingly.

Blinded by their own racial theories and driven by the increasing demands of the war to extract whatever they could from occupied territories, the Axis powers in both Europe and Asia drove civilians into active opposition. Forced labor, punitive taxes, indiscriminate killing and deliberate genocide gave people a stark choice of resisting or probably dying in any case. As armed resistance grew across Asia, from the Philippines to China, and throughout Europe, the Axis powers cracked down ever more severely, the Japanese with such policies as the Three Alls in China and the Nazis with collective punishment for any locality where there were resistance activities. As one German diplomat in occupied Greece said after German forces massacred Greek villagers, "The wonderful result of this heroic deed is that babies are dead; but the partisans continue to live." Ukrainians who had welcomed Nazi troops with the traditional gifts of salt and bread as their deliverers from Soviet rule formed partisan groups as the Nazis started their killings and mass deportations of slave labor to the West.

Resistance in the Second World War was picking up a gun or blowing up railways, but it was also listening to the nightly news bulletins on the BBC, as thousands did all over Europe even though that was punishable by death. Resistance was also printing and distributing information about the occupations and the state of the war. In Belgium around 12,000 people were engaged in putting out and distributing some 300 underground papers. In occupied France audiences clapped British soldiers when they appeared in newsreels and moved if a German sat next to them. In Poland a German officer complained that Polish children were always rude to him. In occupied Denmark citizens gathered in large numbers in the open air to sing Danish folk songs. The Dutch planted flower beds in their national colors. The streets in Prague were empty on the anniversaries of the Munich Agreement, which had destroyed Czechoslovakia. Such gestures may have seemed futile but they helped to keep hope alive.

Individuals did what they could both to preserve memories of their peoples and record the horrors of the present. At the risk of his life, a Muslim librarian in Sarajevo smuggled out a rare illu-

minated Jewish manuscript from the fourteenth century from the
National Museum of Bosnia and Herzegovina to save it from the
Nazis. In Vilna Jewish scholars who were forced by the Nazis to
catalogue a vast hoard of seized Jewish documents smuggled out
what they could and hid them under floorboards and in walls.
Photographers defied Nazi rules to take and preserve pictures of
ghettos and concentration camps. When the Nazis came to power
in Germany in 1933, Victor Klemperer, a professor of Romance
languages in Dresden, decided that he would continue writing his
diary. He makes frequent reference to his health, repeatedly pre-
dicting that he was not long for this world. (He died in 1960 at
the age of seventy-nine.) Klemperer said of himself that he was
not heroic, but to write a record, as he did, of the growing Nazi
control over German society and the regime's many crimes, including the Second World War and the Holocaust, was an act of
great courage. "I shall go on writing," he recorded in 1942. "That is
my heroism. I will bear witness, precise witness!" Although the
Nazis counted him as Jewish despite the fact that his family had
converted to Christianity, he was spared because he was married
to an Aryan woman. As the restrictions tightened around him,
she was still allowed to travel freely and bravely smuggled the
pages of the diary out of the special house for mixed marriages
where they were obliged to live. Equally bravely, a woman doctor
friend hid the material until the war ended.

Where they could, the Allies encouraged and supported armed
resistance. The purpose of the British Special Operations Executive, founded in 1940, was to encourage resisters on the Continent
"to set Europe ablaze." Once Germany invaded the Soviet Union,
European Communist Parties did another reversal and joined in.
Although the Nazis had suppressed communism, much of Party
activity had simply gone underground and communist organization, with its firm hierarchy and self-contained cells, proved
highly adaptable to resistance activities. The growing resistance
networks, communist and non-communist alike, helped Allied

airmen and soldiers escape; provided valuable intelligence, including plans for parts of the Atlantic Wall erected by the Germans to deter Allied landings and detailed information about
Axis troop strengths, organization and movements; and carried
out sabotage in factories, along railway lines and of telegraph and
phone lines. Those who were caught by the occupiers paid a terrible price and often so did innocent bystanders.

What strikes those of us who live in peaceful societies is the
often extraordinary resilience and adaptability of civilians and
civil society to the strange and terrifying world of war in which
they find themselves. People endure privations which would have
seemed unendurable before war came. They make lives in the
ruins, adapt their timetables depending on when it is safe to go
out and sleep in shelters crammed with strangers. They learn to
live without electricity or water and enjoy food—odd cuts of
meat, tins of oily fish, tasteless potatoes, coffee made from
acorns—that they would scorn in peacetime. Nella Last spent the
Second World War in Barrow-in-Furness, some forty miles north
of Liverpool in a shipbuilding region which was a frequent target
of German bombing. Her own beloved house was damaged but
she carried on nevertheless, working for the Women's Voluntary
Service all day and managing her household in a few snatched
hours. She kept chickens and planted out vegetables and took
great pride in stretching her rations as far as possible. She frequently confided to her diary that she was depressed but that she
kept cheerful for the sake of her family and others around her.
She reminded herself of the little Dutch boy who put his finger
in the hole in a dyke and held back the water. "I must keep my
dykes strong enough—or else at times I'd go under."

Women become great improvisers, making dresses out of
curtains—like Scarlett O'Hara in *Gone with the Wind.* In the Second World War women in Great Britain dealt with the shortage
of silk stockings and nylons by painting seams up the backs of
their legs to make it look as though they were wearing them. And

they found themselves doing things that they never thought they were capable of. The author of *A Woman in Berlin* believed that women derived their strength from concentrating on the details of daily life, such as queuing for food. "And for these women," she says of her neighbors, "the task at hand is sausage, and the thought of sausage alters their perspective on things that may be much more important but are nevertheless much further away." She herself takes pleasure in washing her sheets after the Soviets move out—as she says sardonically, "a much-needed change after all those booted visitors."

Libussa Fritz-Krockow came from an old landed family from the east of Germany and made a suitable marriage in 1944 to an officer in the army who went off to fight—she had little idea where—leaving her, her mother and their small household, which was about to include her baby, in the care of her stepfather. Families such as theirs had strong traditions and the values they held dear were largely masculine and military. The men in her world believed in order, discipline and obedience, useful in battle but not in the chaos that was about to engulf them as the Soviet troops advanced and the German front collapsed. In her memoir *Hour of the Women* Fritz-Krockow describes how she and her mother and the maid took over from her stepfather and the other nobly born men of the district. She dealt with the Soviets, bribed officials, scavenged and stole to survive because the men could not: "When it came to ducking your head and crawling on all fours to pick the spinach you needed so as not to starve—with no room for honor and duty—that was where they failed. Such tasks they left to us." She managed to bring her small party of women and her baby safely to the Allied zone in the West and went back to find her stepfather, who was in an improvised prison camp in the Soviet zone. She located him and told him through the barbed wire that she had wire cutters and train tickets to the West. At first he refused to leave, on the grounds that he had given his word as a gentleman and an officer that he would not escape. It was only when she claimed not to know how to travel by herself that he agreed to come. Not surprisingly, when they were safely reestablished in the West she found she could not go back to the old relationship of dependency and submissiveness to the men in her family. The anonymous woman in Berlin has a similar reaction. She now sees men as the weaker sex, miserable and powerless: "Deep down we women are experiencing a kind of collective disappointment. The Nazi world—ruled by men, glorifying the strong man, is beginning to crumble, and with it the myth of 'Man.'" She sees defeat in war as the defeat of the male sex.

War has a way of upending traditional roles and expectations. In Renaissance Europe women in besieged cities were expected to join in their defense. During an eighteen-month siege of the Italian city of Siena between 1552 and 1553 all women, rich and poor alike and between twelve and fifty, were issued with baskets and spades or picks. When the order was cried through the streets, the women were to leave their households and go to work on the city walls. The more total the war, the greater the demands on women's labor and skills. And at the end of the First World War in many countries, including Britain, Canada, Denmark, Germany, Poland and the United States, the contribution made by women to the war effort became a persuasive argument for giving them the vote.

In the First World War the proportion of women working outside the home went up significantly in most of the combatant countries. At the start of the war, women made up 23 percent of the labor force in British industry and transport and by 1918 34 percent. "The Kaiser," said a female Scottish welfare supervisor in a British munitions factory, "handed British women an opportunity which their own fathers and brothers and mothers had ever denied them." Women had worked in offices and factories before the war but they now moved into what had been seen as male jobs. Everywhere women abandoned long skirts for trousers and cut their hair short because it was safer and more convenient.

Women filled in for men as bus conductors or farm laborers (land girls, as they were known in Britain). "Munitionettes" replaced men in the dangerous work at arms factories. Many—"Canary Girls" to the British—turned bright yellow because of the chemicals and sometimes gave birth to babies the same color. In 1915 the Ministry of Munitions instituted its welfare supervisors, themselves women, to look after the health and working conditions of its female workforce, but, perhaps inevitably, the supervisors found themselves dealing with recalcitrant male employers and union officials who did not see why women should be paid the same as men for the same work.

In both world wars working women, especially those in jobs that were traditionally seen as men's, faced challenges in the workplace, particularly from male colleagues who feared that paying women less might provide an excuse for bosses to lower or freeze their own wages, and made it plain they were not wanted. In a Birmingham factory men on the previous shift loosened the nuts on a lathe so that the women taking over would be slowed up. A British woman who gave up hairdressing to become a riveter in the Second World War waited in vain to be assigned a job when she reported for her first day's work along with a group of male recruits. When she asked the foreman what she should do, he replied, "Oh yes! We've forgotten sunshine here!" He showed her a broom: "Here! Take this!" he said. "And sod around!" Managements' reactions to instances such as this and more overt sexual harassment such as banning makeup at work were not always particularly helpful. Boeing caused an outcry when it sent fifty-three women home because their sweaters were too tight and then tried to defend itself by claiming that tight sweaters were a safety hazard because they might get caught in the machinery. The middle-class professions were often no more welcoming to women. When Britain's Institution of Mechanical Engineers admitted its first female full member in 1944, its members protested. Women, wrote one, were too delicate for the "rough and tumble" and coarse language they would inevitably encounter. And, perhaps more to the point, he added, "Professional engineers already have too much competition to face, and après la guerre—well, 'you never can tell.'"

For a lot of women paid work merely added to what they were already doing as mothers and wives, and governments were slow to recognize this. In London women marched through the streets pushing their small children and holding signs saying, "Nurseries for Kids! War Work for Mothers!" As they scrambled to find day care, do the shopping and look after their households, some women found the burden intolerable. Absenteeism among British working women was twice as high as that of men and employers tended to put it down mainly to the women's need to get to the shops before they closed or everything ran out. A Ministry of Food official, one suspects a man, advised unhelpfully, "It should not be beyond the ability of married women war workers to arrange for a neighbor or friend to purchase their food for them." When the United States came into the Second World War, the American government urged women not to be lazy and take up their war work: "It is only in recent years, and mostly in the United States, that women have been allowed to fall into habits of extraordinary leisure."

Josephine von Miklos, who came from an aristocratic background and had a doctorate from the University of Vienna, grumbled about the dirt and boredom of working in a New England munitions factory, but she reminded herself, "Neither did the men of Bataan like their grime or filth. The Chinese and Russian and Australian soldiers haven't any fun fighting, nor do the men at sea." Other women were able to enjoy the experience of making good money for the first time. A Scottish woman who worked during the Second World War in the Rolls-Royce aero-engine plant at Hillington near Glasgow (where women had actually gone on strike over low wages) remembers earning over £5 a week by the end of the war: "I was quite tickled to show them in the house a five pound note. I'd never seen a five pound note." Not all the changes for women were going to be permanent. As men returned from the world wars they moved back into the jobs they had once held; indeed many employers shared the veterans' view that the women had only been temporary replacements. And nor did all the provisions for working mothers, such as day-care centers and crèches, last into the postwar years.

There were gloomy predictions in the press in countries such as the United States and Britain that bringing women out of their homes was likely to lead to immorality and, perhaps as bad, make them unfeminine and overly assertive. For a lot of women, however, being able to work was a form of liberation. They enjoyed the freedom that having their own money gave them and the comradeship at work. "I thoroughly enjoy my four hours working in the afternoon," said a woman who worked part-time in a British factory in the Second World War. "I'm all agog to get here. After all, for a housewife who's been a cabbage for fifteen years—you feel you've got out of the cage and you're free." And, she went on, "Quite a lot of the part-timers feel like that—to get out and see some fresh faces—it's all so different, such a change from dusting." Nella Last confessed to her diary that it was a great relief both to get away from her dull husband and to feel that she was doing something useful. When he complained about his tea not being ready and her not being so "sweet," she snapped back, "Well, who wants a woman of fifty to be sweet, anyway? And besides I suit me a lot better!" The authorities tried to put the Women's Land Army behind the Boy Scouts in Britain's victory parade at the end of the war and the women went on strike. "The army was shattered," said one, "they didn't know what to do with this kind of insubordination, but we were quite determined. If they didn't put us somewhere else, we were going to go home." The army backed down and the Land Army women marched behind the women from the army's Auxiliary Territorial Service.

How war affects civilians depends as much on where they are

as who they are. The rich and powerful can use their money and connections to buy their way out of military service or to acquire scarce luxuries, including food and wine. In occupied Paris Coco Chanel was able to spend a very pleasant war in the Ritz with a handsome German lover. The inhabitants of Leningrad, where food ran so short that there were instances of cannibalism, had a very different war and many of them did not survive it. American servicemen fought and died on the roads to Berlin and Rome and Tokyo, but back home the United States boomed.

War expenditure did in the United States and other Allied countries such as Canada what John Maynard Keynes had been advocating in the aftermath of the Depression. By spending freely and abandoning the sacred cow of balanced budgets, governments got the economy going again. The insatiable appetite of the war for resources and war matériel created new businesses and stimulated existing ones. The *Guardian*'s Washington correspondent, Alistair Cooke, later to be internationally known for his famous BBC series *Letter from America,* persuaded his editors to send him on a road trip across the United States in 1941 just after Pearl Harbor. He visited famous cities such as New Orleans, where Andrew Higgins's new factories and rapidly growing workforce were making thousands of landing craft, as well as an unremarkable small town in Indiana called Charlestown. Before the war it had a population of 939, two churches, a handful of stores and one steak house. In 1940 the federal government decided to build an explosives plant there. By the time Cooke visited, the original inhabitants had been joined by 15,000 people from all over the country, living as best they could in rented rooms and trailers, and Charlestown had new roads, bridges and policemen. In countries such as Britain, the United States and Canada, workers were able to take advantage of their new importance to bid for higher wages and improved benefits. In the Soviet Union, which even in peacetime organized its economy on a war footing, workers were as essential but had far less power. Moreover, the extent of the German advance meant that Soviet industries had been hastily relocated far into the interior and many workers had to live in tents and work long hours in unheated factories through the long, cold winters. The end of the war allowed for a gradual reconstruction of the enormous damage done to Soviet infrastructure, but the new demands of the Cold War meant that Soviet production remained directed toward preparations for war. There was no question of improving workers' rights, allowing them freedom of movement or providing much in the way of consumer goods.

As peace comes and the painful memories of war start to recede, civilians too may experience the nostalgia that combatants can feel for the intensity of comradeship in war. Vera Brittain was a lifelong opponent of war and wrote very movingly about the losses she experienced in the First World War. Yet she could also write, "Whenever I think of the War to-day, it is not as summer but always as winter; always as cold and darkness and discomfort, and an intermittent warmth of exhilarating excitement which made us irrationally exult in all three. Its permanent symbol, for me, is a candle stuck in the neck of a bottle, the tiny flame . . ."

CHAPTER 8

CONTROLLING THE
UNCONTROLLABLE

"It seems to me a funny thing to make rules about war.
It is not a game. What is the difference between
civilized war and any other kind of war?"

—PANCHO VILLA

IN 1827 A YOUNG GERMAN IMMIGRATED TO THE UNITED
States, leaving behind a turbulent career which included fighting
for the Prussian army against Napoleon and a couple of spells in
prison for his liberal views, among them firm and vocal hostility
to the Prussian crown. Franz Lieber was an idealist, polymath,
poet, philosopher and physical fitness enthusiast whose wide circle of friends and acquaintances included Jeremy Bentham, Alexis
de Tocqueville, John Stuart Mill and Daniel Webster. In his new
country he became a prominent intellectual and educator, among
much else editing the first edition of the *Encyclopedia Americana*,
and ending up at Columbia University as the first ever American
professor of political science (a term and discipline he helped to
invent).

When the Civil War broke out Lieber was a staunch supporter
of the Union, but his own family, like so many others, was divided.
One son died fighting for the Confederacy and another was badly
wounded with the Union forces. Lieber became head of the Loyal
Publication Society, but continued his own writing, focusing increasingly on how the two sides should treat each other. He ar-

gued bravely that Confederate prisoners should be treated as combatants, not traitors, and therefore be subject to the customary laws of war. It was, he said, the moral as well as the reasonable thing to do. "When a highway robber asks my purse, and I, being unarmed, consider it expedient to give it, I certainly recognize the robber, it is no more than recognition of a fact." In 1862 Lieber wrote to Henry Halleck, then general in chief of the Union Armies, offering to draw up a code for Union soldiers on how to behave. The result, issued by President Lincoln as General Order #100, was a key document in codifying the modern laws of war, and much that has been done since, such as the Geneva Conventions, has built upon it.

Just over a decade later, in Vienna, Bertha von Suttner, a penniless but beautiful young woman from an old noble family, took a job as a governess in a well-to-do family. As such things sometimes happened, the son of the house fell madly in love with her and, perhaps, she with him. Predictably the parents opposed the marriage and the young couple ran off together, ending up eventually in the Caucasus, newly acquired by Russia. Von Suttner's husband tried one scheme after another, from a timber business, which failed, to designing wallpaper, and eked out a living of sorts as a riding instructor and French teacher. While they both wrote articles for the European press, she became the more renowned. In 1877, when a conflict broke out between Russia and the Ottoman Empire, she saw for herself what war could mean and increasingly devoted her considerable energies to attempting to abolish it. Von Suttner, trailed by her husband, moved westward and became something of a celebrity, devoting her time and her pen to the cause of peace. In 1889 she published her most famous novel, *Lay Down Your Arms*. ("Deep convictions but untalented," said Tolstoy of her.) Overwrought and overwritten, with an improbable plot, its fervent antiwar message nevertheless resounded in a Europe which was becoming increasingly aware of the great destructive capacities unleashed by the Industrial Revolution and the growth of nationalism. Von Suttner met with statesmen including Theodore Roosevelt to beg them to bring an end to war and she also developed a strong partnership with Alfred Nobel, the Swedish industrialist.

An engineer and inventor, Nobel had developed new and powerful explosives initially for mining. Armed forces around the world, however, had been quick to see their potential for better and more deadly weapons. As Nobel's fortunes had grown so had his guilty conscience. He wished, he said, that he could develop a weapon of such "frightful efficacy for wholesale destruction" that war would become unthinkable. Von Suttner persuaded him rather to endow a prize for peace and, since she spent extravagantly, then lobbied shamelessly to receive it. Her goal and that of Nobel and their many like-minded allies was to eliminate war altogether.

Lieber and von Suttner represent two overlapping strands in humanity's long struggle to limit, control or finally eliminate war. One did not necessarily exclude the other. Even pacifists such as von Suttner were prepared to work on developing laws for the making and conduct of war in the hopes that, one day, human beings would come to realize that violence no longer had a place in their affairs. Immanuel Kant, who reflected much on war in his peaceful city of Königsberg on the Baltic, argued that developing internationally accepted laws on war was a step on a long and difficult journey to the goal of getting rid of it altogether—and humanity's own failings might keep it from finally reaching that ideal state.

In 1913 John Reed, a young Harvard graduate already making a name for himself as a radical muckraking journalist, spent four months with the rebel Mexican leader Pancho Villa. Reed happened to show him a pamphlet with the latest rules of war which had been agreed at the Hague Conference of 1907. Villa, reported Reed, spent hours going over it: "It interested and amused him hugely." Villa wanted to know more about the conference and whether there had been a Mexican representative there. Above all he found the whole endeavor absurd: "'It seems to me a funny thing to make rules about war. It is not a game. What is the difference between civilized war and any other kind of war?'"

Villa had put his finger on one of the several paradoxes that confront us when we think about war. How can we talk at all about controlling and managing something where violence is the tool and the domination, if not the total destruction, of the enemy the goal? Yet that has not stopped us from trying repeatedly to do so over the millennia. Like ants with their nests, we laboriously build up a more or less agreed structure only to see it kicked apart by the heavy foot of war. We soldier on to reconstruct what we have come to call the laws of war. These are partly conventions and norms which are widely enough accepted at a particular time and place to have a constraining effect. The Greek city-states fought on some days and not others, in similar patterns on the plains, even though the mountains around them offered possibilities for different sorts of war, and their soldiers generally stopped as the sun went down and one side was declared to be the winner. The Aztecs had their highly stylized "flower" wars, just as the highlanders in New Guinea or the Yanomami in the Brazilian rain forest have in more recent times. Psychological barriers, a sense that some things are taboo or not "done," can be powerful especially, perhaps, when enemies are face to face.

The bleak view of war is that all attempts to control and justify it are futile and pointless. As Machiavelli put it, "War is just when it is necessary." Yet even the powerful and ruthless have looked for reasons or excuses of some sort to justify making war. In 1122 B.C. the duke of Chou in northern China conquered the neighboring state of Shang, arguing that its ruler was a drunkard who oppressed his subjects. Heaven, conveniently for Chou, had therefore withdrawn the Shang ruler's mandate and handed it over to the duke of Chou. The Old Testament is filled with references to the Israelites fighting a righteous war against their enemies. He must kill the Amalekites, God tells King Saul, "men and women, infant and suckling." God himself, says the Book of Exodus, is "a man of war." The Greek and Roman generals usually had religious advisers who would consult the omens before going to battle to see whether the gods were promising victory. Julius Caesar, ruthless even with the gods, said, "The omens will be as favorable as I wish them to be." Aggressors have used religion as an excuse, but the fact that they call on it at all indicates both that they have an uneasy respect for its powers and that they have a need to justify what they are doing.

From its early centuries, the Christian Church accepted that there was a distinction between just and unjust wars but regarded both with disapproval. Its clergy were forbidden to fight and laymen who had taken part in a war had to do penance afterward before they were fully back in the Church. In 1095, however, Pope Urban II made war against infidels both righteous and good for the souls of those who took part. At a council of the Church in Clermont he preached a rousing sermon calling on Europe's feudal knights to recover the holy city of Jerusalem. This was God's will, he said, and the crowd shouted in agreement. He promised the salvation of the souls of those who followed the call, as long as their motives were pure. "Whoever for devotion alone," said the decree issued by the council, "not to gain honor or money, goes to Jerusalem to liberate the Church of God can substitute this journey for all penance." In the First Crusade and the others that followed, Crusaders took vows and were ceremonially given crosses that had been blessed. They were promised both spiritual benefits with forgiveness of their sins and more earthly ones: the Church's protection of their families and their properties, immunity from lawsuits and exemption from paying interest on their debts. This was not the first and not the last time a transcendent purpose unleashed the basest cruelties, as the unfortunate Jews of Europe along the Crusaders' paths were to discover. As the First Crusade slowly moved eastward, its members fell on defenseless

Jewish communities on their way, secure in the conviction that they were waging holy war on God's enemies. In Mainz am Rhein, reported a chronicler, the Crusaders put some 700 Jews—men, women and children—to death. "From this cruel slaughter of the Jews," said a chronicler, "a few escaped; and a few because of fear, rather than because of love of the Christian faith, were baptized."

Religion was never entirely satisfactory in justifying war, because the gods do not always give clear directions: oracles were notoriously ambiguous and signs difficult to interpret. The thinkers of the classical world around the Mediterranean started the process, which has gone on by fits and starts, of disentangling law, ethics and morality from religion in thinking about war. For the Greeks and then the Romans a just war was one which was fought to redress a wrong or an injury. Furthermore, the great Roman orator and writer Cicero argued, war was only permissible when all other means of maintaining peace had been exhausted. "There are two types of conflict," he said, "the one proceeds by debate, and the other by force. Since the former is the proper concern of a man, but the latter of beasts, one should only resort to the latter if one may not employ the former." The conduct of the war itself should involve as little cruelty as possible and have as its aim peace. Plato, who grew up during the Peloponnesian War, argued that war ought to be fought knowing that the two sides will eventually have to be reconciled. His student Aristotle, by introducing the idea of natural law, something that humans could work out for themselves, using their reason, opened the door wider to discussions about moving war away from the religious sphere into the secular world.

While the hugely influential St. Augustine did not devote much of his writings in the fourth and fifth centuries A.D. to war, he reluctantly admitted its existence as part of the human condition. He accepted the Greek and Roman view that war is just when it seeks to right a wrong or is a defense against an enemy who is preparing to use force to achieve unjust demands. Indeed he and the equally influential St. Thomas Aquinas several centuries later saw something positive and redemptive in a war which enforced morality. (Who decides what is a breach of morality or a threat is another matter. In the First World War, for example, all sides claimed to be defending themselves against an immoral enemy.) Augustine also introduced the important proviso that only legitimate authorities could make war. (The issue, however, of what constitutes a legitimate authority is another difficult one which has never really gone away. Is a dictatorship or organization such as Daesh or, to give it the more usual name, Islamic State or ISIS, one?) "It makes a great difference," Augustine wrote, "by which causes and under which authorities men undertake the wars that must be waged." Again like his classical predecessors, Augustine also weighed the goals of a war in deciding whether it was a just one or not. "Peace, as has often been repeated, is the end of war."

In modern war the shadow of Clausewitz, with his insistence that the aim of war should be "the overthrow of the enemy," and the growing capacity of societies to wage all-out war have too often led countries to ignore opportunities for negotiated settlements and to carry on fighting just because they can. Saddam Hussein gave up his weapons of mass destruction after the First Gulf War and was no longer a threat to his neighbors; was it really necessary for the peace of the Middle East to invade Iraq and overthrow his regime in 2003? Michael Walzer, whose *Just and Unjust Wars* is a key text in the modern debate, says, "Many war aims can be achieved well short of destruction and overthrow. We need to seek the legitimate ends of war, the goals that can rightly be aimed at. These will also be the limits of a just war. Once they are won, or once they are within political reach, the fighting should stop. Soldiers killed beyond that point die needlessly, and to force them to fight and possibly to die is a crime akin to that of aggression itself." A rule of thumb is that the means used should be proportionate to the ends. In other words, if the goal—say, a disputed bit of territory or an apology—has been gained, there is no need to go on and obliterate the enemy. The temptation of course is to do just that.

While different cultures developed their own understandings about when and how to fight, the West, appropriately enough since it pioneered so much in modern war, has played a major role in setting international laws and rules about what its scholars called *ius ad bellum* and *ius in bello*—the first the laws governing the initiation and justification of war and the second those of its conduct. Other parts of the world have adopted and adapted these, drawing on their own traditions. While feudal knights were still killing each other's peasants and putting the inhabitants of besieged towns to the sword, for example, Islamic scholars had long been developing rules for how women and children should be treated in war.

The issues raised are not easy ones and have been debated for centuries and still are. What makes a war just and who has the right to wage it? And what principles, if any, should guide the way wars are fought and ended? When it comes to the conduct of war, the questions continue. When is it permissible to attack civilians? And how and which ones? How should prisoners of war be treated? Or conquered peoples?

Even when we think we are making headway we find ourselves in a maze of contradictions. Why do we try and outlaw some weapons and regard others as lawful even though the function of both is to kill and maim? Killing by firebombing or flamethrowers is considered acceptable, but ever since the First World War poison gas or biological warfare has been widely regarded as beyond the pale, even by those who use them. Saddam Hussein gassed his own people in Iraq but either denied it or claimed the Iranians were responsible. As long as war has existed, humans have been arguing about what is allowed and what is not. And each time we appear to be getting closer to an answer, what looks like a certainty dissolves on closer examination or throws up more questions.

One principle that is generally accepted by international society is that unprovoked wars for gain or dominance are illegitimate. Self-defense, however, is not. Yet, following the classical world and medieval thinkers such as Augustine and Aquinas, we like to think that war should be a last resort after all other alternatives have been exhausted. "The Miracle of Holland," as the extraordinarily learned and productive seventeenth-century Dutch scholar Hugo Grotius was nicknamed by Henry IV of France, successfully introduced the idea that war was only just if it was waged by states, to protect themselves, and not by private forces. What that came to mean in practice was that opposing states could each claim to be waging a just war. Furthermore, we have come to believe, governments that resort to war ought to have reasonable grounds for thinking they will prevail; otherwise they would be throwing away their people's lives for nothing. Some experts would add that the victorious nation should not utterly humiliate the defeated one.

Fine-sounding principles, but under closer examination they raise another host of questions for philosophers, ethicists and the rest of us to consider. Is it a just war when a nation, feeling that it might be threatened in the future, decides to wage a preventive war in the absence of an immediate threat? That was the reasoning of the German High Command in 1914 as they anticipated a challenge that might emerge three years in the future—or not at all. And if response to an injury makes a war just, who decides whether there has been an injury in the first place, how great it is and whether war is the only redress possible? Austria was looking for an excuse to destroy its troublesome neighbor Serbia well before the Habsburg heir, Archduke Franz Ferdinand, was assassinated in Bosnia. Although Austria sent a commission of inquiry to Bosnia, it was not able to establish a clear line from the assassins to the Serbian government. Nevertheless, it determined on war, to avenge, in the language of the time, the affront to its honor, and sent Serbia an ultimatum that was designed to be unacceptable. Even so, Serbia accepted the majority of conditions and a settlement might have been possible if the great powers had come together, as they had in previous Balkan crises, to impose one. Instead Europe and the world got the Great War.

The meaning of just war has gradually expanded since Grotius's time. While the Westphalian settlements at the end of the Thirty Years War of the seventeenth century established the principle that states did not interfere in each other's internal affairs, globalization—the spread of liberal ideas and the growth, thanks to modern communications, of an international public opinion— has stimulated and justified the idea of armed humanitarian intervention to protect the defenseless and minorities against their own governments. In the 1850s Tsar Nicholas I of Russia provoked a war with the Ottoman Empire in order, so he claimed, to protect Christians there from unfair and brutal treatment. (The prospect of grabbing territory from the failing Ottoman Empire and getting access for Russia into the Mediterranean from the Black Sea through the Ottoman-controlled straits was also a factor.) In this century the invasion of Iraq by the Anglo-American coalition was justified on humanitarian grounds, as was the more recent and largely unsuccessful American intervention in Syria's civil war. Humanitarian intervention and new doctrines such as the Right to Protect raise questions about who decides what is just and suspicions about the motives and goals of the intervening powers. Critics, many of them from non-Western states, have argued that Western powers are simply cloaking their deep-rooted imperialistic attitudes to the rest of the world in the fashionable new language. "Hypocrisy," as the Duc de La Rochefoucauld remarked, "is a tribute vice pays to virtue."

The West does have a long and shameful history of observing one set of rules for itself and another for those it considers less "civilized." As laws of war became more formalized in a series of understandings and agreements, those peoples, mainly non-European, who were not aware of them or who had not been asked to sign up, did not receive their protection. The "civilized" nations who signed the series of Geneva Conventions dealing with prisoners of war or the Hague agreements on arms limitations before the First World War were quite clear that they applied only to themselves. When Japan modernized and became a Pacific power it was accepted into the circle of the "civilized." "We show ourselves," said a Japanese diplomat, "at least your equals in scientific butchery and at once are admitted to your council tables as civilized men." And scientific butchery, with repeating rifles, machine guns and, after the First World War, the new airplane, was what happened to the "uncivilized" in Africa, Asia, the Philippines, the American West or the Middle East. Western legal experts, politicians and military argued complacently that peoples at an earlier stage of development than the fortunate Europeans or Americans only understood a firm hand. The laws of war, said the 1914 British *Manual of Military Law,* can apply only to a conflict between two civilized nations. "They do not apply," it went on, "in wars between civilized and uncivilized, their place taken by the discretion of the civilized commander and such rules of justice and humanity as recommend themselves in the particular circumstances of the case." The twentieth century brought the gradual acceptance—and we are still not fully there—that all human beings possess the same rights to life and dignity and that international law cannot make such distinctions.

The laws regulating the conduct of war, as they have evolved, are not a legal code as we would recognize it in domestic society. Rather they are a compendium, as Walzer puts it, of "professional codes, legal precepts, religious and philosophical principles, and reciprocal arrangements that shape our judgments of military conduct." In recent centuries formal international agreements, on the treatment of neutral states, for example, have become woven in with the codes of honor of professional soldiers or older, un-

written customs about the treatment of prisoners of war, as well
as with shared views on the sanctity and dignity of human life, to
make a web of understandings about war which can seem
strong—at least, as we have seen time and again, until war comes.

Conventions, in such areas as the exchange or ransom of prisoners of war, can have something close to the power of law, especially when warring parties share a common culture. For centuries,
in European war, officers were usually not confined; it would be
enough to ask them, as gentlemen, to give their word—their
parole—not to escape. After Wellington's victory over the French
at the Battle of Vitoria in 1813, the British officers invited their
defeated French adversaries to their mess. (The officers of their
Spanish allies, whom the British despised, were not treated nearly
so well.) The notion of the officer's honor lingered on into the
twentieth century, as Jean Renoir's wonderful 1937 film *La Grande
Illusion* shows. The French officer gives his word that he will not
try to escape to the German commandant of a First World War
prison (but in fact he does so). In the nineteenth century what
had been customary or the subject of bilateral agreements between two nations—such as a 1675 agreement between France
and Spain setting the rates for ransoming different categories of
soldiers—was elaborated in successive multilateral Geneva Conventions and made part of the newly developing body of international law. The International Committee of the Red Cross took
on responsibility for monitoring the treatment of prisoners of
war, ensuring that they received the agreed amounts of food and
medical care, and transmitting letters and parcels.

The Christmas truce in 1914, when the firing stopped in parts
of the trenches and the opposing sides came out to no-man's-land
to exchange toasts, sing carols or play football, harks back at least
to the medieval tradition of war being suspended on holy days.
The ancient Greeks did not fight during the Olympic Games and
the most warlike among them, the Spartans, had certain sacred
days when they would not fight. And there were long-standing

traditions about how to declare war or sue for a cease-fire. "In-
famy" and "treachery" read the newspaper headlines when the
Japanese attacked Pearl Harbor in 1941, not least because Japan
had not sent a declaration of war first. (When Japan broke precedent in 1904 by attacking Russian ports in the Far East without
warning, Western newspapers admired its boldness. But Japan
was an ally of Britain then and widely regarded as an admirable
modernizing nation.) When Japan capitulated in 1945 it did so in
a radio broadcast by the emperor, but across Asia Japanese forces
signaled their surrender to the Allies through the time-honored
white flag, which is still used on occasion today. Since 1945, however, in one of those inexplicable shifts in fashion, declarations of
war have fallen completely out of favor.

Attempts to control the sorts of tactics and weapons used are
probably nearly as old as war itself. The ancient Greeks tried to
limit acceptable weapons to those suitable for close combat. The
historian Polybius, writing in the second century B.C., claimed
that the Greeks had made an agreement "to use against each other
neither secret missiles nor those discharged from a distance, and
considered that it was only a hand-to-hand battle at close quar-
ters which was truly decisive." In the Middle Ages, Innocent II
tried to ban the crossbow and Roger Bacon tried to bury the secret of how to make gunpowder.

The most productive period, ironically in view of what happened later, in the development of the laws of war applicable to all
nations came in the decades before 1914, reflecting that nineteenth-
century mood of optimism that humanity was improving and
that its darker side, including war, might be brought under control. While the foundations had been laid over many centuries in
the world's religions or the work of philosophers, two main sets of
rules now took shape rapidly. The first was a renewed attempt to
regulate war. In 1856 the Declaration of Paris set rules about when
belligerents could use naval blockades and seize goods that might
be used in war from enemy or neutral ships (although it failed to

define what it meant by contraband), and in 1868 the St. Petersburg Declaration prohibited the use of explosive bullets. These marked an innovation of international relations for they were not bilateral or multilateral treaties among states and nor had they been reached by the great powers which then imposed them, as had happened at the Congress of Vienna in 1815, on smaller states. Instead nations were invited to join in support for a set of proposals. The Declarations and the host of subsequent international agreements on war optimistically assumed a common set of values and a shared goal among peoples.

In 1898 the new young tsar, Nicholas II, sent an open invitation to the world's powers to work together to limit the arms race which was gaining steam. Some twenty-six nations met in The Hague the following year to work on further regulating war. Although the arms agreements reached were something of an anticlimax—merely outlawing asphyxiating gas, the dumdum bullet (which caused gaping exit wounds) and the throwing of projectiles out of balloons—there were other encouraging signs, including agreements on the humane treatment of prisoners of war and the creation of a Permanent Court of Arbitration. Peace activists continued to hope that the civilized parts of the world, at least, were moving away from war. In 1907, a second Hague Conference, this time with forty-four nations represented, made some minor changes to the earlier agreements and attempted to regulate war at sea, banning, for example, certain kinds of submerged contact mines, which were increasingly posing a threat to shipping, both naval and merchant. In 1910 the Declaration of London finally provided a working definition of contraband. Since the British then turned around and refused to accept a declaration which they had helped to draw up, it remained on the books. The initiative started in The Hague has never died away, however. As new weapons—bombers, chemical and biological, more deadly landmines, nuclear weapons—have appeared, the world has endeavored, and still does, to limit or ban their use. And individual powers still choose to ignore or fail to ratify provisions they do not like, as the British and others once did.

"The Hague Conventions" has become a shorthand way of describing the rules of war, just as Geneva has given its name to the other main set of conventions. These also originated in the nineteenth century but in this case were intended to protect the victims of war, both those who do the fighting and civilians. In 1859 Henri Dunant, a young Swiss businessman wearing a white summer suit, stumbled onto the battleground at Solferino in northern Italy, where the French and their Sardinian allies had just defeated the Austrians in a decisive battle in the Italian Wars of Unification. The cause may have been glorious; the results were horrific. New and improved weapons had caused some 30,000 casualties. None of the contending armies had made even the most elementary arrangements for the care of the wounded who lay among the dead, as Dunant later wrote, "helpless on the naked ground in their own blood." Horrified, he joined local volunteers in trying to bring the wounded water, bandage their wounds and carry them on crudely improvised stretchers off the field.

Dunant came to think that God had guided him to the battlefield that day. In his subsequent book, *A Memory of Solferino,* he painted the misery of war and called on societies of volunteers everywhere and their governments to undertake medical aid to all soldiers in war irrespective of which side they were on. His work had a huge impact on public opinion across Europe at a time when many, thanks to modern communications, were becoming more aware of how badly soldiers were treated. Dunant also got support within Switzerland, which, as a neutral country, was well positioned to be impartial among opposing sides. In 1863, with the help of well-connected supporters, he established the International Committee for Relief to Wounded Soldiers, which promptly invited the European powers to send representatives to a conference in Geneva. A year later, at a second conference, twelve states' representatives signed the Geneva Convention for the Amelioration of the Condition of Wounded in Armies in the Field. Volunteers on or near the battlefields were to be protected by a symbol, the red cross, which was an inversion of the colors in the Swiss flag. (It has since been joined by the red crescent and the red diamond in countries where it might look too much like a Christian cross.) The International Committee of the Red Cross has grown into a formidable nongovernmental organization. From that moment onward, successive Geneva Conventions, signed by an increasing number of nations, have amplified and expanded the original mission, to include civilians as well as combatants.

The idea that civilians should be distinguished from combatants and spared where possible goes back a long way into history. An ancient Indian text gave a list: "Those who look on without taking part, those afflicted with grief . . . those who are asleep, thirsty, or fatigued or are walking along the road, or have a task on hand unfinished, or who are proficient in fine art." In the twelfth century the great Jewish scholar Maimonides laid down rules that banned wasteful destruction of, for example, fruit trees, or stipulated that a city should be besieged only on three sides so that those who wanted to could escape. While women have often been treated as prizes in war, they have also been singled out among civilians for special treatment. It is all right, says the Old Testament Book of Deuteronomy, for you, as a victorious man, to carry away a woman if you like her and will make her your wife. But, the passage goes on, "if thou have no delight in her, then thou shalt let her go whither she will; but thou shalt not sell her . . . for money, thou shalt not deal with her as a slave."

When Lieber wrote his famous Code during the American Civil War he was drawing both on Judeo-Christian morality and long-accepted practices in European warfare. "Men who take up arms against one another in public war do not cease on this account to be moral beings, responsible to one another and to God," he argued. It was not therefore permissible in war to inflict unnecessary suffering, take revenge, wound or maim the defenseless or use torture to extract confessions. He prohibited rape but, interestingly, did not make a distinction between the sexes when it came to punishment for offenses "concerning the spy, the war-traitor or the war-rebel."

Yet Lieber also acknowledged that he was dealing with modern warfare where the means of destruction were greater than in the past and the distinction between civilians and combatants was already porous. And, despite himself, he was going to blur it still further. "Military necessity, as understood by modern civilized nations," he said in Clause 14, "consists in the necessity of those measures which are indispensable for securing the ends of the war, and which are lawful according to the modern law and usages of war." He then goes on to list the sorts of things, from people to property, that can be legitimately destroyed. Necessity, he argues, "allows of all destruction of property, and obstruction of the ways and channels of traffic, travel, or communication, and of all withholding of sustenance or means of life from the enemy." Indeed, echoing Clausewitz, he argued that waging war must be taken to the limit (the positive side, he pointed out, was that it might therefore end sooner). Civilians cannot always be spared: "It must never be forgotten that the whole country is always at war with the enemy . . ."

Lieber's Code distinguished between units of the enemy's army remaining behind in occupied territory and what he called "armed prowlers" and "war rebels" who organized themselves to attack the occupying forces. The former came under the rules of war and if captured, for example, should be treated as any other prisoners of war; the latter were like ordinary criminals and could be put to death. Although his Code was widely copied, this did not settle the issue of what to do with civilians who took up arms to defend themselves and their territory against an invading force. Were they combatants under the laws of war or something else? The question has become increasingly important in the last two centuries with the spread of nationalism and total war. Where European governments and elites in the eighteenth century saw war very much as the occupation of professional soldiers, by the start of the nineteenth century they were starting to see civilians as part of the war effort and as a resource. Napoleon's forces easily defeated the regular Spanish army in 1807 but found themselves fighting a debilitating and protracted series of engagements against Spanish rebels. This "little war"—*guerrilla*—helped Spain become what Napoleon called his "ulcer." In Prussia patriots talked of a "national state of emergency" when their incompetent king led the supposedly invincible Prussian army to defeat at the hands of Napoleon and organized themselves to resist the French. When Napoleon invaded Russia in 1812, there was spontaneous resistance by the population and landowners destroyed their own property in a scorched-earth policy before fleeing. In the face of such civilian resistance, the military tended to react harshly, arguing, as they have often done since, that civilians had no business being soldiers and that acts of resistance in occupied territories are illegal. In Spain the French refused to call the guerrillas soldiers; rather they were "bandits and brigands."

Later in the century, the Prussians, whose forebears had once resisted Napoleon's occupation, reacted with fury when the French did the same during the Franco-Prussian War of 1870–71. In parts of the occupied French provinces of Alsace and Lorraine, soon to be taken from France, German notices were torn down and isolated German soldiers attacked. When French prisoners of war marched by, the watching crowds burst into "La Marseillaise." The *francs-tireurs,* those French there and elsewhere in France who organized themselves into armed militias, were treated by the German occupiers as having no rights at all and were often shot out of hand. In a foretaste of what was to happen in the two world wars, communities suspected of harboring them were subject to harsh reprisals. A popular German novel later depicted the *francs-tireurs* as cowardly, treacherous and, perhaps most damning of all, ill-disciplined. As a result of their experiences in France, the German military remained set on severe measures against civilian resistance; the army's manual on tactics advised, "*Francs-tireurs* are strung up on the next best tree without further ado."

The two international conferences at The Hague raised questions which we are still debating today. When is it legitimate for civilians to attack invading and occupying forces? What can those forces do in response? And who counts as a soldier and therefore deserves to be treated under the Geneva and other conventions and who is merely a criminal or a traitor? At The Hague the Germans held out for the narrowest possible definition of civilian fighters, insisting that the only legitimate forces were those in clearly identifiable uniforms and that resistance was allowable only during an invasion and not when an occupation had been established. When it came to what that last meant, the Germans suddenly wanted the widest possible definition, arguing that it was enough that the regular troops of the invading army be around but not necessarily visible. The British, thinking perhaps of the success of the guerrilla war in Spain during the Napoleonic Wars, and the French, with their revolutionary tradition of the *levée en masse*, as well as some of the smaller nations, wanted to leave room for spontaneous uprisings of citizens in the face of an invasion. The 1899 Hague Conference saw a compromise: collective penalties against civilian populations were banned but enemy individuals who committed "illegitimate acts of war" might be punished. The 1907 Conference spelled out more clearly what constituted a recognized resistance force: its members must be organized, distinguished by uniforms or badges, carry their weapons openly and fight according to the laws of war.

Enough progress had apparently been made on protecting civilians for Andrew Carnegie, the American philanthropist who devoted a large part of his fortune to the cause of peace, to say in a speech in 1905 that noncombatants were now spared in war and prisoners of war well cared for: "If man has not been busily striking at the heart of the monster War, he has at least been busily engaged in drawing some of its poisonous fangs." And he expected that under "the blessed law of evolution" things could only get better.

Like so many others before 1914, Carnegie was far too optimistic. As in earlier times, the exigencies of war tore holes in the web of laws and conventions intended to contain it. Whether the Germans in Belgium, the Austrians in Serbia or the Russians in Galicia, the occupiers terrorized and brutalized local populations during the First World War. The actions of the British in Iraq in the early 1920s, where the new tool of air power was used to bomb rebellious districts into submission, of the Italian and German air forces in the 1930s in Spain during the Civil War or of the Japanese in China after 1937 demonstrated that, as much as the international community might deplore attacks on civilians in general and on their resistance in particular, the powers ignored international agreements when it suited them.

In the Second World War the savage reprisals carried out against civilians by the Germans, Italians and Japanese helped to highlight the issue afresh and there were real advances in the law during and after the war. In their 1942 London Declaration of War Crimes, the Allies defined hostage-taking or the execution of civilians by occupying powers as a war crime. Since 1945 a new category of war, and of fighters, has entered the international vocabulary: wars of national liberation. Were the members of the National Liberation Front (the FLN) in Algeria criminals, as the French maintained, or soldiers? The older provisions dealing with partisans specified that they must wear some form of uniform or visible badge, but wars of liberation also used guerrillas who, as Mao Zedong put it, swim among the people like the fish in the sea. Were fighters who pretended to be ordinary civilians protected by the laws of war? The French military's view in its long struggle in Indochina was brutally clear. "Never forget," said the motto on the wall of their counterinsurgency training school, "the enemy does not fight this war in accordance with French Army Rules." Was it all right, then, in the name of some common good, to torture the enemy prisoners in such counterinsurgency wars or was that a war crime and a crime against humanity? The so-called War on Terror has raised similar questions today. Did the Geneva Conventions apply to the prisoners held by the Americans at Abu Ghraib in Iraq and do they apply to those at Guantánamo? And in addition were what was called "enhanced interrogation techniques" (a euphemism worthy of Orwell's *Nineteen Eighty-Four*) a violation of the prisoners' human rights? Memoranda from the United States Justice Department in 2003 argued that American interrogators were allowed to do what they did; American courts and much of the public have disagreed. The debate will go on.

Making the laws is one thing; enforcement another. Nations have police forces, courts and prisons. Those who break the law can be judged and punished. The international order so far has only achieved the beginnings of such a system and recent history is full of examples of nations breaking the laws of war when it suits them and they think they can get away with it. Before 1939, Germany had signed up to the various protocols about treating prisoners of war and the Nazis did observe them in the West with peoples they considered their racial equals, such as the British or the French. In the East, however, where the German forces were dealing with Poles or Russians, who, according to Nazi ideology, were racial inferiors, they allowed themselves a free hand to brutalize and murder their prisoners. Even democratic regimes have found that, when defeat is imminent or victory just out of reach, it is tempting, even necessary, to bend the rules. After all, it can be dangerous to fight with one hand tied behind your back. The British and the Americans overcame their initial reluctance and used mass bombings of civilians in the Second World War to try to hasten its end and spare the lives of their own citizens. Were they right to do so? The question is one which still stirs up strong disagreements.

Even determining who is guilty for waging an unjust war and how such persons can be dealt with has proved difficult and is still evolving. In 1815 the great powers did not think in terms of an offense against international law when it came to dealing with Napoleon. All they knew is that they wanted him well out of the way so that he could not escape, as he had done from Elba, and set Europe in turmoil again. The Prussians suggested that the simplest solution was to assassinate him but the British had reservations. Perhaps, they hoped, the French would try their former ruler themselves on the grounds that, by returning to France, Napoleon had defied the new, legitimate, Bourbon ruler, but the French government not surprisingly showed little enthusiasm for this. The British fell back on declaring that Napoleon was a prisoner of war who could be held indefinitely because it was clear that he was never going to stop trying to make war. To reinforce a flimsy legal argument, Parliament passed an act saying that his imprisonment was "necessary for the Preservation of the Tranquility of Europe." To everyone's relief, except of course that of Napoleon himself and his remaining loyal supporters, the British firmly removed him to the remote island of St. Helena in the South Atlantic, where he died.

A hundred years later, the great powers were again thinking of how to deal with those they held responsible for war and they now had a more fully developed set of assumptions. The codification of various international rules about how wars should be fought, as well as arms agreements, had given rise to the assumption—perhaps no stronger than that—that there was an international community which ought to react strongly in the name of all humanity to unjust wars and unjust conduct in war. In 1915, for example, Britain and France issued a declaration to the Ottoman government that it would be held responsible for "crimes against humanity and civilization" for its massacres of the Armenians. When the Great War ended, the public and many of the leaders on the Allied side demanded that someone or something should be punished for the catastrophe that had struck Europe. The leading statesmen spent considerable time before and during the Paris Peace Conference debating about who among the defeated leaders and military should be tried for having started the war and for crimes committed in its course. The obvious figure was Kaiser Wilhelm II of Germany and possibly some of his advisers. (The Austrian Empire had ceased to exist and its old emperor, Franz Joseph, had long since joined his ancestors in the Imperial Crypt in Vienna.) France, Italy and Britain agreed before the Peace Conference opened to set up an international court. "Justice," said their agreement, "requires that the Kaiser and his primal accomplices who designed and caused the war with its malignant purpose, or who were responsible for the incalculable sufferings inflicted on the human race during the war, should be brought to trial and punished for the crimes." The United States objected to an international tribunal, as it continues to object today to the International Criminal Court, although its president, Woodrow Wilson, did join in the speculation about where Wilhelm might be exiled if found guilty. Bermuda was too close to the United States for comfort, the American thought, and Lloyd George offered the Falkland Islands. In the end, Wilhelm remained in the Netherlands, where he had taken refuge at the end of the war, since the Dutch refused to surrender him. The Allies' loud demands for trial and punishment of those guilty of war crimes and their list of over 1,000 war crimes said to have been committed by Germany petered out in a few trials of German officers the German government was obliged to hold at Leipzig.

In the interwar years, humans, as they had done so often before, drew on what they perceived to be the lessons of the past in renewed attempts to control or even abolish war. A Geneva Convention of 1925 prohibited trade in chemical and biological weapons and another in 1929 prohibited their use in war altogether. Still another, signed in 1928, fleshed out the rules governing prisoners of war. The Washington Naval Conference of 1921–22 was successful, for a time, in cooling down a naval race in the Pacific and in setting up new security guarantees there. The London Conference of 1930 extended the Washington Agreements until 1936, at which point both Japan and Italy refused to sign an extension. The new League of Nations worked throughout the 1920s on a more general disarmament conference which finally met in Geneva in 1932, only to collapse into impotence and insignificance when Germany's new Chancellor, Adolf Hitler, pulled his country out of both the conference and the League of Nations.

The scale and destructiveness of the Second World War brought renewed attempts to strengthen the international regime controlling war. The Atlantic Charter which Churchill and President Franklin Delano Roosevelt signed off the coast of Newfoundland in 1941 looked forward to a lasting peace where all nations could be free from the threat of aggression. The following year the Allies, including the Soviet Union, signed up to the United Nations Declaration, in which they promised to fight together until their enemies were defeated, and endorsed the principles of the Atlantic Charter.

While the Allies were looking to the future, they were also considering how to punish those responsible for the war. Germany, Japan and Italy, it was agreed then and since, had all initiated the war and, unlike with the First World War, a legal basis to charge their leaders existed in the various prewar conventions and agreements. The Allies already had evidence too of atrocities committed by their enemies during the war, although the full horror of what had been happening in the death camps or to civilians in occupied territories and to prisoners of war was not fully evident until the end of the fighting. On the other hand, the Soviet Union, now on the side of the virtuous, had connived with Hitler to carve up the center of Europe. And it could be argued, and has been, that the Allies had also broken the law and committed crimes, in their submarine warfare and their mass bombing of civilians. The trials of German and Japanese leaders by special tribunals at

Nuremberg and Tokyo remain nevertheless an attempt, if flawed, to bring the perpetrators of war crimes to justice. The defendants were charged with breaking international agreements and violating the laws of war, and, in the case of the Germans, under a new heading of "crimes against humanity." The trials also established the important precedent that it was not sufficient defense to say that those on trial were simply following orders.

A commission of the new United Nations later elaborated the Nuremberg Principles, covering crimes against peace, war crimes and crimes against humanity. Affirmed in a resolution of the General Assembly in 1950, these have formed the basis for the further expansion of international law. And the new language and agreements on human rights have also strengthened the argument that war cannot be the excuse for armed forces to deprive fellow human beings of fundamental rights such as the right not to be held illegally or be tortured. The challenge, of course, as it has always been, is enforcement. Since 1945 we have used sanctions or United Nations or NATO forces for peacekeeping, and we have tried to develop international law and international courts to try aggressors, such as Slobodan Milošević of Serbia, but such measures have only been effective when the powers want them to be. And when the most powerful country in the world holds prisoners illegally in sites around the world or does not accept the jurisdiction of the International Criminal Court—which was set up to punish unjust wars, among other crimes against humanity—others will be tempted to follow its example.

Yet we continue to hope, as people have done through the centuries, that we can do more than control war and mitigate its effects—that we can abolish it altogether. In Europe's Middle Ages the Church tried repeatedly to impose the Peace of God and outlaw war, except for the holy cause of the Crusades. From the tenth century to the twelfth bishops called on local nobles to attend councils where they would take vows not to plunder local churches and monasteries, hurt unarmed priests or steal from peasants. The list got longer with time: crimes came to include attacking merchants or someone on the way to or from church, or uprooting vines. In the eleventh century the Church also attempted to forbid fighting on certain days: for example, from the end of the evening prayers, Vespers, on Wednesdays until sunrise the following Monday, or during sacred seasons in the Christian calendar such as Easter and Christmas. Understandably, there was much popular enthusiasm for the Church's measures, but the nobles and their retainers kept on their lawless ways even under threat of excommunication. The Bishop of Le Puy in southern France took more effective action in A.D. 990 when he asked local nobles to take an oath to keep the peace and to give back what they had taken from the poor and the Church. When they refused, he called in troops he had previously concealed and, said the chronicler, "with the help of God" the nobles decided to swear the oath after all. The Church also tried, with some success, to direct noble violence outward, toward the Crusades. While religions have, like the medieval Church, a mixed record when it comes to war, certain sects have produced more than their share of antiwar activists. After the Napoleonic Wars, British dissenters and evangelicals established the Society for the Promotion of Permanent and Universal Peace and Quakers and Mennonites have been active in antiwar movements up until the present.

Others have put their hope in reason rather than religion. Christine de Pisan, a prominent poet and thinker of the fifteenth century, wrote that, if a prince feels wronged, he should assemble a "great council of wise men . . . and not only will he assemble those of his own realm, but in order there be no suspicion of failure, he will also call upon some from foreign countries that are known not to take sides, elder statesmen as well as legal advisers and others." Kant, in his *Perpetual Peace: A Philosophical Sketch*, hoped that "crooked timber of humanity" might grow straighter in the ways of peace. The nineteenth century, with its evident signs of material progress, especially in Europe and the Americas, gave rise to hopes that there would be a similar transformation of the moral nature of humanity. "Peace," that indefatigable crusader Bertha von Suttner wrote, "is a condition that the progress of civilization will bring about by necessity . . . It is a mathematical certainty that in the course of centuries the warlike spirit will witness a progressive decline." (Over a century later, Steven Pinker is expressing the same hope in his *Better Angels of Our Nature: Why Violence Has Declined.*) The equally evident progress in weaponry and the growth in the military added incentive to think of ways to move beyond the use of war. Sir Henry Maine, the great nineteenth-century British jurist, remarked, "War appears to be as old as mankind, but peace is a modern invention." True, there were still wars, even in Europe, but increasingly the powers were resorting to arbitration to settle disputes. There were some 300 arbitrations between 1794 and 1914 and more than half of those were between 1890 and 1914, which seemed to indicate a clear trend. Moreover, the spread of representative government and the widening of the franchise appeared to be fulfilling Kant's hope that governments based on the consent of the people and operating by consensus would follow the same principles in dealing with other nations. (What came to be called the democratic peace theory in the twentieth century, with its assumption that democracies would not fight each other, still has a powerful hold on our imaginations, even though history offers examples of countries with a fair degree of democracy, such as Germany and Britain in the First World War, fighting each other.) By 1914 many Europeans had come to think of war as obsolete, something that only the less civilized did. Looking back on his childhood, the Austrian writer Stefan Zweig recalled, "People no more believed in the possibility of barbaric relapses, such as wars between the nations of Europe, than they believed in ghosts and witches."

There appeared to be sound economic arguments against war as well. As the British journalist Norman Angell pointed out in his wildly popular *The Great Illusion,* war no longer made economic sense. In the past nations had fought each other for loot; in the modern world they got what they needed at much less cost through trade and investment. The nations of the early twentieth century were so economically interdependent that a war would hurt even the most powerful among them. And that interdependence should be encouraged. Free trade was not just good for all, it brought good. As the great British radical of the early nineteenth century Richard Cobden had said, free trade was like gravity in keeping the earth stable, "drawing men together, thrusting aside antagonisms of race and creed, and language, and uniting us in bonds of eternal peace." A similar hope lay behind the creation of the Bretton Woods institutions at the end of the Second World War and again behind the US push to lower international trade and investment barriers after the end of the Cold War.

The world was being knitted together before 1914 in other ways too, through travel—the second half of the nineteenth century saw both mass tourism and mass movements of migrants—and by the growth of international organizations, from the International Committee of the Red Cross to the Inter-Parliamentary Union. By the start of the twentieth century there was an International Peace Bureau in Berne and also peace crusades and peace petitions. The two disarmament conferences in The Hague drew hordes of observers, including von Suttner, whose hotel flew a white flag in her honor, and a Russian financier, Ivan Bloch, who handed out copies of his massive study of war, which showed how it would be madness for the advanced powers to fight. "There will be no war in the future," he told his British publisher, "for it has become impossible, now that it is clear that war means suicide."

Although few countries had yet given them the vote, women were increasingly active in the peace movement and were going to be again after the First World War. In Britain in the 1920s and 1930s, the Women's Co-operative Guild with its 72,000 members was a strong supporter of the Women's International League for Peace and Freedom (WILPF) and women were active in the

Peace Pledge Union. The WILPF eventually had chapters in fifty different countries. After the Second World War women peace activists were involved in the Campaign for Nuclear Disarmament (CND) in the 1950s and 1960s and in the 1980s ran their own women-only demonstrations to protest against the deployment of American cruise missiles in the United Kingdom, most notably at Greenham Common in Berkshire. In Northern Ireland Betty Williams and Mairead Maguire (formerly Corrigan) founded the Community for Peace People in the 1970s after witnessing sectarian violence firsthand. In 1976 they won the Nobel Peace Prize. We always need to remember, though, that other women have been cheerleaders for war.

The statesmen, and increasingly stateswomen, have not always liked it, but from the nineteenth century they have had to deal with international public opinion and, as the franchise widened in many countries, more and more voters at home. When Tsar Nicholas II suggested the first disarmament conference in The Hague, his fellow heads of state and their ministers were not particularly enthusiastic. "Conference comedy," said the Kaiser, and Edward VII called the idea "the greatest nonsense and rubbish I ever heard of." The public felt otherwise (a petition in favor of disarmament in Germany, for example, got over 1 million signatures) and so the powers agreed to send delegations to the Netherlands. The German one, which included a professor who had just written a pamphlet condemning the whole peace movement, was under orders to oppose any measures that would impede Germany's ability to wage war. The British, whose delegation included Admiral Jacky Fisher, who was in the midst of overhauling and strengthening the navy, refused to contemplate any measures that would affect their ability to use a blockade in war. The Americans expressed support for peace but said that their own forces were so small there was no point in limiting them.

And perhaps Tolstoy had a point when he criticized arms limitation as a dangerous diversion from the real cause, which was getting rid of war altogether. In *War and Peace,* on the eve of the Battle of Borodino, in which he will be mortally wounded, his hero Prince Andrey reflects on attempts to make war less cruel:

> But playing at war, that's what's vile; and playing at magnanimity and all the rest of it. That magnanimity and sensibility is like the magnanimity and sensibility of the lady who turns sick at the sight of a slaughtered calf—she is so kind-hearted she can't see blood—but eats fricasseed veal with a very good appetite. They talk of the laws of warfare, of chivalry, of flags of truce, and humanity to the wounded, and so on. That's all rubbish.

Or, as the slogan of the interwar Peace Pledge Union put it more tersely, "Wars Will Cease When Men Refuse to Fight."

Memories of the First World War and growing fears of another one gave renewed purpose and vigor to those who would abolish war. The League of Nations, said President Wilson, and many around the world agreed with him, was "the only hope for mankind." An organization of free nations, he told the Senate in July 1919 when he presented the Treaty of Versailles, which incorporated the League's Covenant, "would make wars of aggression and spoliation such as this that has just ended forever impossible." The League of Nations would provide sufficient collective security for its members to deter attacks by outsiders and sort out disputes among its members peacefully. If members refused to engage in discussion or submit to arbitration, Wilson believed, the solution was economic sanctions. "No, not war but something more tremendous than war. Apply this economic, peaceful, silent, deadly remedy and there will be no need for force." Wilson also hoped that international public opinion would serve to isolate and shame aggressive nations.

Although the United States did not join the League, its representatives worked closely with League bodies in Geneva and public support for ending war remained strong throughout the interwar years. In Britain the League of Nations Union had 400,000 members by the start of the 1930s. Some 11.5 million British men and women, nearly 40 percent of the adult population, voted in a peace ballot held between 1934 and 1935, providing huge majorities in support of the League and disarmament. In 1928 the French Foreign Minister, Aristide Briand, and the American Secretary of State, Frank Kellogg, created what many at the time hoped would mark a giant stride for humanity away from war. Nations signing their Pact of Paris promised to renounce war as an instrument for settling disputes among themselves. Eventually sixty-one nations signed up, including Germany, Italy and Japan. There was, as skeptics pointed out at the time, no way of enforcing the pact and the outbreak of war in 1939 showed that they were right to be skeptical.

Under pressure from President Roosevelt, Allied planning started during the war for a new body to supersede the League and for new economic organizations, which, it was hoped, would help to knit the world's nations together and minimize the danger of future war. In April 1945, just after Germany's surrender but while the fighting continued in the Pacific, forty-six nations met in San Francisco to create the United Nations. It has not lived up to its promise of getting rid of war once and for all—that was always too much to hope for—but it has brokered a series of arms-limitation agreements and has helped through peacekeeping and peace-building and the activities of its various bodies, such as the World Health Organization, to mitigate and alleviate some of the effects of war.

The Cold War between the United States and the Soviet Union which followed the Second World War again focused humanity's attention on the dangers of war, which, certainly by the 1960s, was threatening to bring the long story of human beings to a close. Novels, films and television programs such as *On the Beach, Dr. Strangelove* and *The Day After* gave terrifying pictures of the impact of nuclear war and the ease with which it might occur. Somehow, and that is more to do with the nuclear balance between the two superpowers during the Cold War, the possibility of mutually assured destruction, with its all too apposite acronym MAD, meant that the United States and the Soviet Union avoided going to war with each other, although at times they came close. That does not mean that the world has been free of war since 1945: the superpowers and some lesser ones fought proxy wars and fueled, as they still do, civil wars. And violence need not be committed by the latest high-tech weapons; out-of-date, cheap weapons can do great damage. In Rwanda before Hutu militias started their slaughter of the Tutsi, the country imported enough machetes for every third Rwandan male to have a new one. Those machetes were not used for farming. As we look around the world, we need to remember that war and all the others since 1945. War and the threat of war are still very much with us.

1. A Roman sarcophagus from the third century A.D. which shows Roman soldiers triumphing over the less-well-armed barbarians, the term for peoples who were not part of Roman civilization. The sculptor reflects a view common among Romans that their success came from their discipline and war-like spirit. It was common for well-to-do civilians to be buried in such sarcophagi since Rome, like many other societies, admired military virtues and triumphs.

2. A page from an eighteenth-century history of the life of Nurhaci, founder of the Manchu Qing dynasty that conquered the Ming and ruled China from 1644 to 1911. Cavalry played an important role in warfare throughout history until the twentieth century. Mounted warriors such as the feudal European knights or the Mongols have mobility and, as this illustration shows, can overwhelm and scatter foot soldiers.

3. Albrecht Dürer's *The Four Horsemen of the Apocalypse,* 1498, one of the most famous woodcuts by the German artist. He made it as part of a series to illustrate the Book of Revelation. It shows the coming of, from left to right, Death, Famine, War and Pestilence. In his depiction, as is often the case in war, the four are intimately linked and trample the helpless civilians without mercy.

4. *Napoleon Crossing the Alps* by Jacques Louis David. One of five versions done by David to celebrate the glory and heroism of Napoleon on his way to defeat the Austrians in the north of Italy, it gives a highly idealized version of the journey. Napoleon, like war leaders before and since, understood the power of propaganda and enlisted the services of artists and writers. Like David, many were ready to offer their talents.

5. *The Battle of San Romano* by Paolo Uccello, ca. 1438. It shows forces from the city-state of Florence defeating those from its rival Siena. Here the Florentine commander Niccolò Mauruzi da Tolentino, who had a reputation for reckless bravery, leads a cavalry charge.

6. Francisco Goya, "And they are like wild beasts," plate five of *The Disasters of War*. The Spanish painter made a series of prints between 1810 and 1820 to show the horrors and cruelties afflicting Spain during the revolution against the Bourbon kings and the French invasion of 1808 and the subsequent Peninsular War. Civilians resisted the invaders too and here Spanish women, one carrying an infant on her waist, attack French soldiers.

7. Félix Vallotton, a naturalized French citizen, had volunteered to fight for France at the start of the First World War, but was rejected because of his age. Part of a series he did in 1917 of the battlefronts, *Verdun* shows the struggle around the great French fortress where more than 600,000 soldiers died during a prolonged attack by German forces.

8. A. Y. Jackson, *Gas Attack, Liévin*. Canadian painter Jackson admitted to a friend that there was a strange beauty about the battlefields of the Western Front at night. The sky is lit by flares as clouds of poison gas rise. In the First World War a number of governments commissioned official war artists although they did not always approve of their graphic depictions of the front.

9. Käthe Kollwitz, *The Grieving Parents*. The left-wing German artist lost her son in October 1914, and she and her husband mourned him until their own deaths. In her work she returned repeatedly to the themes of loss and mourning, and made these sculptures for their son's grave in Belgium. Although they were originally placed far apart, the figures have since been moved closer, and yet they each remain locked in their own grief.

10. Albin Egger-Lienz, *Den Namenlosen*, or *The Nameless*. This example of Austrian war art from the First World War is a depiction of modern, industrialized war with little of the supposed glory of premodern ones. Not an official war artist, Egger-Lienz managed to paint at the front. Here he sees the soldiers as dehumanized and anonymous figures marching toward enemy fire as if into a storm.

11. Henry Moore, *Figures in a Shelter*. Primarily known for his sculpture, Moore did a series of sketches of civilians enduring the Second World War. Mainly in shades of gray with occasional muted colors, they capture the drabness but also the danger of daily life in 1941, when London was still being heavily bombed. Here people sleep helter-skelter in an underground shelter.

12. George Grosz, *Christ with Gas Mask*. Like Goya before him, the German artist Grosz used his art to attack war. This sketch from 1926, one of several he did on the same theme, uses the image of Christ on the cross to criticize those who profited from the war. He was tried for blasphemy and later still condemned as a degenerate artist by the Nazis.

13. Graham Sutherland, *Devastation, 1941: An East End Street.* Sutherland was employed by the British government to record the impact of the Second World War on the British Isles; his *Devastation* series shows the outcome of aerial bombing on cities and towns as Nazi Germany tried to break the capacity and the will of the people. This scene is of an ordinary, now ruined, row of houses in the East End of London which was particularly hard hit.

14. Eric Ravilious, *Spitfires at Sawbridgeworth, Herts.* Another British war artist, Ravilous painted the coastal defenses and the planes the British relied upon to blunt a German attack. The Spitfire fighter planes depicted here played a critical part in the Battle of Britain in 1940 in preventing Germany from achieving dominance in the air.

CHAPTER 9

WAR IN OUR IMAGINATIONS AND OUR MEMORIES

ORGIVE US, SAYS THE CHORUS, AT THE START OF ACT IV OF
Shakespeare's *Henry V:*

> *Where—O for pity!—we shall much disgrace*
> *With four or five most vile and ragged foils,*
> *Right ill-disposed in brawl ridiculous,*
> *The name of Agincourt. Yet sit and see,*
> *Minding true things by what their mockeries be . . .*

In the scenes to come, Shakespeare will bring to the audience both the tragedy and the glory of war. The night before the battle a pensive King Henry wanders incognito among his troops. Williams, an ordinary soldier, talking to his friends, says simply he does not expect they will live out the coming day. Henry probes: Are they not happy to be with the king when his cause is such a just one? he asks. Well, says Williams, that may be, but those who die will go to their deaths cursing, crying out for help, or worrying about the wives and children they leave behind. "I am afeard," he says, "there are few die well that die in a battle . . ." Henry replies with a long, reasoned and not particularly comforting speech, about responsibility in war and how every soldier should prepare his conscience so that he is ready to die a good death and achieve salvation. The next morning, however, he makes a different sort of speech. The coming battle, he tells his men, is their chance for glory. The day, he reminds them, is the feast of the twin saints— Crispin and Crispian.

> *He that outlives this day, and comes safe home,*
> *Will stand a tip-toe when the day is named,*
> *And rouse him at the name of Crispian.*
> . . .
> *And Crispin Crispian shall ne'er go by,*
> *From this day to the ending of the world,*
> *But we in it shall be remember'd;*
> *We few, we happy few, we band of brothers . . .*

A company commander in the East Yorkshire Regiment read extracts from Henry's stirring speeches to his men over the landing craft's loudspeaker as they neared Sword Beach on D-Day in 1944 and as the 1st Special Service Brigade disembarked their imposing commander, Lord Lovat, led them with his personal piper, Bill Millin, wading through the water onto the beach playing "Highland Laddie" and "Road to the Isles." The great commanders, Alexander, Julius Caesar, Napoleon, MacArthur, Montgomery, had the ability of great actors to reach out and make their men feel that their commanders knew them, cared about them and were speaking directly to them. They grasped what Shakespeare had, that war is a sort of theater, and that theatrical gestures play their part. The giant cannon which the Ottomans made in the fifteenth century to guard the Dardanelles, the elephants brought to Italy by Hannibal or used by the Mughals in India, the nuclear bombs developed by the two sides in the Cold War—all were designed to terrify and intimidate the enemy as much as for actual war-fighting. Shock and Awe was what the coalition called the invasion of Iraq in 2003. We use our arts in war but how we think about and wage it is, in turn, affected by our artistic representations of it.

Plays, poems, novels, paintings, sculptures, photographs, music and films shape how we—warriors and civilians alike—imagine and think about war. The arts can give us war's many aspects: from the heroic and glorious to the cruelty and horror. They can convey something of war's excitement and passions as well as its craziness, its tedium and pointlessness. They remind us of the power and the complexity of war and of our own ambiguous feelings about it. The arts can urge us toward war as they did before the First World War or help turn us against it as they did afterward. They help us process, remember and commemorate war.

The currents between the arts and war run both ways: war changes those who are creating its images and stories. Writers struggle to find new language and painters experiment with styles. Goya abandoned color for *The Disasters of War* and the long tradition of celebrating the victorious or heroic side of war to show its baseness, the moments of gratuitous cruelty, the shattered, mutilated bodies. The First World War, a cultural review said in 1916, was impossible to capture in pictures: "No artist can give us a total impression of the things that go on in night and fog, under the earth and above the clouds ... The death-defying men who march past and pounce on the enemy in battlefield canvases of the old school have disappeared; communication trenches have swallowed them up." The Swiss painter Félix Vallotton, who fought in the French army, said, "From now on I no longer believe in bloodsoaked sketches, in realistic painting, in things seen, or even experienced. It is meditation alone which can draw out the essential synthesis of such evocations." His *Verdun*, that ghastly battle of attrition between the French and the Germans, is a pattern of flames, black and white clouds of gas and smoke, beams of light, shattered landscapes and falling rain—with no human beings to be seen. Perhaps it was merely a coincidence that in different cities across Europe and in the New World artists were experimenting before 1914 with forms that suited the battlefields to come. The Cubists were developing a new idiom to capture the fragmentation of the world around them, while the Futurists tried to find ways to paint movement itself. In England, the Vorticists wanted to smash the existing order to pieces and that, for them, meant a new geometric style that reflected the jagged nature of the modern world. Paul Nash, the British artist who was much influenced by the Vorticists, was soon to find himself sketching and painting smashed battlefields. Did they all somehow sense the catastrophe that was about to strike European society? Their experimentation was sadly all too well suited to the shattered landscapes of the battlefields and the play across them of light, rocket bursts and waves of gas.

Yet when we try to imagine war or rely on the imagination of others, we run up against the perennial question: Can the reality of war ever be pinned down, its experience confined within the pages of a book or a picture frame or a strip of film? In *The Sorrow of War* by Bao Ninh, who fought for the North Vietnamese forces in the Vietnam War, his protagonist, himself a veteran, tries obsessively and doggedly to write his story of love and war: "These flimsy pages represented Kien's past; the lines told stories that were sometimes clear, but most were at best obscure and as vague and pale as twilight. They told stories from the precariously fine border dividing life from death, blurring the line itself and finally erasing it. Ages and times were mixed in confusion, as were peace and war." When the book first came out it was condemned by the communist authorities and Ninh has published very little since. The American writer Tim O'Brien, who fought on the other side, says in *The Things They Carried*, "To generalize about war is like generalizing about peace. Almost everything is true. Almost nothing is true." And can we, he asks, ever get at the meaning of war? "In a true war story, if there's a moral at all, it's like the thread that makes the cloth. You can't tease it out. You can't extract the meaning without unraveling the deeper meaning. And in the end, really, there's nothing much to say about a true war story, except maybe 'Oh.'" Yet he has kept trying, as so many others have done before him and will do in the future. Wilfred Owen wrote to his mother of the "very strange look" he had seen on the faces of soldiers in 1917 at the huge British base of Étaples: "an incomprehensible look, which a man will never see in England . . . It was not despair or terror, it was more terrible than terror, for it was a blindfold look, without expression, like a dead rabbit's. It will never be painted, and no actor will ever seize it. And to describe it, I think I must go back and be with them." In the Korean War the American photographer David Douglas Duncan talked about trying to capture that soldiers' look, which he called "the thousand-yard stare."

Although much of the art produced by and about war focuses only on one side, the artist's own, a war will often provoke responses which transcend borders. *All Quiet on the Western Front* by the German writer Erich Maria Remarque says the same things about the futility of trench war, the comradeship among the soldiers and the gulf between them and the home front as do antiwar English-language novels such as Frederic Manning's *The Middle Parts of Fortune* and Robert Graves's *Goodbye to All That*. O'Brien and Ninh were on different sides in Vietnam but the jungle, the heat, the fear and the hauntings are there in the work of both. What Ninh said of his main character, whose life so resembles his own, could as easily have been said of O'Brien's narrator: "And into the stories also went the atmosphere of the dark jungle with its noxious scents, and legends and myths about the lives of ordinary soldiers, whose very deaths provided the rhythm for his writing."

Certain wars stimulate more and better art than others. The First World War brought great novels and poems in several languages, as well as great paintings and music. It is hard to think of a comparable outpouring from the Second World War. Vasily Grossman's *Life and Fate* is the great novel, but where are the others? And why did Vietnam but not the two world wars or Korea have such a galvanizing impact on the arts in the United States?

In popular music it was a golden age, with Creedence Clearwater Revival, Bruce Springsteen, Country Joe and the Fish, Bob Dylan and the Doors writing and recording songs about the war. In addition to O'Brien and his body of work, there are Philip Caputo's *A Rumor of War,* Michael Herr's *Dispatches* and Karl Marlantes's *Matterhorn* or the extraordinary range of films such as *Platoon, Born on the Fourth of July* and *Apocalypse Now.* It is surely no coincidence that these, like the great works of art from the First World War, are almost all critical of the war. For the Americans, Vietnam did what the First World War did for the Europeans; it shook their confidence in themselves and their civilization. Perhaps the need to get at the terrifying mystery of how *we,* who are good and moral people, could get involved in such a war and do such dreadful things explains the impact of both wars on artists.

Yet it is too easy to say that great art grows only out of the horror and futility of war. Against Benjamin Britten's *War Requiem,* Tolstoy's *War and Peace* or Remarque's *All Quiet on the Western Front* we can counterpoise the *Winged Victory of Samothrace,* the *Iliad* or Ernst Jünger's *Storm of Steel.* John Ruskin, Victorian England's most influential art critic and a leading intellectual, may have surprised young officer cadets at Woolwich in a lecture on war in 1865 when he told them, "No great art ever yet arose on earth but among a nation of soldiers." Peace, he argued, brought prosperity and contentment but it also brought the withering away of the arts, because men were not being raised to their highest state, which only war could do: "For it is an assured truth that, whenever the faculties of men are at their fullness, they *must* express themselves by art." And so, he concluded, "When I tell you that war is the foundation of all the arts, I mean also that it is the foundation of all the high virtues and faculties of men."

As some of those who fight realize, there can be beauty in war itself. The Canadian painter A. Y. Jackson wrote near the end of the First World War, "I went with Augustus John one night to see a gas attack we made on the German lines. It was like a wonderful display of fireworks, with our clouds of gas and the German flares and rockets of all colors." Shortly afterward he painted his *Gas Attack, Liéven,* one of the most famous Canadian paintings of the period, and it too is a thing of beauty, with its somber dark foreground of blasted land, the hovering bluish-gray clouds and the green and pink streaks of light. So is the opening shot of *Apocalypse Now,* with the graceful palms of the pristine green jungle gently swaying and the thock-thock-thock of helicopters drifting by. A few wisps of smoke curl up, then more, and then suddenly the whole scene goes up in flames. (And such was the madness of the making of the film that an actual jungle was burned.) All the while the Doors are singing "The End." It is breathtaking, perhaps one of the greatest film openings ever. Its director, Francis Ford Coppola, set out to make an antiwar film—it was based on Joseph Conrad's indictment of Western imperialism *Heart of Darkness*—but he makes parts of the war exhilarating and beautiful.

Artists can deliberately glorify war, whether because they are paid to do so or because they believe in what they are doing, or both. Using art to depict and celebrate war goes back far into human history. So much of what has survived from the ancient world—sculptures, triumphal arches and columns, mosaics, decorated vases, tombs—deals with war. The Elgin Marbles show men fighting the centaurs—half horse, half man. One of the treasures of Germany's Pergamon Museum, its great altar from the city of the same name, shows the legendary battle between the Giants and the gods on Olympus. The Bayeux Tapestry records the Norman conquest of Britain. Giant stylized paintings of past victories on land and sea came to fill Europe's palaces and government buildings in the Renaissance and the rulers' orchestras played celebratory pieces such as Handel's *Music for the Royal Fireworks,* composed in 1749 to mark an English triumph, in this case the Treaty of Aix-la-Chapelle in 1748 at the end of the War of the Austrian Succession. The crucial Battle of Lepanto of 1571, when the Catholic states of the Holy League defeated the Ottomans, inspired works by Veronese, Tintoretto, Titian and a host of lesser-known artists, poems and music. The Battle of San Romano between Florence and Siena in the fifteenth century is now remembered mainly because of Paolo Uccello's triptych. Horses rear, men exchange blows, broken spears, discarded helmets and bodies litter the ground, but there is no blood, no smashed heads or severed limbs.

Such depictions can remove war's terror, its chaos and the human costs of fighting. Mughal paintings commissioned by rulers such as Akbar show sieges, battles, guns, soldiers and cavalry, all very beautifully colored and decorative, even the corpses. The famous 1945 Joe Rosenthal photograph *Raising the Flag on Iwo Jima* (which was posed sometime after a smaller flag had been raised) captures a moment of triumph, but there is no hint of the 26,000 American casualties that victory cost. In eighteenth-century Europe, which prided itself on being in the Age of Reason, artists, with very few exceptions, showed battles as orderly games, chess perhaps, with human pieces. In 1745, in the long War of the Austrian Succession, British forces with their Dutch and Hanoverian allies attacked the French at Fontenoy, now in Belgium. The battle, which resulted in a French victory, left some 5,000 men dead and another 10,000 wounded. Louis XIV commissioned a painting of the day by Pierre L'Enfant (whose son would design the plans for Washington, DC). The soldiers are drawn up and are attacking in neat lines. There are puffs of smoke from the guns, men on horseback gallop about and a handful of bodies lie decoratively on the ground. Paintings of the deaths of individual heroes in battle, Wolfe at Quebec or Nelson on his flagship, also show death coming decorously as the dying man lies in a graceful pose surrounded by his mourners. The arts can make even the tools of war look pretty. Suits of armor, swords, scimitars, pikes, the early pistols and cannon were often beautiful objects, embellished with precious metals and jewels in demonstrations of the skill and vision of the craftsmen who designed and made them. It is a fashion we have lost, at least for military weapons; it is hard to imagine machine guns with inlaid decorations playing musical tunes.

As it does with others of society's resources, whether human, material or spiritual, war co-opts the arts for its own needs, and artists can co-opt themselves. Jacques-Louis David, a great painter with a strong instinct for survival, started out and prospered under the ancien régime in France, adapted quickly to the French Revolution and then became Napoleon's favorite painter. In his famous *Napoleon Crossing the Alps*, David shows a heroic figure on a rearing stallion ascending the slopes on his way to his victories in Italy. On stones by the horse's feet the names of Hannibal and Charlemagne can be made out, but it is only Bonaparte's name that is spelled out clearly. In the First World War artists and intellectuals rushed to condemn their counterparts on the other side. The war, said the prominent French philosopher Henri Bergson, in a speech on August 8, 1914, was between French civilization and German barbarism. The German writer Thomas Mann also saw the war as a clash of different value systems, but in his case it was German *Kultur*, vibrant, vital, deeply human, as opposed to "civilization," which was mild, polite and based on reason, not emotion. "The entirety of Germany's virtue and beauty," he proclaimed, "unfolds only in war. Peace is not always becoming to it—in peacetime one could sometimes forget how beautiful Germany is." In the Second World War Noël Coward wrote, directed and starred in the film *In Which We Serve*, which praises the quiet heroism of the Royal Navy. The British government helped to pay for Laurence Olivier's stirring film *Henry V,* in which he also starred. It came out in 1944, not long before the invasion of Normandy, and his Henry is courageous and noble, fighting in the right cause. (The screenplay leaves out such scenes as Henry's threatening speech to the citizens of Harfleur.) The Hollywood star John Wayne made *The Green Berets* at his own expense in support of the Vietnam War. In the last scene a small Vietnamese boy, a war orphan who has been taken care of by one of a Special Forces team—the Green Berets—weeps as he discovers his friend has been killed. "What will happen to me now?" the boy asks the colonel, played by Wayne himself. Wayne gives the child the beret of the dead soldier. "You let me worry about that, Green Beret," he says. "You're what this thing's all about." The two walk into the sunset as "The Ballad of the Green Berets" plays on the soundtrack.

Wayne's film stands out because it was one of the few to show an increasingly unpopular war in a favorable light. In the First World War, by contrast, artists on all sides overwhelmingly sup-ported their countries' war efforts, at least in the early years of the conflict. Edward Elgar wrote patriotic music, including a score for Kipling's *The Fringes of the Fleet,* a 1915 booklet of poems and essays about the lesser-known heroic moments of British sea power, although he came to hate the way that his prewar *Pomp and Circumstance Marches* had been given more bombastic words. The vast majority of novels and poems produced among all the belligerents were patriotic; some, like Thomas Hardy's "Men Who March Away" (which promises that "Victory crowns the just"), by established poets, others by enthusiastic unknowns. In August 1914 alone a major Berlin newspaper was getting 500 patriotic poems submitted a day. "We love as one, we hate as one / We have one foe and one alone— / ENGLAND!" said the wildly popular Ernst Lissauer's "Hymn of Hate."

With the growing size and demands of modern war, govern-ments came to realize how they could use the arts just as they did science or industry in order to mobilize their societies. In the First World War the British government commissioned well-known artists to camouflage freighters. The "dazzle ships" were covered with crazy designs to make it difficult for German sub-marines to estimate their speed and direction. A new Department of Information developed a series of projects employing artists to record the war and create propaganda for the home front. In the new industry of filmmaking British and French studios turned out films on a wide range of subjects, from keeping the home fires burning to the iniquities of the Germans. The latter were shipped to neutral countries in attempts, often quite successful, to win people over to support the Allied cause. The German film industry, under tight government control, was slow to realize the power of the new medium and its exported films had little impact. German films showing the front featured contented soldiers reading their post and eating, some lightly wounded recovering in hospitals or German troops rebuilding churches that had been destroyed by the enemy. There were no battle scenes, which would have been difficult to film, and no dead. When German troops at the front were given showings they roared with laughter. (In the Second World War German propaganda was much more effective; its chief, Joseph Goebbels, said he had learned a lot from the British.) Yet another front of struggle opened up when arts produced by the enemy came under attack as so many Trojan horses. In France, again in the First World War, Camille Saint-Saëns and others formed the Ligue Nationale pour la Défense de la Musique Française to campaign for a ban on the performance of contemporary German music. "After the massacres of women and children," Saint-Saëns asked, "how can the French listen to Wagner? It is necessary to make this sacrifice of not reading or hearing the works of Wagner, because he thought Germany could use his work to conquer souls." In Britain the press attacked orchestras for performing Beethoven, Brahms or Bach.

As Lord Lovat understood, music has a particular role to play on the battlefield. In *The Drums of the Fore and Aft*, one of his powerful stories about British soldiers on the frontiers of empire, Kipling may have been drawing on an incident from the Second Afghan War when a British force initially falls back in the face of an Afghan attack. In his story, a pair of reprobate drummer boys, hard-drinking thugs at the age of fourteen, are left behind in the retreat. Having shared out their purloined rum, they pick up drum and fife and march out toward the Afghan lines playing "British Grenadiers." Shamed by the boys, the Fore and Aft rejoin the battle, coldly and efficiently stabbing and killing until victory is theirs. The boys are buried along with the other British dead.

According to Thucydides, the Spartans went into battle singing their war songs. He describes them advancing slowly toward the Argives and their allies in 418 B.C. during the Battle of Mantinea to the music that came from flute players in their ranks: "This custom of theirs has nothing to do with religion; it is designed to make them keep in step and move forward steadily without breaking their ranks, as large armies often do when they are about to join battle."

In war as in dance, music helps to train soldiers so that movements become automatic and they stay together, even in battle. The great eighteenth-century soldier Maurice de Saxe, whose drilling was famous, said, "Have them march in cadence. There is the whole secret, and it is the military step of the Romans ... Everyone has seen people dancing all night. But take a man and make him dance for a quarter of an hour without music and see if he can bear it ... Movement to music is natural and automatic. I have often noticed while the drums were beating for the colors, that all the soldiers marched in cadence without intention and without realizing it. Nature and instinct did it for them." Sunzi advised commanders to use gongs and drums, as well as banners, to keep their troops together while marching, maneuvering and charging and to focus their attention on one particular point. On premodern battlefields, before field telephones, radios or electronic communications, music was one of the few ways for commanders to signal orders. As European armies were to discover, high-pitched woodwinds and brass can carry over much battlefield noise. In the Napoleonic Wars, infantry regulations for the British army listed a variety of messages that could be sent by music: advance, retreat, even warnings about the approach of enemy cavalry or infantry. And music could have a psychological impact on attackers and defenders alike. A British veteran of Wellington's Peninsular Wars against the French said that, when the French drummers beat the *pas de charge* at the Battle of Waterloo for the quickened step at the start of an attack, the sound was something "few men, however brave they may be, can listen to without a somewhat unpleasant sensation."

In peacetime, as they did in the decades in Europe before the First World War, the arts can prepare the public psychologically for war. Military bands playing in bandstands in parks all over Europe, naval reviews on summer days, horse guards jingling down avenues in their dress uniforms, these were entertainment for the masses but they were also powerful propaganda for war. In poems, heroic young men rallied their troops in far-off places against savage foes and went to their deaths with happy memories of home. Barbarossa slept in his mountain and Drake in his hammock, waiting for the call to awaken and save their countries. Upper- and middle-class boys, particularly in Britain, dreamed of glorious combat such as they had read about in Homer or Livy or Julius Caesar. Across Europe the Middle Ages were being rediscovered, or rather a particular part, with chivalry and knights in armor and Crusades. Popular fiction and magazines for boys largely wrote about the heroic deeds of the past. In Germany the most popular subjects were the nation's great triumphs, whether the Battle of the Teutoburg Forest in the first century A.D., when Germanic tribes defeated a Roman army, or victory over the French at Sedan in 1870. G. A. Henty, the popular British novelist, wrote over eighty books whose heroes were almost always decent British boys who overcame adversity and made their names in war. "To inculcate patriotism in my books," he said, "has been one of my main objects, and so far as it is possible to know, I have not been unsuccessful in that respect." Europe's young went to war in 1914 hoping for a chance to measure themselves against their heroes.

Because of their education and their familiarity with literature, history and myth, members of that generation—novelists, poets and memoirists such as Robert Graves, Siegfried Sassoon and Wilfred Owen in Britain, Frederic Manning in Australia or Henri Barbusse in France—were particularly well equipped to express their shock and disillusionment. (They also resented attempts by civilian writers—"eye-wash," said a French writer—to describe the front.) We always need to remember, however, that the antiwar writers were much less popular, at least immediately after the war, than those like Jünger who talked about its heroic side. In the late 1920s, *All Quiet on the Western Front* sold 1.2 million copies in German (before the Nazis banned it), but the memoirs of the flying ace Manfred von Richthofen, the Red Baron, sold as many. One scholar estimates that only 5 percent of books produced about the war in the interwar years were pacifist.

During the war the authorities understood, and tried to use, the power of the arts while at the same time managing portrayals of the front so that the true nature of industrialized war did not horrify the public. British war artists were told not to include the bodies of the dead in their pictures. When Christopher Nevinson showed a pair of corpses lying facedown on the ground in his 1917 work *Paths of Glory,* the censors would not pass it. Nevinson slapped a large "censored" sign over the picture, leaving only the sole of a boot and a helmet for the viewer's imagination. The German artist George Grosz did a savage engraving of Christ in a gas mask saying, "Shut your mouth and do your duty." His fellow German Otto Dix produced a series of horrific prints after the war, of the dead and the mutilated, and a painting, *The Trench,* which showed bodies blown apart after an artillery attack. The new Nazi Party denounced him and, when it came to power, gave this work and others of his a prominent place in their *Degenerate Art* exhibition, held in Munich in 1937.

The struggle between those who would sanitize war and those who would show its brutality is a very old one and the arts have a way of escaping or sliding away from controls. The British painter Paul Nash was an official war artist in the First World War but his paintings from the front, such as *The Menin Road* and the ironically named *We Are Making a New World,* are a haunting testament to the loss and destruction. These are not the lovely British landscapes he had done before the war but their reverse, with shattered trees, mud and pools of putrid water. No happy picnickers here or cheerful peasants but the lonely figures of advancing soldiers. "I am no longer an artist interested and curious," he wrote to his wife in November 1917. "I am a messenger who will bring back word from the men who are fighting to those who want the war to go on for ever. Feeble, inarticulate, will be my message, but it will have a bitter truth, and may it burn their lousy souls."

Francisco Goya created his great series of prints *The Disasters of War* between 1810 and 1820, when Spain was afflicted by a weak government, French invasion, revolution, civil war and a war between the French and the British. While he continued to work as painter to the Spanish court and also painted portraits of the French and British officers, he quietly made his prints. Published long after his death, they are a searing and powerful indictment of all sides in the wars and show the cruelty of which humans are capable. The *Wild Beasts* shows Spanish women, one with an infant on her arm, killing French soldiers, while *Barbarians!* shows French soldiers shooting a monk tied to a tree as other soldiers look on indifferently. Goya's captions are terse but telling. "One can't look"; "This is bad"; "This is worse"; "This is the worst." And, he insists, "I saw this"; "This is how it happened." Goya's work moved a long way from the orderly pictures of war of the eighteenth century and his influence over later artists such as Otto Dix and Salvador Dalí would be considerable. The war photographer Don McCullin said, "When I took pictures in war, I couldn't help thinking of Goya."

Picasso also thought of Goya, whom he revered, and in 1937 he created one of the greatest antiwar paintings of the twentieth

century. The Republican Spanish government, fighting for its survival against General Franco's Nationalist rebels, commissioned
Picasso to provide a mural for Spain's pavilion at the World's Fair
in Paris. In April he found his subject when German aircraft
bombed Guernica. Picasso's painting of the event marked a significant shift in war paintings from concentrating on the military
victims of war to the civilians. Working at high speed, he covered
a large canvas with scenes of chaos and fear. Screaming people
and a horse are flying apart. A woman carries her dead child. As
he was painting, he issued a statement: "In the panel on which I
am working, which I shall call Guernica, and in all my recent
works of art, I clearly express my abhorrence of the military caste
which has sunk Spain in an ocean of pain and death." There is a
story, which may be true, that a Gestapo officer visited Picasso in
German-occupied Paris during the Second World War and saw a
photograph of *Guernica*. "Did you do that?" he asked. "No," Picasso replied, "you did." Picasso would not allow the painting to
return to Spain until its democracy had been restored. From 1981
it has been in Madrid, where it is seen as a national treasure.

Not everyone has shared in the admiration for it. On the left,
the communists, under the heavy hand of the Soviet Union,
greeted it with faint praise and deplored it for not being realistic
enough. The guide the Nazis produced for the World's Fair called
it "a hodgepodge of body parts that any four-year-old could have
painted" and when the painting went on tour in the United States
before the Second World War an American conservative said it
was "Bolshevist art controlled by the hand of Moscow." Can we
appreciate a work of art if we disagree strongly with the views and
purpose of the person who made it? Richard Wagner was an anti-
Semite who wrote superb music and Leni Riefenstahl was a committed Nazi who made innovative and powerful films. These have
been difficult questions, especially in Israel. How we react to
works of art depends on who we are, where we are standing and
when we encounter them. Robert Graves was surprised that his

Goodbye to All That was taken as an antiwar manifesto when he had only intended to describe the war—he was proud of his war service—and perhaps to make some much-needed cash. But his book came out at the end of the 1920s, when disillusionment with the First World War and skepticism about the peace that followed were growing and the future looked increasingly bleak. If we do not know much or anything about the creator, such questions matter less, and the passage of time has a way of removing the emotions and ideas that surrounded works of art when they were new. Homer—if he existed—may have been admirable or dreadful, a lover of war or of peace. We will never know and so we can read the *Iliad* and the *Odyssey* without having to take a stand on their creator. In Spain *Guernica* is now a national treasure but if Picasso had agreed to Franco's request to send it back after the Second World War it might have been received differently.

From the middle of the nineteenth century photography and then film have increasingly taken their place beside painting to depict war. Whether or not what the new mediums show is somehow more authentic is another question. Cameras can select and distort as much as the artist's eye does and again it matters who you are and from what place you are looking. Although the earliest cameras could not show action, they could show the faces and the consequences of war. The successful photographer Mathew Brady decided to make as complete a record of the American Civil War as possible. In 1862 Alexander Gardner took what became the most famous series in the collection at the battlefield of Antietam, the bloodiest day of the Civil War. In one photograph the crumpled bodies of soldiers stretch along an ordinary country road as it meanders into the distance. Does it make his photographs any the less moving if we know that he often staged his scenes, moving bodies about? In 1916 the British government broke with its practice of using film for anodyne and rather dull propaganda pieces and made a film of the first days of the Battle of the Somme. Because the military authorities had expected the opening attacks to break through the German lines, they had allowed unprecedented access to the cameramen. The cameras catch the soldiers preparing in their trenches, fitting bayonets to their rifles and disappearing over the tops of the trenches into no-man's-land. The filming stops there: the early film cameras were too heavy to carry and it was too dangerous for the cameramen to stand up, as they needed to if they were to film the battlefield. The producers spliced in shots of training film to portray the actual attack and then used real footage of the return of the wounded. Even so the impact was deeply moving and troubling for British audiences, who, for the first time, got an approximation of what was happening on the Western Front. Nearly a quarter of the population had seen the film by the end of its first six-week run in the summer of 1916, while the fighting in France went on. People wept and some fainted.

The other significant innovation in recording war was the appearance of the cheap still camera, which made it possible for every combatant to be his own artist. By the middle of the First World War a small Kodak camera cost a dollar and could fit in a uniform pocket. The authorities tried to censor the photographs as they did soldiers' letters and the Canadians attempted to ban soldiers from carrying cameras, both unsuccessfully. As the technology continued to improve and camera equipment got much lighter, photographers were able to move about the battlefronts and capture fleeting instants, as Robert Capa did in his famous photograph of the Loyalist soldier at the moment he was shot in the Spanish Civil War. Today soldiers in conflict zones such as Afghanistan and Iraq use their mobile phones.

After the Vietnam War, the American military drew the conclusion that public support had waned because of the impact of the print and visual reports by the journalists, photographers and writers who had been allowed to move quite freely through the war zones. Such pictures as that of the Vietnamese child burned by napalm running down a road, the enemy soldiers seizing the perimeter of the American embassy in Saigon during the Tet Offensive or the Saigon police chief shooting a captured North Vietnamese soldier in the head in its aftermath persuaded significant numbers of Americans that the war was unwinnable and wrong. The military had a point, but it is debatable whether reporting was the major factor in turning public opinion against the war. The conflict was already unpopular and so was the draft, and many Americans never understood why their country was fighting a long-drawn-out struggle in a small country on the other side of the world.

Tim O'Brien may be right that we can never really get at the truth about war, but the arts help us to deal with it and to try to understand what may, in the end, be inexplicable. That is true as much of those who have fought as of those who have not. The Greeks saw Homer as a "doctor of the soul." Philip Caputo gets letters from Vietnam veterans who have found that reading his *A Rumor of War* unlocked their bottled-up memories and feelings. A recent French study has looked at what ordinary French soldiers were reading in the trenches in the First World War. Many had only an elementary education but they sent to their families and to booksellers for books such as Tolstoy's *War and Peace*. And perhaps they found not just greater understanding but some comfort from the fact that there was something of beauty or importance that might outlast the misery of the present. The British writer Rebecca West was in a restaurant in Serbia in 1937 having an unpleasant argument with a fanatical German nationalist when someone turned the radio on and a Mozart symphony poured out. "How could we hope that it [art] would ever bring order and beauty to the whole of that vast and intractable fabric, that sail flapping in the contrary winds of the universe?" she asked. "Yet," she went on, "the music promised us, as it welled forth from the magic box in the wall over our heads, that all should yet be well with us, that sometime our life should be as lovely as itself."

Creating and consuming works of art can be an act of defiance as much as of hope. In the two world wars, prisoners of war staged plays and concerts. Olivier Messiaen, the French composer who became a German prisoner of war in 1940, discovered three fellow professional musicians—a clarinetist, a violinist and a cellist—in his camp. He managed to obtain some paper and a small pencil from a sympathetic guard and some battered old instruments, including a piano for himself. On January 15, 1941, out of doors in the rain, the quartet played the premier of his *Quatuor pour la fin du temps*. He later recalled, "Never was I listened to with such rapt attention and comprehension." In eight parts, his work is based on the New Testament's Book of Revelation and deals with the end of time and the coming of the Angel of the Apocalypse. It ends with "Praise to the immortality of Jesus." "It is all love," said Messiaen. "Its slow ascent to the acutely extreme is the ascent of man to his god, the child of God to his Father, the being made divine toward Paradise." That promise and that defiance of the present are there too in one of the most memorable photographs of the Second World War, of St. Paul's Cathedral still standing amidst the fires and destruction of the Blitz.

The arts give us individual voices sometimes from centuries past. One of the world's earliest poems, from Sumer in the third millennium B.C., mourns the consequences of defeat:

> *The foe trampled with his booted feet into my chamber!*
> *That foe reached out his dirty hands toward me!*
> *. . . That foe stripped me of my robe, clothed his wife*
>   *in it,*
> *That foe cut my string of gems, hung it on his child,*
> *I was to tread the walks of his abode.*

In the *Iliad* when Andromache, wife of the great Trojan warrior Hector, learns that Achilles has killed him, she cries out:

> *Now you go down*
> *To the House of Death, the dark depths of the earth,*
> *and leave me here to waste away in grief, a widow*

lost in the royal halls—and the boy only a baby,
the son we bore together, you and I so doomed.

Käthe Kollwitz was a left-wing artist who, with her doctor
husband, ran a clinic in a poor part of Berlin before the First
World War. When Peter, their eighteen-year-old son, wanted to
volunteer for the German army in August 1914 she did not try to
stop him. He left for the front on October 12 and was dead ten
days later. She never stopped mourning him and kept his bed-
room just as he had left it. Peter was, she said, "seed for the plant-
ing which should not have been ground." In time she made a
memorial in granite for the German cemetery at Roggevelde in
Belgium, where he was buried. *The Grieving Parents,* as originally
installed, showed the parents far apart, isolated in their grief. The
mother has her head bowed and has wrapped her arms about
herself. The father is upright but he too has his arms wrapped
around himself. In 1955 the cemetery was moved into a larger
nearby one and the Kollwitz figures now stand closer together.

Mourning in the First World War drew on older rituals—the
Greek columns or the statues resembling ancient warriors, the
wearing of black or the prayers for the dead—but it also seemed to
need something new because of its scale and the ways in which the
war had affected so many people. Fabian Ware, the hard-driving
visionary who effectively created the Imperial War Graves Commission for the British, insisted on three key principles: the men
should be buried in the countries where they fell; there should
be no distinction of rank, unlike in previous wars; and each man
should get the same simple headstone. Although private citizens
had always remembered their dead in their own ways, they now
took the initiative in creating local rituals and memorials and
also in shaping official ones. Towns and villages across Europe
and in parts of the empire raised local subscriptions for a variety
of memorials: from monuments to parks, libraries, fountains, village halls and hospitals. St. John's, Newfoundland, built a Memo-

rial University. In Cambridge, near the railway station, a bronze statue of a striding soldier has a curiously short torso on long legs because the funds raised were not enough and the size had to be reduced. The obelisk was a popular shape for a memorial because it was cheap and easy to make. Eventually there were going to be 60,000 memorials in Britain and France alone.

In 1919 the British authorities asked the prominent architect Sir Edward Lutyens, who had helped to design cemeteries for the British war dead, to make a temporary cenotaph for the Victory Parade that July along Whitehall, in the heart of London. The symbol of an empty tomb was particularly fitting for the First World War, since the remains of so many of those who had died as a result of artillery fire could never be found and identified. Lutyens's cenotaph, made of wood and plaster, attracted huge public attention and the government had to leave it standing longer than planned as hundreds of thousands visited it, leaving flowers and wreaths. The two-minute silence, first observed on November 11, 1919, Armistice Day, and then annually during the 1920s and 1930s, was similarly embraced by the public. People gathered together in public spaces across the country; traffic spontaneously came to a stop; and telephone operators pulled the plugs out of their switchboards.

Giving way to popular demand, the government asked Lutyens to design a permanent cenotaph in stone, which was unveiled in November 1920, the same day that the body of the Unknown Soldier arrived from the Western Front and was brought ceremonially through the streets on its way to Westminster Abbey. This, like the Cenotaph, was a brilliant and simple way of dealing with the absence of bodies to be mourned. Everyone whose dead lay in anonymous graves now had a focus for their grief. Again the authorities had to modify their plans and allow much greater public participation than they had intended. The grave at Westminster Abbey remained open for two weeks and 1.25 million people filed past it, in a silence broken only by shrieks and weeping. In the 1920s Paris, Rome, Washington, DC, Brussels, Prague, Belgrade, Bucharest and Vienna followed suit, but Berlin and Moscow did not. The Second World War produced its own memorials, but in many cases the ones from the previous war were simply adapted, with the names of the next generation of dead being added in. Today, in most countries which participated in the world wars, the commemoration of the dead includes all those who have died in war in the twentieth and twenty-first centuries. And the public still continue to shape official remembrance in their own fashion. Veterans and their families come to the Vietnam War Memorial in Washington and leave tributes—bottles of beer sometimes, flowers, teddy bears—at the foot of the wall. At the exhibition in 2014 of the more than 800,000 poppies, one for each of the British and Empire war dead in the First World War, the railings at the Tower of London were festooned with notes and photographs.

How we remember and commemorate war reflects both the nature of war itself and the societies involved, and also who is doing the remembering. Veterans remember their dead comrades; women their lost loved ones. The children of those who fought remember differently from the grandchildren, if they remember at all. While not all veterans want to remember, many join associations and go to reunions or make pilgrimages to former battlefields such as the Normandy beaches or Vietnam. They do not necessarily glorify war or support future wars. After the First World War French veterans took the lead in criticizing what they thought were militaristic school curricula and former enemies, including French, German and British veterans, came together at the Conférence Internationale des Associations de Mutilés de Guerre et Anciens Combattants to work for improved benefits and peace. On the other hand, right-wing veterans' associations in both France and Germany did their best to keep the wartime hatreds alive and turned on what they saw as traitors at home, variously the Left, liberals and Jews.

Our attitudes to past wars are also influenced by what has happened since. The Second World War, which is so often cast as a clear-cut struggle of good against evil (conveniently overlooking the fact that the Western powers were allied with the Soviet Union, one of the world's greatest tyrannies), has shaped present thinking about the First World War, which now appears morally ambiguous, foolish and futile. The men who fought and died between 1914 and 1918 are now pitied rather than admired. "Lions led by donkeys," as the British politician Alan Clark falsely claimed a German general had said of British soldiers. The popular view today, and not just among the British, is that those who fought in the First World War were dupes, lured to the battlefields by irresponsible elites wielding slogans about fighting for civilization or king and country or the home fires. We should be careful about condescending to those who lived in the past. The dead had ideas and beliefs just as we do. We may not agree with them, but we should respect them. Those who went off to the First World War did think they were fighting for something worthwhile, more usually their loved ones than abstractions such as democracy or empire.

In the 1920s those remembering the First World War, on the Allied side certainly, tended to see it as a sacrifice but a necessary one. Germans did not so much question the rightness of the war itself but the injustice, as they saw it, of the peace. "How did the heroes die?" asked a plaque at a cemetery in Tübingen. "Fearlessly and loyally" was the answer. Across Germany local communities planted "heroes' groves." In Britain inscriptions on memorials, including the Cenotaph in London, referred to "The Glorious Dead" and at the annual services of commemoration congregations were reminded "They Did Not Die in Vain." Canada's war memorial at Vimy Ridge mourned Canada's dead, but it also showed what they had died for: stone figures represent faith, justice, peace, honor, charity, truth, knowledge and hope. When it was unveiled, speakers referred to the site as hallowed ground.

Field Marshal Sir Douglas Haig is now widely seen as a cold-hearted butcher, but in the 1920s he was a hero. Huge numbers of veterans turned out for his funeral in 1928.

It was only in the 1930s, as the possibility of another war grew ever more likely, that people in Britain and France began to wonder if the First World War had been worth it and the works of Sassoon, Graves and others seen as antiwar started to resonate with the public. The poetry of Wilfred Owen, now seen as the preeminent poet of the war, was known only to a small circle before 1945. The vast majority of the works published in the interwar years regarded the war as a just one and opinion still remained divided on its meaning even after the Second World War. Until the 1970s there were enough veterans to give a range of views on the war, from its futility to its validity. When they disappeared from the scene, views in Britain swung firmly around to seeing the First World War as an appalling mistake which it seemed pointless to go on commemorating. Popular television programs such as the 1989 *Blackadder Goes Forth* served to reinforce the tendency to see the war as a monumental folly.

In many countries that had participated in that war there was talk of canceling remembrance ceremonies. In Australia the Left was criticizing Anzac Day for glorifying the war and empire, and for being an excuse to get drunk. Only 2,000 people were turning out for the Dawn Service at the War Memorial in Canberra. In Canada very little attention was paid to the anniversaries of the taking of Vimy Ridge and the memorial in France, put up in the 1930s, was crumbling and discolored. In Britain there was talk in the 1980s of dropping Remembrance Day services in churches and ending the November 11 ceremonies. Yet between 2014 and 2018, as a series of anniversaries for the war fell due, public interest and engagement in Britain was high. Hundreds of thousands came to see the ceramic poppies at the Tower of London and many more saw them when they went on tour around the country. In 2015 the public demand for places at the Gallipoli commemorations in Turkey was so high that the Australian and New Zealand governments had to hold a lottery. In 2019 more than 35,000 came to the annual Dawn Service at the War Memorial in Canberra. What had happened between the 1970s and the present?

Part of the answer may be that, at least in certain countries, well-organized lobby groups have pushed for government support for commemorations and to make such symbolic gestures as the wearing of the poppy every November mandatory for television presenters. In 1997 the Spice Girls launched an appeal on behalf of the British Legion to raise funds but also to push for the reintroduction of the two-minute silence on November 11 and to encourage young people to wear poppies. "Millions of people died so that we could be free," said Sporty Spice. The group got a certain amount of criticism when it launched a new album the following week along with a host of paraphernalia for sale to their fans.

The First World War also resonates in a world where we are experiencing rapid change, as Europe was before 1914, where globalization has brought both winners and losers, and where the international scene appears increasingly troubled and unstable. Europe's leaders may have started the First World War by accident, not seeing where it might lead and what its costs would be. Are we in danger of the same thing happening today? As the historian Dan Todman argues, we face a number of questions today that were raised by that war: "What was the relationship of individuals to the vast, faceless organizations of which they were part? Could individuals control their fates or were they just cogs in the machine? With the advent of greater democracy, how did the citizen relate to the government?"

As we tend to paint the past with broad brushstrokes, we also fix on certain episodes to stand in for the whole. In recent commemorations for the First World War the British focused largely on the first day of the Battle of the Somme, which has come to represent the huge costs of the war to Britain and the beginning of the end for the British Empire as the world's leading power. Australians remembered Gallipoli, when Australian lives were wasted in a poorly planned attack, while for Canadians it is Vimy Ridge, when Canadian forces successfully took a German strong point which had resisted all earlier attacks. The French commemoration of the First World War was centered on Verdun, the site of that long battle of attrition which drew in such a large part of the French army. Such memories are often highly selective. New Zealanders, as they point out, were there at Anzac Cove as part of the Australian and New Zealand Army Corps and the Canadians at Vimy fought beside British troops.

Not all the former belligerents felt the need to stage large-scale commemorations. The American commemorations were slow to start and remained low-key, largely driven by volunteers. For the United States the Second World War is the one that really counts, when the country fought a gigantic struggle around the globe and emerged as a world power. The Russians have paid relatively little attention to the First World War because for them its legacy is very mixed. The collapse of the old regime during the war brought to power the Bolsheviks, who have themselves now vanished, so how to remember, and what, is problematic. The Great Patriotic War, as the Russians call the Second World War, above all its Battle of Stalingrad, is a much more important commemoration for the Russians. The Germans and the Japanese bear a heavy burden of guilt from the Second World War and seem to have little interest in commemorating the earlier war. India sent millions of troops to both wars but the struggle for independence plays a much greater part in public and official memory. For Poland, on the other hand, the First World War is the time of its rebirth, when all three of its enemies, Germany, Austria-Hungary and Russia, were defeated.

While the British, the Americans and the Russians have remembered the Second World War with pride, the French responses have been more mixed. For decades French scholars and writers stayed away from the reasons for France's collapse in 1940 or the subsequent collaboration of so many French, not least the Vichy government, with the Nazis. The key works were written by British or American historians. The Resistance, however, did receive French attention. When General Charles de Gaulle, the leader of the Free French, arrived in Paris just after its liberation in 1944, he spoke at the city hall. Paris, he said, was "Liberated by itself, liberated by its people ... with the support and the help of the whole of France." It was a wild distortion of the truth but he was trying to paper over the divisions in French society and build a shared narrative to serve the cause of French unity. When Marcel Ophüls made his shocking documentary *Le chagrin et la pitié* (*The Sorrow and the Pity*) in 1969, exploring both collaboration and resistance and the involvement of French people in the persecution and removal to the death camps of French Jews, it was banned from French television. When the network's director general appealed to de Gaulle, the general apparently replied, "France does not need truths, she needs hope." The film was finally shown in 1981, after de Gaulle had died.

Remembrance of past wars often gets tangled up with current social and political debates. Much of the Left would prefer not to teach about war at all unless it shows the folly and wickedness of the past. Conservatives tend to decry the teaching of history which, in their view, concentrates too much on their country's past mistakes and not enough on its great victories. As Michael Gove argued when he was in charge of British education, British schools were giving too much of the *Blackadder* view of the First World War and not pointing out that it was a good and necessary struggle. Museums draw particular fire; while they may be founded as centers of education and research, the public tends to see them as memorials. Australia has dealt with that by having a war memorial which is also a museum. In Washington in the 1990s the Smithsonian ran into trouble when it put on an exhibition featuring the *Enola Gay,* the plane that had dropped the atomic bomb on Hiroshima, in which the curators tried to call attention to the human costs on the ground and the moral issues surrounding the bomb's use. In the ensuing uproar, conservatives, veterans and armed forces' associations all weighed in and the Smithsonian canceled the exhibition.

In the continuing discussions among the British over whether to stay in or leave the European Union, the Leave side in particular have used the example of Dunkirk. Indeed the prominent Leaver, Nigel Farage, has said that everyone should see the recent movie of that name. The British, he and others argue, fought alone then and endured to triumph in the end. Such a version of the past conveniently ignores the fact that Britain had the support of its empire, that there were many overseas troops fighting in both France and the Middle East, and that the Royal Air Force was filled with foreign pilots, including Poles. Moreover, it ignores the crucial role of the Soviet Union and the United States in defeating the Germans. The Russians make a similar use of Stalingrad as a symbol of the unbowed Russian nation. President Trump tried to demonstrate his and the Republicans' commitment to the American armed forces at the Fourth of July celebrations in 2019 by using the War of Independence, although he spoiled the effect by getting key details wrong.

The president is only the latest in a long line of leaders appealing to past wars to build political support and to promote a particular view of the nation. In the decade before the First World War, at a time of heightened nationalism, Europe saw a series of big state-sponsored commemorations of anniversaries of past triumphs—Trafalgar for the British in 1905, Borodino for the Russians in 1912 and in 1913 at Leipzig for the Germans—with a series of events that included a display by some 275,000 gymnasts. A new cathedral is being built today outside Moscow which will use German military hardware captured by the Red Army in the Second World War to build the main steps. The Defense Minis-

ter, Sergei Shoygu, said the cathedral was to serve God and the
country and that he wants "every square meter" to be symbolic.

War can also be a vehicle for reconciliation, however. In Slovenia's Kobarid, once called Caporetto and the site of Italy's most
devastating defeat in the First World War, a museum commemorates all the men who died there. The Historial de la Grande
Guerre (Museum of the Great War) at Péronne in France, near
the Western Front, commemorates the Battle of the Somme as a
shared experience for the British, French and Germans. It was,
says the American Jay Winter, who was one of the three senior
historians involved, "a transnational project from the start." The
exhibits are designed to show the commonalities, not the differences, between soldiers and civilians on all sides, and to show that,
whichever trench you were in, your sufferings would have been
much the same.

As war undergoes yet another revolution in the twenty-first
century, we will continue to probe its mysteries. Our artists will
continue to grapple with its horror and beauty, its baseness and its
nobility, its boredom and excitement, its devastation and its cre-
ativity. And all of us will wonder how best to commemorate and
remember war.

CONCLUSION

Those who knew
what was going on here
must make way for
those who know little.
And less than little.
And finally as little as nothing.

In the grass that has overgrown
causes and effects,
someone must be stretched out
blade of grass in his mouth
gazing at the clouds.

—WISŁAWA SZYMBORSKA,
"THE END AND THE BEGINNING"

A FEW YEARS AGO I VISITED A SMALL TOWN IN THE SOUTH of France, near the border with Spain. In the church's graveyard were leaning, crumbling tombstones marking overgrown grassy hummocks, the graves of British soldiers who had died nearby in one of Wellington's battles as he chased Napoleon's forces north-ward. It was a very peaceful spot and you could imagine that in a few more years the stones would have merged with the earth and there would be little trace left of the graves. Perhaps that is what we should be doing with past wars, letting them slide away into oblivion and allowing the shades of all those who died finally rest. Perhaps we are making a mistake when we commemorate the anniversaries of wars, build our war museums, reenact battles or carefully tend war cemeteries and war memorials. Do we risk making war a commonplace, something that is part of being human and an ever-present force in our histories and our societies? A tool that can rightfully and necessarily be used by states? Something we might even be proud of? And, above all, by studying and thinking of war do we make it more likely?

Western societies today have a curiously mixed attitude to war. We commemorate it and have a huge appetite for war stories, movies and games. But, for the most part, we do not want to fight wars. The high costs of two world wars have left us unwilling to contemplate such casualties ever again. We mourn over our soldiers who die in conflicts in Afghanistan or Iraq; and even casualties of a few hundreds, where once we accepted many thousands, seem too much. The military and their civilian masters are well aware of this and invest heavily in weapons and other defensive measures which will minimize, as much as possible, the danger to our fighters. Germany and Japan, where the military dominated and their values permeated society, are now peaceable and peace-loving. Except among a small subgroup of military families, the military is no longer seen as a desirable career. Students at leading universities dream of careers on Wall Street or in the City of London or in the media, not in armies or navies or air forces. Perhaps we need not worry about the power of the past; we may have moved beyond war. Our political leaders may shrink from starting hostilities if they know we will not fight or support a war.

And yet . . . the West is only a part, and a shrinking part, of the world and its assumptions and values are not necessarily universal ones. Apprehension over losses did not bother the Chinese communist leadership when they ordered human wave attacks in the Korean War or the North Vietnamese in the long struggle against the French and then the Americans or the ayatollahs in the Iran–

Iraq war, when they sent their troops out across the Iraqi mine-fields. The substate actors such as Al Qaeda or ISIS, with their international networks of fanatical volunteers, do not care about casualties, either their own or those of innocent civilians. And while the West has enjoyed peace at home the world has seen, depending on how you count them, between 150 and 300 armed conflicts since 1945. Some, such as the Korean or Iran–Iraq wars, have been, like many earlier ones, between states, but by far the greatest number have been inside states, whether struggles for in-dependence against imperial rulers, as in Algeria or Indonesia, or civil wars. And outside powers have frequently joined in, express-ing the highest principles and acting all the while to further their own interests. As political structures, often fragile to begin with, splinter, war becomes an ever-shifting game, where the stakes are life and death, played between relatively sophisticated bodies such as states or religious movements at the one extreme and criminal gangs and mercenaries at the other. Ending such wars, as Europe's Thirty Years War in the seventeenth century showed and Afghan-istan and Somalia show today, is a hard and long task. And the factors that produce war—greed, fear, ideology—will continue to work among us as they always have. The impacts of climate change such as the struggle for scarce resources and the large-scale movements of peoples, the growing polarization within and among societies, the rise of intolerant nationalist populisms and the willingness of messianic and charismatic leaders to exploit these will provide, as they have in the past, the fuel for conflict.

Predictions about the future shape of war are like betting on the horses or guessing where new technology is going. You can weigh all the apparent factors but a sudden obstacle or change of direction, a mistake by the jockey or a chief executive, an unfore-seen glitch or unexpected reactions on the part of the public or the markets can produce surprising results. Past predictions of war offer a rich history of people getting it wrong. Military plan-ners thought the First World War would be a war of movement and offensives and that the Second World War would be a defensive one. Naval experts in both wars looked for the decisive battle when great navies clashed and underestimated the submarine, the torpedo and the humble mine. "The least successful enterprise in Washington, DC" was how Major General Bob Scales, a former commandant of the US Army War College, recently described attempts to determine the nature and character of future wars. That has not stopped us trying and nor should it.

It is possible at the very least to identify trends in war. The future, like the present, will hold two levels of war, the one employing professional forces and high technology, with all the power of advanced economies and organized societies behind them, and the other will be fought with loosely organized forces using low-cost weapons. And what is also sure is that the two sorts of war will overlap. The president of the United States, the world's greatest military power by far, can threaten to bomb Afghanistan until there is no one left to fight or hunt down the members of ISIS, but he will still not be able to keep American citizens free from threats. Just as the battlefields expanded in the twentieth century to include the home fronts, now the distinctions between the fronts, as well as the lines between war and peace, are disappearing. Americans, and indeed many of the rest of us, cannot be sure that we will be safe when we travel abroad. Terrorists or rogue states can bring down airplanes, blow up nightclubs on peaceful beaches or rake tourist buses with machine-gun fire. And their weapons are often simple ones, a suicide bomber with an explosive vest or a truck with a tankful of gas. We cannot be certain that we will be any safer at home. The threats may come, as in older wars, from bombers, rockets or blockades, but today and in the future they will also come from amorphous ever-changing international networks of self-proclaimed warriors. An enemy without uniforms or even bases, whose members often recruit themselves on the internet, cannot be defeated by expensive jet fighters, tanks or aircraft carriers.

A second security threat that is expanding and challenging the capacity of the military is urban warfare. In the past armies tried to take enemy cities for their strategic, political and economic importance; today the enemy is often within, in the form of home-grown armed urban gangs who control whole districts. More and more people will live in cities—by 2050, according to one estimate, two-thirds of the world's population—and the challenges for governance and the basic provision of law and order will be huge. In such cities as Rio de Janeiro, Guatemala City, Dhaka and Kinshasa, governments have already had to use armed force, not always successfully, to try to reestablish their authority, and the military in many countries are investing time and money in counterinsurgency and urban warfare.

We should not assume, however, that massive wars between states are no longer possible. One of the many wrong predictions in the 1990s was that the age of the nation-state, with its pronounced identity and strong central government, was disappearing in an increasingly internationalized world where borders were becoming meaningless. However, the United States, China, India and Russia have not disappeared into what Trotsky rudely called the dustbin of history, and they are continuing to plan and spend heavily on their war-making capacities against similarly prepared and armed foes. Their defense budgets continue to climb. China's spending has gone up as much as eight times in the past two decades. The United States allocates nearly two-thirds of its discretionary budget (those funds not mandated for paying the interest on national debt and entitlements such as social security) to defense. It spends as much as the next eight spenders combined, even though six are friendly nations or allies—Saudi Arabia, France, Britain, Germany, India and Japan—and only China and Russia, at the moment, can be seen as serious potential enemies.

We are also living through a time of rapid technological change which may make the international order more unstable. While it is always difficult in history to distinguish between what is truly new and what is not, war is acquiring new tools and moving into new dimensions, as it once did into the air and below the seas. As happened in the past with the introduction of metal weapons, the horse or gunpowder, the powers will have to adapt their organization, strategy and tactics or risk being left behind. The international agreement that space should not be militarized is fraying as the powers contemplate space-based weapons or countermeasures against each other's communications satellites.

A whole other dimension for war has opened up, with dizzying speed, in cyberspace. As the world, its peoples and its things, from refrigerators to intercontinental ballistic missiles, have become linked through the internet, the possibilities of disruption have grown. In 2007 Estonia's websites, including those of the parliament, its banks and its government ministries, were flooded with waves of fake messages and a new term, "denial of service," entered our language. The Stuxnet computer virus coming from some unknown source disabled much of Iran's nuclear program in 2010. In 2017 North Korea had a series of failures as it tried to test its rockets. No one claimed responsibility but, as with the Stuxnet virus, it is suspected that the United States may have had something to do with it. And if war is also about undermining the faith of the enemy's people in their own institutions and leaders or interfering in their internal politics, then cyberspace is an active battlefield there too.

Meanwhile the older battlefields are getting new and improved weapons which must be absorbed and countered. At one extreme are gliding missiles which fly at the speed of intercontinental ballistic missiles but have much greater accuracy. At the other are tiny self-propelling devices. The American army has ordered Black Hornet drones, at thirty-two grams about the same weight as an ordinary letter, for its soldiers to use for surveillance of their surroundings. And the United States, China, Israel, South Korea, Russia and the United Kingdom are all developing killer robots or, as the military prefer to call them, fully autonomous weapons.

These will direct themselves, rather like self-driving cars, and be programmed to learn and make adjustments as they go. As with all new computerized systems, we would be wise to expect bugs. Self-driving cars have crashed and even run people down; imagine what an intercontinental ballistic missile or fighter plane could do. And systems, as we know, can be hacked. Or what if, by simple human error, someone feeds in the wrong code or instructions? In theory killer robots should still be responsive to human control, but whether they will always be is open to question. And, like other new weapons in the past, they raise issues about morality. What does it mean, as already happens, to have operators sitting in their offices on one side of the world directing robots to kill or destroy targets on the other? Are we in the countries which possess such advanced technologies dangerously detached from the reality of war and too inclined to treat it as a game with no flesh and blood consequences? And what happens if and when human beings are removed from the command chain altogether? Human Rights Watch and other groups are already waging a Campaign to Stop Killer Robots. The past record of such campaigns achieving their goals is not encouraging.

Along with spending and the development of new technologies and tactics goes the planning. Yes, the military must plan for all contingencies, but the danger is that the plans come to focus on one or a few enemies and then guide future spending and thinking. By the time of the First World War, the Japanese navy was fixing on the United States as its chief future enemy, and its policies, including pushing its government to acquire Germany's islands in the Pacific, were intended to prepare for that eventuality. Japan's actions provoked a response in the United States, where some strategists were already identifying it as a future enemy, and so the Americans also began to act on assumptions. War became more likely because it was contemplated as a serious possibility. Today in both Beijing and Washington they are making war plans to deal with the other power. Neither side may want war but they do not rule out the possibility. And, as we know from previous wars, arms races can raise tensions to a dangerous level or accidents can happen which push people over a line they had not intended to cross.

To go back to the peaceful graveyard in France, we cannot let all memories of war slip away. We need to pay attention to war because it is still with us. We need to know about its causes, its impact, how to end it and how to avoid it. And in understanding war we understand something about being human, our ability to organize ourselves, our emotions and our ideas, and our capacity for cruelty as well as for good. We fight because we have needs, because we want to protect what we hold dear or because we can imagine making different worlds. We fight because we can. But that long intertwining of war and society may be coming to an end or ought to—not because we have changed but because technology has. With new and terrifying weapons, the growing importance of artificial intelligence, automated killing machines and cyberwar, we face the prospect of the end of humanity itself. It is not the time to avert our eyes from something we may find abhorrent. We must, more than ever, think about war.

ACKNOWLEDGMENTS

THIS BOOK HAS BEEN on my mind for many years. If you teach and write about modern history and international relations, as I have done and still do, you cannot escape the deep impact of war on human affairs—and vice versa. I was prompted to get down to it by a meeting in July 2017 with Gwyneth Williams, then controller of BBC's Radio Four. She had asked if I would mind dropping by Broadcasting House for a quick chat and to my considerable surprise I found myself with an invitation to give the 2018 Reith Lectures. It was an honor, if a daunting one. In the lectures and now the book which builds on them, I start with a question: Are war and humanity inextricably interwoven? In trying to answer that and understand why and how we humans fight, I have accumulated many debts.

I am privileged to be part of two great universities, Oxford and Toronto, where I have benefited from the learning and conversation of their faculties and students and used their outstanding libraries. I will never be able to repay the experts who know much more about war and human society than I ever will or the audiences and friends who asked such good questions and made such good suggestions. The historians of war have been unfailingly generous in welcoming me into their field. Max Hastings, Peter Wilson, Adrian Gregory, Hew Strachan and Roger Sarty provided models of historical writing and gave me much valuable advice. I also owe much to colleagues at Oxford, among them Paul Betts and Ivor Roberts. Hermione Lee helped me with the shape of my book when I felt stuck. Anthony Bicknell kindly let me see his thesis on women and war and Chris Parry helped me to understand naval war. Peter Snow, former defense correspondent for the BBC and my kind brother-in-law, and Dan Snow, my equally kind nephew, gave me ideas and suggested readings. Stephen Sedley shared with me his marvelous collection of First World War soldiers' songs. Margaret Bruce, Margaret Bent and Katherine Lochnan helped me to understand the relationship between war and the arts. David Thomson generously gave me access to his rich collection of war photographs at the Archive of Modern Conflict and Ed Jones, Timothy Prus and Lizzie Powell there were very helpful indeed. I owe a particular debt to the great historian of war Michael Howard. I knew and admired his work long before I met him and I came to value deeply his wisdom, kindness and friendship. His death, at the end of 2019, was a great loss.

At the BBC I was fortunate to have the excellent advice and help of Gwyneth Williams, Jim Frank, Hugh Levinson and their colleagues. I am equally fortunate to have such publishers as Andrew Franklin at Profile Books and his wonderful colleagues, including Penny Daniel, Lesley Levene and Valentina Zanca, and, in the United States, particular thanks are due to Kate Medina and Noa Shapiro and the excellent team at Random House, including Gina Centrello, Avideh Bashirrad, Benjamin Dreyer, Steve Messina, Robbin Schiff, Barbara Bachman, Karen Fink and Ayelet Gruenspecht, and in Canada particular thanks to Diane Turbide and her excellent team at Penguin, including Shona Cook, David Ross and Kate Panek. Caroline Dawnay remains a peerless agent and friend, and it has been a pleasure to work with her colleagues Sophie Scard and Katherine Aitken. I am privileged indeed to have a large, generous and kind family. They made sure that some of them were at every Reith Lecture and, as they have always done, encouraged me as I got down to researching and writing this book. Particular thanks for reading parts of my manuscript and offering such constructive comments to my sister Ann MacMillan, my brothers Tom and David, my sister-in-law Marie-Josée Larocque and my niece-in-law Margot Finlay.

I want to thank them all most sincerely for helping me make the lectures and the book. Any faults or shortcomings are of course mine alone.

BIBLIOGRAPHY

HERE IS A VAST LITERATURE ON WAR AND I HAVE PUT down here only the books and articles which I found particularly useful and which the reader might enjoy if he or she wishes to explore the subject further. For each chapter, I have also listed the works I particularly drew on.

NONFICTION

Armitage, David, *Civil Wars: A History in Ideas,* New Haven: Yale University Press, 2017
———, "Civil Wars, from Beginning . . . to End?," *American Historical Review,* 120, 5, December 2015, pp. 1829–37
Beard, Mary, *S.P.Q.R.: A History of Ancient Rome,* London: Profile Books, 2015
Beevor, Antony, *Berlin: The Downfall, 1945,* London: Penguin, 2003
Bell, David A., *The First Total War: Napoleon's Europe and the Birth of Modern Warfare,* London: Bloomsbury, 2007
Bessel, Richard, *Violence: A Modern Obsession,* London: Simon & Schuster, 2015
Best, Geoffrey, *War and Law Since 1945,* Oxford: Clarendon Press, 1994
Blanning, T. C. W., *The Pursuit of Glory: Europe, 1648–1815,* London: Allen Lane, 2007
Bond, Brian, *The Victorian Army and the Staff College, 1854–1914,* London: Eyre Methuen, 1972
———, *War and Society in Europe 1870–1970,* London: Fontana, 1984
———, *Britain's Two World Wars against Germany: Myth, Memory and the Distortions of Hindsight,* Cambridge: Cambridge University Press, 2014
Bourke, Joanna, *An Intimate History of Killing: Face-to-face Killing in Twentieth Century Warfare,* London: Granta Books, 2000
Braybon, Gail, and Summerfield, Penny, *Out of the Cage: Women's Experiences in Two World Wars,* London: Routledge, 2013

Brewer, John, *The Sinews of Power: War, Money and the English State, 1688–1783,* New York: Alfred A. Knopf, 1989

Brodie, Bernard and Fawn M., *From Crossbow to H-Bomb,* Bloomington: Indiana University Press, 1973

Browning, Peter, *The Changing Nature of War: The Development of Land Warfare from 1792 to 1945,* Cambridge: Cambridge University Press, 2002

Caputo, Philip, "Putting the Sword to the Pen," *South Central Review,* 34, 2, Summer 2017, pp. 15–25

Catton, Bruce, and McPherson, James M., *American Heritage History of the Civil War,* Rockville, MD: American Heritage Publishing, 2016

Chickering, Roger, Showalter, Dennis, and van de Ven, Hans (eds.), *The Cambridge History of War: War and the Modern World, 1850–2005,* Cambridge: Cambridge University Press, 2012

Coates, A. J., *The Ethics of War,* Manchester and New York: Manchester University Press, 2007

Collingham, Lizzie, *The Taste of War: World War Two and the Battle for Food,* London: Penguin, 2011

Costello, John, *Love, Sex and War: Changing Values, 1939–45,* London: Collins, 1985 (US edition, *Virtue Under Fire: How World War II Changed Our Social and Sexual Attitudes,* Boston: Little, Brown, 1985)

Cox, Mary Elisabeth, *Hunger in War and Peace: Women and Children in Germany, 1914–1924,* Oxford: Oxford University Press, 2019

Danchev, Alex, *On Art and War and Terror,* Edinburgh: Edinburgh University Press, 2011

Dash, Mike, "Dahomey's Women Warriors," Smithsonianmag.com, September 23, 2011

Diamond, Jared, *Guns, Germs, and Steel: The Fates of Human Societies,* New York: W. W. Norton & Company, 1977

Echevarria II, Antulio J., *Imagining Future War: The West's Technological Revolution and Visions of Wars to Come, 1880–1914,* Westport: Praeger Security International, 2007

Edgerton, David, *Britain's War Machine: Weapons, Resources and Experts in the Second World War,* London: Penguin, 2012

Elshtain, Jean Bethke, *Women and War,* Chicago: University of Chicago Press, 1995

Emerging Technology from the arXiv, "Data Mining Adds Evidence That War Is Baked into the Structure of Society," *MIT Technology Review,* January 4, 2019

English, Richard, *Modern War: A Very Short Introduction,* Oxford: Oxford University Press, 2013

Fall, Bernard, *Hell in a Very Small Place: The Siege of Dien Bien Phu,* London: Pall Mall Press, 1967

Ferguson, Niall, *The Cash Nexus: Money and Power in the Modern World, 1700–2000*, New York: Basic Books, 2001

Finkelman, Paul, "Francis Lieber and the Law of War," *New York Times*, March 2, 2013

Freedman, Lawrence, *The Future of War: A History*, New York: Public Affairs, 2017

——— (ed.), *War*, Oxford: Oxford University Press, 1994

Frevert, Ute, *Emotions in History: Lost and Found*, New York: Central European University Press, 2011

Gabriel, Richard, *Between Flesh and Steel: A History of Military Medicine from the Middle Ages to the War in Afghanistan*, Washington, DC: Potomac Books, 2016

Gat, Azar, *War in Human Civilization*, Oxford: Oxford University Press, 2006

Goldstein, Andrea N., "'Why Are You Trying to Destroy the Last Good Thing Men Have?' Understanding Resistance to Women in Combat Jobs," *International Feminist Journal of Politics*, 20, 3, April 2018, pp. 385–404

Goldstein, Joshua S., *War and Gender: How Gender Shapes the War System and Vice Versa*, Cambridge: Cambridge University Press, 2001

Goldsworthy, Adrian, *Pax Romana: War, Peace and Conquest in the Roman World*, New Haven and London: Yale University Press, 2016

Hale, J. R., *War and Society in Renaissance Europe, 1450–1620*, London: Fontana Press, 1985

———, *Artists and Warfare in the Renaissance*, New Haven: Yale University Press, 1990

Hastings, Max, *Overlord: D-Day and the Battle for Normandy, 1944*, London: Pan, 1999

———, *Warriors: Extraordinary Tales from the Battlefield*, London: HarperCollins, 2005

———, "Wrath of the Centurions," *New York Review of Books*, 40, 2, January 25, 2018

Herwig, Holger, et al., *Cassell's World History of Warfare*, London: Cassell Military, 2003

Herzog, Dagmar (ed.), *Brutality and Desire: War and Sexuality in Europe's Twentieth Century*, Basingstoke: Palgrave Macmillan, 2009

Heuser, Beatrice, *The Evolution of Strategy: Thinking War from Antiquity to the Present*, Cambridge: Cambridge University Press, 2010

Hobbes, Thomas, *Leviathan*, Oxford: Oxford University Press, 2012

Horne, John, and Kramer, Alan, *German Atrocities 1914: A History of Denial*, New Haven: Yale University Press, 2001

Howard, Michael, *The Franco-Prussian War: The German Invasion of France, 1870–1871*, London: Methuen, 1981

———, *The Causes of War and Other Essays*, London: Unwin Paperbacks, 1984

————, *The Invention of Peace and the Reinvention of War*, London: Profile Books, 2002

————, *Captain Professor: The Memoirs of Sir Michael Howard*, London and New York: Continuum, 2006

————, *War in European History*, Oxford: Oxford University Press, 2009

———— (ed.), *Theory and Practice of War: Essays Presented to Captain B. H. Liddell Hart*, London: Cassell, 1965

———— (ed.), *Restraints on War*, Oxford: Oxford University Press, 1979

Hull, Isabel V., *A Scrap of Paper: Breaking and Making International Law during the Great War*, Ithaca: Cornell University Press, 2014

Hynes, Samuel, *The Soldiers' Tale: Bearing Witness to Modern War*, London: Allen Lane, 1997

Jackson, Julian, *France: The Dark Years, 1940–1944*, Oxford: Oxford University Press, 2001

Jordan, David, et al., *Understanding Modern Warfare*, Cambridge: Cambridge University Press, 2016

Kagan, Donald, *On the Origins of War and the Preservation of Peace*, New York: Doubleday, 1995

————, *The Peloponnesian War*, New York: Viking, 2003

Keegan, John, *The Face of Battle*, New York: Viking, 1976

Kello, Lucas, *The Virtual Weapon and International Order*, New Haven and London: Yale University Press, 2017

Kennedy, David, *Of War and Law*, Princeton: Princeton University Press, 2006

Kierman Jr., Frank A., and Fairbank, John K. (eds.), *Chinese Ways in Warfare*, Cambridge, MA: Harvard University Press, 1974

Knox, MacGregor, and Murray, Williamson (eds.), *The Dynamics of Military Revolution, 1300–2050*, Cambridge: Cambridge University Press, 2001

Kramer, Alan, *Dynamic of Destruction: Culture and Mass Killing in the First World War*, Oxford: Oxford University Press, 2007

LeBlanc, Steven, *Constant Battles: The Myth of the Peaceful Noble Savage*, New York: St. Martin's Press, 2003

Lee, Steven P., *Ethics and War: An Introduction*, Cambridge and New York: Cambridge University Press, 2012

Lee, Wayne, *Waging War: Conflict, Culture, and Innovation in World History*, Oxford: Oxford University Press, 2016

Leonhard, Jörn, *Pandora's Box: A History of the First World War*, trans. Patrick Camiller, Cambridge, MA: The Belknap Press of Harvard University Press, 2018

Levy, Jack S., and Thompson, William R., *The Arc of War: Origins, Escalation, and Transformation*, Chicago: University of Chicago Press, 2011

Lowe, Keith, *The Fear and the Freedom: How the Second World War Changed Us,* London: Viking, 2017

Lynn, John A., *Battle: A History of Combat and Culture,* New York: Basic Books, 2008

Maalouf, Amin, *The Crusades Through Arab Eyes,* New York: Schocken Books, 1984

McNeill, William, *Keeping Together in Time: Dance and Drill in Human History,* Cambridge, MA: Harvard University Press, 1995

McPherson, James M., *Crossroads of Freedom: Antietam,* Oxford: Oxford University Press, 2002

Malešević, Siniša, *The Sociology of War and Violence,* Cambridge: Cambridge University Press, 2010

Matthews, Jessica T., "America's Indefensible Defense Budget," *New York Review of Books,* 66, 12, July 18, 2019

Mayor, Adrienne, *The Amazons: Lives & Legends of Warrior Women across the Ancient World,* Princeton: Princeton University Press, 2014

Mazower, Mark, *Governing the World: The History of an Idea,* London: Penguin, 2013

Moore, Aaron William, *Writing War: Soldiers Record the Japanese Empire,* Cambridge, MA: Harvard University Press, 2013

Morris, Ian, *War! What Is It Good For? Conflict and the Progress of Civilization from Primates to Robots,* London: Profile Books, 2014

Murray, Williamson, Knox, MacGregor, and Bernstein, Alvin (eds.), *The Making of Strategy: Rulers, States, and War,* Cambridge: Cambridge University Press, 1994

Nolan, Cathal, *The Allure of Battle: A History of How Wars Have Been Won and Lost,* Oxford: Oxford University Press, 2017

Paret, Peter (ed.), *Makers of Modern Strategy: From Machiavelli to the Nuclear Age,* Princeton: Princeton University Press, 1986

Parker, Geoffrey (ed.), *The Cambridge History of Warfare,* Cambridge: Cambridge University Press, 2005

Piketty, Thomas, *Capital in the Twenty-first Century,* trans. Arthur Goldhammer, Cambridge, MA: The Belknap Press of Harvard University Press, 2014

Pinker, Steven, *The Better Angels of Our Nature: The Decline of Violence in History and Its Causes,* London: Allen Lane, 2010

Rabb, Theodore, *The Artist and the Warrior: Military History Through the Eyes of the Masters,* New Haven: Yale University Press, 2011

Rhea, Harry M., "The Commission on the Responsibility of the Authors of the War and on Enforcement of Penalties and Its Contribution to International Criminal Justice after World War II," *Criminal Law Forum,* 25, 1–2, June 2014, pp. 147–69

Ricks, Thomas E., *Fiasco: The American Military Adventure in Iraq*, New York: Penguin, 2006

Ring, J., *How the Navy Won the War: The Real Instrument of Victory, 1914–1918*, Barnsley: Seaforth Publishing, 2018

Roland, Alex, *War and Technology: A Very Short Introduction*, Oxford: Oxford University Press, 2016

Roshwald, Aviel, and Stites, Richard (eds.), *European Culture in the Great War: The Arts, Entertainment, and Propaganda, 1914–1918*, Cambridge and New York: Cambridge University Press, 2002

Rothenberg, Gunther, *The Art of Warfare in the Age of Napoleon*, Bloomington: Indiana University Press, 1980

Rousseau, Jean-Jacques, *The Major Political Writings of Jean-Jacques Rousseau: The Two Discourses and The Social Contract*, translated and edited by John T. Scott, Chicago and London: University of Chicago Press, 2012

Scheidel, Walter, *The Great Leveler: Violence and the History of Inequality from the Stone Age to the Twenty-first Century*, Princeton: Princeton University Press, 2017

Sheehan, James J., *Where Have All the Soldiers Gone? The Transformation of Modern Europe*, Boston: Houghton Mifflin, 2008

Sheffield, G. D. (ed.), *War Studies Reader: From the Seventeenth Century to the Present Day and Beyond*, London: Bloomsbury, 2010

Sidebottom, Harry, *Ancient Warfare: A Very Short Introduction*, Oxford: Oxford University Press, 2004

Sorabji, Richard (ed.), *The Ethics of War: Shared Problems in Different Traditions*, Aldershot: Ashgate, 2006

Spiers, Edward M., *The Army and Society, 1815–1914*, London: Longman, 1980

Stargardt, Nicholas, *The German War: A Nation Under Arms*, London: The Bodley Head, 2015

Stevenson, David, *With Our Backs to the Wall: Victory and Defeat in 1918*, Cambridge, MA: The Belknap Press of Harvard University Press, 2011

Strachan, Hew, *European Armies and the Conduct of War*, London: George Allen and Unwin, 1983

Strachan, Hew, and Scheipers, Sibylle (eds.), *The Changing Character of War*, Oxford: Oxford University Press, 2011

Summers, Harry, *On Strategy: The Vietnam War in Context*, Carlisle Barracks, PA: Strategic Studies Institute, US Army War College, 1981

Thucydides, *History of the Peloponnesian War*, trans. Rex Warner, London: Penguin, 1972

Tierney, Dominic, "Mastering the Endgame of War," *Survival*, 56, 5, October–November 2014, pp. 69–94

Tilly, Charles (ed.), *The Formation of National States in Western Europe*, Princeton: Princeton University Press, 1975

Todman, Dan, *The Great War: Myth and Memory*, London: Continuum, 2007

Townshend, Charles (ed.), *The Oxford History of Modern War*, Oxford and New York: Oxford University Press, 2005

Tyerman, Christopher, *The Crusades: A Very Short Introduction*, Oxford: Oxford University Press, 2006

Van Creveld, Martin, *Supplying War: Logistics from Wallenstein to Patton*, 2nd ed., Cambridge: Cambridge University Press, 2004

Verhey, Jeffrey, *The Spirit of 1914*, Cambridge: Cambridge University Press, 2000

Walzer, Michael, *Just and Unjust Wars: A Moral Argument with Historical Illustrations*, New York: Basic Books, 2015

Weinberg, Gerhard, *A World at Arms: A Global History of World War II*, New York: Cambridge University Press, 2005

Wilson, Peter, *Europe's Tragedy: A History of the Thirty Years War*, London: Allen Lane, 2009

Winter, Jay (ed.), *The Cambridge History of the First World War*, 3 volumes, Cambridge: Cambridge University Press, 2016

————, *War Beyond Words: Languages of Remembrance from the Great War to the Present*, Cambridge: Cambridge University Press, 2017

Wintringham, Tom, and Blashford-Snell, John, *Weapons and Tactics*, London: Penguin Books, 1973

Wrangham, Richard, *The Goodness Paradox: The Strange Relationship Between Virtue and Violence in Human Evolution*, New York: Pantheon Books, 2019

MEMOIRS AND DIARIES

Alexievich, Svetlana, *The Unwomanly Face of War: An Oral History of Women in World War II*, trans. Richard Pevear and Larissa Volokhonsky, New York: Random House, 2017

[Anonymous], *A Woman in Berlin: Diary 20 April 1945 to 22 June 1945*, trans. Philip Boehm, London: Virago, 2011

Brittain, Vera, *Testament of Youth: An Autobiographical Study of the Years 1900–1925*, London: Virago, 2014

Caputo, Philip, *A Rumor of War*, New York: Ballantine Books, 1978

Douglas, Keith, *Alamein to Zem Zem*, London: Faber and Faber, 1966

Fraser, George MacDonald, *Quartered Safe Out Here: A Recollection of the War in Burma*, London: Harvill, 1992

Goodall, Jane, *Reason for Hope: A Spiritual Journey*, New York: Warner Books, 1999

Gordon, Huntly, *The Unreturning Army: A Field Gunner in Flanders, 1917–18*, London: Bantam, 2015

Graves, Robert, *Goodbye to All That*, Harmondsworth: Penguin, 1960

Grenfell, Julian, *Soldier & Poet: Letters and Diaries, 1910–1915*, Hertford: Hertfordshire Record Society, 2004

Herr, Michael, *Dispatches*, New York: Avon, 1978

Jünger, Ernst, *Storm of Steel*, trans. Michael Hofmann, London: Penguin, 2004

Klemperer, Victor, *I Will Bear Witness: A Diary of the Nazi Years, 1933–1941*, trans. Martin Chalmers, New York: Modern Library, 1999

——, *I Will Bear Witness, 1942–1945: A Diary of the Nazi Years*, trans. Martin Chalmers, New York: Modern Library, 2001

Last, Nella, *Nella Last's War: The Second World War Diaries of Housewife, 49*, London: Profile Books, 2006

Lussu, Emilio, *A Soldier on the Southern Front*, trans. Gregory Conti, New York: Rizzoli Ex Libris, 2014

Makdisi, Jean Said, *Beirut Fragments: A War Memoir*, New York: Persea Books, 1990

Parry, Chris, *Down South: A Falklands War Diary*, London: Viking, 2012

Reith, J., *Wearing Spurs*, London: Hutchinson, 1966

Richards, Frank, *Old Soldiers Never Die*, London: Faber and Faber, 1964

Ritchie, Charles, *Siren Years: Undiplomatic Diaries, 1937–1945*, London: Macmillan, 1947

Sassoon, Siegfried, *Memoirs of an Infantry Officer*, London: Faber and Faber, 1965

Twain, Mark, "The Private History of a Campaign That Failed," in David Rachels (ed.), *Mark Twain's Civil War*, Lexington: University Press of Kentucky, 2007

Von Krockow, Christian, *Hour of the Women*, trans. Krishna Winston, Boston: Faber and Faber, 1993

Yeates, V. M., *Winged Victory*, London: Buchan and Enright, 1985

FICTION

Gilloux, Louis, *Blood Dark*, trans. Laura Morris, New York: New York Review of Books, 2017

Grossman, Vasily, *Life and Fate*, trans. Robert Chandler, London: Vintage Books, 2006

Heller, Joseph, *Catch-22*, New York: Simon & Schuster Paperbacks, 2011

Kipling, Rudyard, *Soldier Stories*, New York: The Macmillan Company, 1896

Manning, Frederic, *The Middle Parts of Fortune: Somme and Ancre, 1916*, London: Penguin Classics, 2014

March, William, *Company K,* London: Apollo, 2017

Ninh, Bao, *The Sorrow of War: A Novel,* trans. Phan Thanh Hao, London: Minerva, 1994

O'Brien, Tim, *The Things They Carried,* New York: Mariner Books, 2009

Remarque, Erich Maria, *All Quiet on the Western Front,* trans. A. W. Wheen, Boston: Atlantic Books, 1995

Tolstoy, Leo, *War and Peace,* trans. Constance Garnett, London: Penguin Classics, 2016

OTHER

Homer, *The Iliad,* trans. Robert Fagles, New York: Penguin Books, 1991

Stallworthy, Jon (ed.), *The New Oxford Book of War Poetry,* Oxford: Oxford University Press, 2015

Szymborska, Wisława, *View with a Grain of Sand: Selected Poems,* trans. Stanisław Barańczak and Clare Cavanagh, New York: Harcourt, Brace and Company, 1995

WEBSITES

Uppsala Conflict Data Program, https://www.pcr.uu.se/research/ucdp/

War on the Rocks, https://warontherocks.com/

CHAPTER 1: HUMANITY, SOCIETY AND WAR

Beard, *S.P.Q.R.*

Bell, *The First Total War*

Brewer, *The Sinews of Power*

Emerging Technology from the arXiv

Ferguson, *The Cash Nexus*

Gabriel, *Between Flesh and Steel*

Goldstein, Joshua, *War and Gender*

Goldsworthy, *Pax Romana*

Goodall, *Reason for Hope*

Hobbes, *Leviathan,* Chapter 13

Kagan, *On the Origins of War and the Preservation of Peace*

Kierman and Fairbank (eds.), *Chinese Ways in Warfare*

LeBlanc, *Constant Battles*

Morris, *War!*

Nolan, *The Allure of Battle*
Parker (ed.), *The Cambridge History of Warfare*
Piketty, *Capital in the Twenty-first Century*
Pinker, *The Better Angels of Our Nature*
Rousseau, *The Social Contract*
Scheidel, *The Great Leveler*
Sidebottom, *Ancient Warfare*
Thucydides, *History of the Peloponnesian War*
Uppsala Conflict Data Program
Wrangham, *The Goodness Paradox*

CHAPTER 2: REASONS FOR WAR

Armitage, *Civil Wars*
——— , "Civil Wars, From Beginning . . . to End?"
Bell, *The First Total War*
Bernstein, Alvin, "The Strategy of a Warrior-State: Rome and the Wars against Carthage, 264–201 B.C.," in Murray, Knox and Bernstein, *The Making of Strategy*
Costello, *Virtue Under Fire*
Frevert, *Emotions in History*
Goldstein, Joshua, *War and Gender*
Kagan, *On the Origins of War and the Preservation of Peace*
——— , "Athenian Strategy in the Peloponnesian War," in Murray, Knox and Bernstein, *The Making of Strategy*
Lee, Wayne, *Waging War*
Lynn, John, "A Quest for Glory: The Formation of Strategy Under Louis XIV, 1661–1715," in Murray, Knox and Bernstein, *The Making of Strategy*
Parker (ed.), *The Cambridge History of Warfare*
Ricks, *Fiasco*
Roland, *War and Technology*
Tierney, "Mastering the Endgame of War"
Tyerman, *The Crusades*
Wintringham and Blashford-Snell, *Weapons and Tactics*

CHAPTER 3: WAYS AND MEANS

Brodie, *From Crossbow to H-Bomb*
Diamond, *Guns, Germs, and Steel*
Heuser, *The Evolution of Strategy*

Howard, *War in European History*

Kagan, *On the Origins of War and the Preservation of Peace*

Lee, Wayne, *Waging War*

Lynn, *Battle*

Lynn, John, "Forging the Western Army in Seventeenth-Century France," in Knox and Murray (eds.), *The Dynamics of Military Revolution*

Morris, *War!*

Murray, Williamson, "On Strategy," in Murray, Knox and Bernstein (eds.), *The Making of Strategy*

Parker (ed.), *The Cambridge History of Warfare*

Ranft, Bryan, "Restraints on War at Sea before 1945," in Howard (ed.), *Restraints on War*

Roland, *War and Technology*

Sidebottom, *Ancient Warfare*

Wintringham and Blashford-Snell, *Weapons and Tactics*

CHAPTER 4: MODERN WAR

Bell, *The First Total War*

Bessel, *Violence*

Bond, *The Victorian Army and the Staff College*

Browning, *The Changing Nature of War*

Collingham, *The Taste of War*

Elshtain, *Women and War*

Goldstein, Joshua, *War and Gender*

Howard, *The Franco-Prussian War*

———, *War in European History*

——— (ed.), *Theory and Practice of War*

Knox and Murray (eds.), *The Dynamics of Military Revolution*

Lynn, John, "Forging the Western Army in Seventeenth-Century France," in Knox and Murray (eds.), *The Dynamics of Military Revolution*

Pinker, *The Better Angels of Our Nature*

Scheidel, *The Great Leveler*

Sheehan, *Where Have All the Soldiers Gone?*

Spiers, *The Army and Society*

Summers, *On Strategy*

Townshend (ed.), *The Oxford History of Modern War*

Van Creveld, *Supplying War*

Verhey, *The Spirit of 1914*

CHAPTER 5: MAKING THE WARRIOR

Alexievich, *The Unwomanly Face of War*
Dash, "Dahomey's Women Warriors"
Elshtain, *Women and War*
Goldstein, Andrea, "'Why Are You Trying to Destroy the Last Good Thing Men Have?'"
Goldstein, Joshua, *War and Gender*
Gordon, *The Unreturning Army*
Hale, *War and Society in Renaissance Europe*
Hastings, "Wrath of the Centurions"
Hynes, *The Soldiers' Tale*
Jackson, *France*
McNeill, *Keeping Together in Time*
McPherson, *Crossroads of Freedom*
Mayor, *The Amazons*
Moore, *Writing War*
Sidebottom, *Ancient Warfare*

CHAPTER 6: FIGHTING

Alexievich, *The Unwomanly Face of War*
Beaupré, Nicolas, "Soldier-Writers and Poets," in Winter (ed.), *The Cambridge History of the First World War*, Vol. III, *Civil Society*
Bourke, *An Intimate History of Killing*
Costello, *Love, Sex and War*
Fall, *Hell in a Very Small Place*
Fraser, *Quartered Safe Out Here*
Grenfell, *Soldier & Poet*
Homer, *The Iliad*
Jünger, *Storm of Steel*
Lowe, *The Fear and the Freedom*
Lussu, *A Soldier on the Southern Front*
Manning, *The Middle Parts of Fortune*
Moore, *Writing War*
O'Brien, *The Things They Carried*
Parry, *Down South*
Reith, *Wearing Spurs*
Richards, *Old Soldiers Never Die*

Ritchie, *Siren Years*
Yeates, *Winged Victory*

CHAPTER 7: CIVILIANS

[Boehm, Philip,] *A Woman in Berlin*
Beevor, *Berlin*
Bessel, *Violence*
Bond, *Britain's Two World Wars against Germany*
Braybon and Summerfield, *Out of the Cage*
Cox, *Hunger in War and Peace*
Downs, Laura Lee, "War Work," in Winter (ed.), *The Cambridge History of the First World War*, Vol. III, *Civil Society*
Horne and Kramer, *German Atrocities 1914*
Iacobelli, Teresa, "The 'Sum of Such Actions': Investigating Mass Rape in Bosnia-Herzogovina Through a Case Study of Foca," in Herzog (ed.), *Brutality and Desire*
Klemperer, *I Will Bear Witness*
Last, *Nella Last's War*
Makdisi, *Beirut Fragments*
Stargardt, *The German War*
Von Krockow, *Hour of the Women*
Walters, John Bennett, "General William T. Sherman and Total War," in Sheffield (ed.), *War Studies Reader*

CHAPTER 8: CONTROLLING THE UNCONTROLLABLE

Best, *War and Law Since 1945*
Best, Geoffrey, "Restraints on War by Land before 1945," in Howard (ed.), *Restraints on War*
Coates, *The Ethics of War*
Finkelman, "Francis Lieber and the Law of War"
Howard (ed.), *Restraints on War*
Kennedy, *Of War and Law*
Lee, Steven, *Ethics and War*
Mazower, *Governing the World*
Quataert, Jean H., "War-Making and the Restraint of Law: The Formative Years, 1864–1914," in Chickering, Showalter and van de Ven (eds.), *The Cambridge History of War*

Ranft, Bryan, "Restraints on War at Sea before 1945," in Howard (ed.), *Restraints on War*

Rhea, "The Commission on the Responsibility of the Authors of the War . . ."

Roberts, Adam, "Against War," in Townshend (ed.), *The Oxford History of Modern War*

Sorabji (ed.), *The Ethics of War*

Tyerman, *The Crusades*

Walzer, *Just and Unjust Wars*

CHAPTER 9: WAR IN OUR IMAGINATIONS AND OUR MEMORIES

Beaupré, Nicolas, "Soldier-Writers and Poets," in Winter (ed.), *The Cambridge History of the First World War,* Vol. III, *Civil Society*

Becker, Annette, "Art," ibid.

Caputo, "Putting the Sword to the Pen"

Danchev, *On Art and War and Terror*

Jelavich, Peter, "German Culture in the Great War," in Roshwald and Stites (eds.), *European Culture in the Great War*

Leonhard, *Pandora's Box*

McNeill, *Keeping Together in Time*

Ninh, *The Sorrow of War*

O'Brien, *The Things They Carried*

Scates, Bruce, and Wheatley, Rebecca, "War Memorials," in Winter (ed.), *The Cambridge History of the First World War,* Vol. III, *Civil Society*

Winter, *War Beyond Words*

CONCLUSION

Echevarria, *Imagining Future War*

Freedman, *The Future of War*

Jordan et al., *Understanding Modern Warfare*

Kello, *The Virtual Weapon and International Order*

Matthews, "America's Indefensible Defense Budget"

ILLUSTRATION CREDITS

——

15.   American Army military police escorting a Taliban prisoner to his cell in Camp X-Ray at the American Naval Base at Guantánamo Bay, Cuba, 2002. Image © Shane McCoy/Mai/The LIFE Images Collection via Getty Images/Getty Images

16.   China's National Day military parade. Image © Sovfoto/Universal Images Group via Getty Images

INSERT 2: ART

1.   Roman art: Ludovisi sarcophagus with battle scene from the third century A.D. Image © Luisa Ricciarini/Bridgeman Images

2.   A page from an eighteenth-century history of the life of Nurhaci, founder of the Manchu Qing dynasty. Image © British Library Board. All Rights Reserved/Bridgeman Images

3.   Albrecht Dürer's *The Four Horsemen of the Apocalypse* (1498, woodcut). Image © Bridgeman Images

4.   *Napoleon Crossing the Alps* by Jacques Louis David. Image © Bridgeman Images

5.   *The Battle of San Romano* by Paolo Uccello. Image © Luisa Ricciarini/Bridgeman Images

6.   Francisco Goya, "And they are like wild beasts," plate five of *The Disasters of War* (1810–14). Image © Index Fototeca/Bridgeman Images

7.   *Verdun* by Félix Vallotton (1917). Image © Photo Josse/Bridgeman Images

8.   *Gas Attack, Liévin* by A. Y. Jackson (1918). Image © SOCAN, Montreal, and DACS, London, 2020/image courtesy of Bridgeman Images

9.   *The Grieving Parents* by Käthe Kollwitz. Image © David Crossland/Alamy Stock Photo

10.   *Den Namenlosen* by Albin Egger-Lienz (1916). Image © Fine Art Images/Heritage Images via Getty Images

11.   *Figures in a Shelter* by Henry Moore (1941). Image © The Henry Moore Foundation. All Rights Reserved, DACS/www.henry-moore.org. Image courtesy of Lefevre Fine Art Ltd., London/Bridgeman Images.

12.   *Christ with Gas Mask* by George Grosz. Image © Estate of George Grosz, Princeton, N.J./DACS 2020. Image courtesy of Topfoto

13.   *Devastation, 1941: An East End Street* by Graham Sutherland. Image © Tate

14.   *Spitfires at Sawbridgeworth, Herts* by Eric Ravilious (ca. 1942). Image © Eric Ravilious/Imperial War Museums via Getty Images

INDEX

armed forces (*cont'd*):
  honor of officers, 214
  increase in size of standing,
    104–105
  Industrial Revolution enabled fast
    mass movement of, 97–98, 99
  led to growth of states, 18, 73–74,
    75–76
  memorials to dead, 255–257
  mercenaries, 125–126, 142–143
  motivating, 108
  nationalism and mass mobilization
    of citizens, 84, 90, 91
  need to plan for future wars, 268,
    271–272
  in oligarchic societies, 52
  organization necessary to
    support, 68
  parading before public, 111–113
  prisoners of war, 223, 225–226,
    253–254
  private, 70
  professionalization of, 77
  rape of women by, 133, 176–178,
    182–183
  reasons for fighting, 123–130,
    141–142
  respect for enemy, 166–167
  size of, during First World War,
    85, 86
  size of German, in Franco-
    Prussian War, 86
  social bonds among soldiers and
    effectiveness of, 69–70
  soldiers' feelings in literature, 253
  state spending on, 110–111
  swift movement of, by railways, 25,
    97, 99, 100
  training for new technology,
    75–76
  treatment of prisoners of war, 223,
    225–226
  undermining of states by, 18
  uniforms, 87
  veterans' organizations, 257

women as cheerleaders of, 139–141
women as equals in, 134
women in, during Second World
  War, 135–137
Armenians, Ottoman massacres of,
  224
Arm of Iron, 184
armor, disadvantages of, 70
Arndt, Ernst Moritz, 35
The Art of War (Sunzi), 61
arts. *See also* literature; specific works
  of art
  architecture, 16, 255–257
  attempts at depicting horrors of
    war, 249–250
  attempt to get at meaning of war,
    238–239
  boycotting works by nationals
    from enemy countries, 245
  changes in view of First World
    War as depicted in postwar,
    259–261
  dance, 246
  depictions of weapons, 242–243
  different perspectives in portraying
    war, 151
  effect of different wars on output
    of, 239–244, 243–244
  effect of peace on, 240
  glorification of war by, 241–243
  help people to process, remember,
    and commemorate war, 237
  inability to predict public reaction
    to, 250–251
  mourning through, 255–257
  museum exhibits, 262–263, 264
  music, 240, 244, 245–247, 253–254
  as part of governments' war efforts,
    244–245
  photography, 251, 252–253
  portrayals of naval and aerial
    warfare, 152
  prisoners of war and, 253–254
  produced during First World War,
    151–152, 238–239, 240–241, 243, 244

loss of Americans' support for,
109–110
media coverage of, 111
memorials, 257
photography and, 252–253
use of drugs, 158
Viking women warriors, 132
Villa, Pancho, 203, 205–206
violence
as distinguished from war, 6
reconciliation of war with
unwillingness to tolerate, xxii
trend away from, in society and
toward more deadly wars, 7–8, 10
Voigt, Wilhelm, 113–114
von Falkenhayn, Erich, 115
von Moltke, Helmuth, the Elder, 95,
96, 153
von Suttner, Bertha, 204–205, 229,
230

W
Wagner, Richard, 250
Wallace, Mike, 148–149
Waller, Sir William, 43–44
Walzer, Michael, 209, 213
Wang Jingwei, 192
War and Peace (Tolstoy), 153, 232
War of the Austrian Succession, 242
War on Terror, 223
war(s). *See also specific wars*
advantages of defense over offense,
87–88
advantages of offense over
defense, 88
attempts to abolish, 227
"cabinet," of eighteenth century, 78
changes society, xiv, 25–26
current attitude of Western and
non-Western societies toward,
266–267
decision to enter, 68
declarations of, 214–215
determining if and expanding
meaning of just, 211–212

discovery of artifacts from past,
xix–xx
economic arguments against,
229–230
as getting less cruel, 78
as having gotten more violent, 7–8
inability to get to truth of, 253
as last resort when all other means
of maintaining peace have been
exhausted, 208
momentum factor, 47–48
of national liberation, 222–223
as necessary and sanctifying
nation, 93–94
nuclear, 233–234
number of armed conflicts since
1945, 267
peace as aim of just, 208, 209
planning for, but not planning for
peace, 45–46
powerful polities' ability to
regiment society for, 23–24
as product of less civilized people,
187
rewriting and recalling, over time,
261–264
state as making, and as being made
by, 20
treaty renouncing, 233
trends in, 268–271
Wars of the Roses, 120–122, 123
Wayne, John, 243–244
weapons
during American Civil War,
86, 97
arms limitation as diversion from
ending war, 231–232
crossbows, 71–72, 79, 215
disarmament conferences, 225–226,
231
drones, 270
of earlier wars as depicted in
paintings, 242–243
fully autonomous, 270–271
halberds, 71

ABOUT THE AUTHOR

MARGARET MACMILLAN is emeritus professor of international history at the University of Oxford and professor of history at the University of Toronto. She received her PhD from Oxford University and became a member of the history faculty at Ryerson University in 1975. In 2002 she became Provost of Trinity College at the University of Toronto, and from 2007 to 2017 she was the Warden of St. Antony's College at Oxford University. Her previous books include *Paris 1919*, *The War That Ended Peace, Nixon and Mao, Dangerous Games*, and *Women of the Raj*.

margaretmacmillan.com